FootprintItalia

Sardinia

D1022718

Eliot Stein

Listings

Introducing the island

About the island

Cagliari & the south

Oristano & the west

Nuoro & Ogliastra

The Gallura

Sassari & the northwest

Practicalities

Contents

RETIRÉ DE LA COLLECTION UNIVERSELLE
Bibliothèque et Archives nationales du Québec

About the author

Eliot Stein was born in Washington, DC and 'adopted' by a Neapolitan neighbour soon after who cultured him in all things Italian, much to the amusement of his parents. He has since hosted an Italian-language radio show in Siena, guided university students from Sicily to Veneto and kayaked around the Tuscan archipelago. Utter curiosity led him to Sardinia years ago, and he's stayed ever since. Eliot regularly contributes travel articles and photographs to a variety of publications and has written extensively about Sardinia as a contributing editor for *The American* magazine.

Acknowledgements

Writing this guide was a real labour of love for me and it never would have been possible without the help of many wonderful people, starting with Maria Trunnell. Special thanks go to Alan Murphy for believing in this project, Davina Rungasamy for fitting Sardinia into 300 pages, Sophie Jones for her patience and keen editorial eye, and all the great folk at Footprint.

My deepest gratitude and warmest wishes to my Sardinian family: Daniela, Michela, Mama Mura, Marcello and the lovely Manuela. Your hospitality and kindness are beyond words and testify to what makes this island truly special.

Many thanks to Michele Vascellari, Franciscu Sedda, Pierluigi Montalbano and Antonella, Fabio and Roberta at Itzokor for helping make sense of giants' tombs, fairies' houses and 1,500 years of invasions. I'm especially indebted to Sardinia's greatest living archaeologist, Giovanni Ugas, for his patience and counselling regarding the Nuraghic society.

Many thanks are owed to my friend and mentor, Christopher Winner, for allowing me to grow as a writer, 800 words at a time. I'd also like to thank Sean O'Neill for his generosity, encouragement and a Guinness.

Thank you to Paolo Todde for his friendship, Judy Raggi-Moore for allowing me to fall in love with Italy, and Sabrina Ravani for her generosity.

Special thanks to Andrea Trincas and his wonderful family in Cabras. Additional thanks to Nicoletta Adamo for trusting me with her Smart Car, and my constant companion, Lavazza, for pushing me onward with each €0.80 *tazza*.

Extreme thanks go to the thousands of Sardinians on the street, in hotels, eating dinner, in tourism offices, and throughout the island whose local insight seeped into these pages.

Most importantly, thank you to my family whose unwavering love and support was with me throughout this journey, especially the man who bought me my first journal: a tireless editor, brilliant writer and the next Edward Albee.

About the book

The guide is divided into four sections: **Introducing the island**; **About the island**; **Around the island** and **Practicalities**.

Introducing the island comprises: **At a glance**, which explains how the island fits together by giving the reader a snapshot of what to look out for and what makes this island distinct from other parts of the country; **Best of Sardinia** (top 20 highlights); **A year in Sardinia**, which is a month-by-month guide to pros and cons of visiting at certain times of year; and **Sardinia on screen & page**, which is a list of suggested books and films.

About the island comprises: **History**; **Art & architecture**; **Sardinia today**, which presents different aspects of life in the region today; **Nature & environment** (an overview of the landscape and wildlife); **Festivals & events**; **Sleeping** (an overview of accommodation options); **Eating & drinking** (an overview of the region's cuisine, as well as advice on eating out); **Entertainment** (an overview of the island's cultural credentials, explaining what entertainment is on offer); **Shopping** (the island's specialities and recommendations for the best buys); and **Activities & tours**.

Around the island is then broken down into five areas, each with its own chapter. Here you'll find all the main sights and at the end of each chapter is a listings section with all the best **sleeping**, **eating & drinking**, **entertainment**, **shopping** and **activities & tours** options plus a brief overview of public **transport**.

Map symbols

ℹ	Informazioni Information	**▥**	Monumento Monument
○	Luogo d'interesse Place of Interest	**☗**	Stazione Ferroviaria Railway Station
🏛	Museo/Galleria Museum/Gallery	**👢**	Escursioni a piedi Hiking
🎭	Teatro Theatre	**Ⓜ**	Metropolitana Metro Station
○	Negozi Shopping	**🍎**	Mercato Market
✉	Ufficio postale Post Office	**🎞**	Funicolare Funicular Railway
†	Chiesa Storica Historic Church	**✈**	Aeroporto Airport
◖	Giardini Gardens	**🎓**	Universita University
......	Percorsi raccomandati Recommended walk		

Sleeping price codes

€€€€	over €300 per night for a double room in high season.
€€€	€200-300
€€	€100-200
€	under €100

Eating & drinking price codes

€€€€	more than €40 per person for a 2-course meal with a drink, including service and cover charge
€€€	€30-40
€€	€20-30
€	under €20

Picture credits

Eliot Stein pages 2, 3, 4, 9, 24, 37, 40, 41, 53, 67, 69, 80, 82, 83, 84, 86, 93, 95, 97, 101, 104, 105, 106, 109, 110, 111, 113, 123, 128, 134, 136, 138, 140, 144, 145, 146, 147, 148, 149, 150, 151, 153, 155, 156, 160, 166, 169, 171, 172, 173, 174, 180, 183, 186, 189, 198, 203, 206, 209, 212, 220, 221, 222, 223, 229, 230, 233, 235, 237, 238, 240, 241, 243, 244, 245, 248, 249, 250, 251, 253, 256, 257, 259, 261, 263, 264, 266, 267

Fotolia.com page 62: alberto maisto; page 197: Birgit Lampe; page 103: carodani; page 219: Comugnero Silvana; page 254: daulton; page 90: Discover Sardinia; pages 199, 200: lucien82; page 31: Luka76; page 234: Małgorzata; page 206: Massimo Putzu; page 44: maurizio loi; pages 45, 280: Michele Campini; page 193: puck; page 71: quadricromia; page 231: Razielss; page 92: Reinhold Einsiedler; page 90: Stefano Salemi; pages 158, 224, 273: Stormcab; page 177: Visionär

Hemisphere pages 12, 13, 15, 18, 33, 38, 46, 47, 48, 64, 139, 152, 175, 176, 179, 184, 265, 277, 279: Bruno Morandi; pages 50, 165, 216, 281: Franco Barbagallo; page 226: Jean Du Boisberranger; page 98: Maurizio Borgese; pages 2, 9, 10, 15, 22, 28, 52, 58, 74, 99, 100, 119, 124, 135, 142, 255, 270, 280, 281: Philippe Renault

Marina Spironetti pages 2, 3, 9, 26, 42, 56, 66, 78, 132, 201, 268

Shutterstock pages 1, 2: CaptureLight; pages 11, 15, 117: Elisa Locci; pages 102, 104: Filip Fuxa; page 196: federico stevanin; pages 3, 9, 194, 213: Shutterschock; pages 14, 275: Tamara Kulikova; page 164: Vaara

Superstock pages 16, 30, 34, 126, 167: age footstock; pages 54, 59, 211: Mauritius

Tips Images pages 2, 9, 72: Alberto Pugliese; pages 89, 228, 271: Alberto Rossi; page 17: Bildagentur RM; page 43: Arco Digital Images; pages 44, 137, 141, 215: Bruno Manunza; page 59: Food & Drink; page 105: Hermes Images; page 19: Mark Edward Smith; pages 6, 55, 65, 68, 103, 204, 205, 214, 225: Paolo Curto; page 75: Roberto Casagrande; page 192: Stefano Scata; page 246: Tommaso Di Girolamo

- -

Marina Spironetti front cover

age Fotostock/SuperStock back cover
Marina Spironetti back cover

Contents

Isola di Spargi, Arcipelago della Maddalena.

Introducing the island

Introduction

Mix jagged mountain ranges with flowering bougainvillea, combine glitzy jet-set coastal resorts with Wild West towns rooted in banditry, soak it in nearly 2,000 km of lonely Mediterranean coastline and then bake it all in a six-month summer. This enchanting recipe of striking beauty and rugged brawn is one that Sardinia has guarded fiercely until recently.

Sardinia is the least Italian region in terms of character. With 2,000 Neolithic 'fairy house' graves, more than 7,000 Bronze Age towers, 'giants' tombs' and hundreds of Spanish watchtowers, the island is a virtual outdoor museum, where its tangled past meets its colourful present. Nowhere else could you find bands of nomadic shepherds, three-storey yachts, pink flamingos, myrtle-scented liquor, pagan celebrations and medieval churches within a 30-minute drive of each other. So pack your snorkel, lace up your hiking boots and get ready for one of Italy's last truly unspoiled corners.

Bosa.

At a glance
A whistle-stop tour of Sardinia

According to Sardinian legend, after God created the Earth, He gathered all the leftover pieces from everywhere else, threw them in the sea and stepped on them to create Sardinia or, as the Greeks called it, *Ichnusa*, meaning 'footprint'. Since then, the island has been walked on by anyone who has ever sailed through the Mediterranean. Invaded in name but never conquered in spirit, Sardinia has managed the clever trick of absorbing a cultural buffet of influences while holding its head high with a resolutely independent pride.

Lying 178 km from the nearest mainland, slightly closer to Tunisia than Italy, no other island is as marooned in the Mediterranean as Sardinia; a fact that has shaped the island's unique character. Although the Sardinians, or Sardi, have adopted the Italian tongue of their latest landlords, they cling fiercely to their native language, Sardo, and are recognized as a distinct ethnic group from their mainland countrymen, who drop anchor in droves each summer to splash around the island's beaches. Sardinia boasts the Romanesque churches, mosaics, medieval castles and fine wines associated with Italy but also pulsates with an unsullied and unscripted spirit that the mainland lost long ago.

From the Phoenicians to the Romans to tourists today, foreigners have usually found it difficult to move beyond Sardinia's coasts, and for good reason. The island is ringed by a shimmering shoreline of jaw-dropping beauty. But to limit your visit to the beaches is to miss the essence of an island whose people have traditionally turned their backs to the sea, fearful of those coming to exploit them and, until fairly recently, of the malaria outbreaks that plagued the coastal lagoons.

The lowdown

Money matters
Depending on when, where and how you travel, Sardinia can be one of Italy's most expensive getaways or cheapest finds. Accommodation prices rise in high season (July to September), peaking in August. Hotel rooms average between €80-250 for a double and are more expensive than B&Bs or *agriturismi*. You can eat lunch comfortably for less than €15 and dinner for under €35 a person. With bus and train fares hovering at roughly €20 from one end of Sardinia to the other, budget-conscious travellers with plenty of time and patience can easily squeeze by on less than €100 a day per person. Those seeking to loosen their belts in style can spend upwards of €300, depending on their accommodation.

Opening hours & holidays
Most sights grant discounted or free admission to children, students or senior citizens, so always carry your ID. Stores and museums generally close between 1300 and 1600 for lunch and all day on Sundays. However, the main tourist sights in heavily visited areas are often open all day during July and August but may close down completely in the winter months.

Unlike those in Venice or Rome, most Sardinian churches keep irregular hours with long gaps between morning and evening openings, although, as a general rule, most are more accessible before lunch. (Where churches have fixed hours, they are listed in this book.)

Tourist information
Larger towns generally have their own tourist office with English-speaking volunteers. Tourist offices in provincial capitals and popular destinations often carry information for the surrounding region. For further information consult sarnow.com, ciaosardinia.com, sardinia.net, goingtosardinia.com and discover-sardinia.com.

Carloforte.

Instead, many Sardinians have long sought refuge in the island's interior, a landscape of deep chasms, impressive massifs and impenetrable macchia (maquis) brush that nurtures the Sardi's defiant character and hides the most compelling evidence of their secret history: more than 7,000 nuraghi (stone towers) built by one of the world's most advanced and mysterious Bronze Age societies.

Cagliari & the south
Sardinia's capital, Cagliari, makes a natural starting point for a tour of the island. Refreshed by a laid-back breeze from Sardinia's southern gulf, the island's largest city combines a fascinating look back at the island's past with a dynamic modern social scene. Three historic districts shelter the city's steep medieval heart, the Castello, where a warren of tight cobblestone alleyways lead to Sardinia's most important museum with its displays of miniature *bronzetti* statues made by the island's inspired Bronze Age artisans. Outside, admire the Pisans' architectural ingenuity from the top of the Bastione or head out to the city's beach, Poetto.

Away from the capital, Sardinia's southern third is a mosaic of contrasting landscapes draped in prickly pears, wheat fields and colourful oleanders. To the east, the lonely Gerrei region hides under the seven peaks of the Sette Fratelli park and is one of Sardinia's most secluded pockets as well as the source of fine pecorino cheese. Nearby, the Sarrabus produces Sardinia's best citrus crop and endures its highest temperatures from which the turquoise waters of the Costa Rei provide welcome respite. North of Cagliari, you'll find the Su Nuraxi and Arrubiu nuraghi in the dusty plains of the central Campidano. Their ancient stones make the ninth-century BC Phoenician settlement of Nora to the south seem young in contrast. To the west, the island of Sant'Antioco has a proud Punic past, and the island of San Pietro retains its Ligurian heritage with Genoese recipes and a blood-thirsty tuna-catching festival. Don't leave the south without visiting the Spanish-accented town of Iglesias and the surrounding abandoned mines and ghost towns of the Iglesiente.

Oristano & the west

The town of Oristano lends its name to Sardinia's smallest province, nestled in the island's western corner. The region lets its hair down for a string of daredevil horseback acrobatics in Sedilo and Santu Lussurgiu that will leave you gasping in amazement. On the coast, the Sinis Peninsula is a watery oasis, where over 10,000 pink flamingos winter on Europe's largest lagoon between September and June. The peninsula is still guarded by the evocative Punic-Roman city of Tharros and is famed for its *bottarga* (mullet roe). Quartz beaches pave the way north to Bosa, a beautiful medieval town in a fairytale setting, while the Montiferru mountain to the west yields Seneghe's artichoke-flavoured olive oil, San Vero Milis' *novello* wines and the region's prized *bue rosso* steaks.

Nuoro & Ogliastra

To the east, the provinces of Nuoro and Ogliastra tuck their towns in to the craggy nooks and crevices of the Supramonte and Gennargentu mountain ranges, which shield them from too much outside attention. The tall massifs serve as a bastion, protecting some of Sardinia's ancient rites and traditions, which modernity has yet to sweep away. You can see examples of native costumes in the ethnographic museum in Nuoro. Elsewhere, Orgosolo is Sardinia's bandit capital, famous for harbouring and hiding outlaws in its mountainous

Golfo di Orosei.

Costa Verde.

folds; now it is equally known for the abstract murals on its cinderblock walls. Sardinia's two best hiking routes will take you deep into the island's interior: up to the mystifying settlement of Tiscali buried inside a mountainous sinkhole, and into the depths of Gola Gorroppu, Europe's deepest ravine. If you only have one day to stretch out on Sardinia's shores, take a boat trip along the Golfo di Orosei.

The Gallura

The northeast is best known as the location of the world-famous Costa Smeralda, known as the *Costa Rubata* (stolen coast) by locals. Developed by Arabs with Mediterranean panache, there's hardly anything Sardinian about this 55-km stretch of coast between Liscia Ruja and Poltu Cuatu, but it remains fabulous nonetheless. Pop Cristal with Russian oligarchs at Club Billionaire and tan next to football stars along the coast's kaleidoscope of shimmering beaches.

Elsewhere, nature has carved Gallura's coastline with deep, dramatic bays and sculpted its granite into supple, wind-whipped natural art. Nowhere is this more evident than around Santa Teresa, where spring erupts in a palette of wild flowers, and around the La Maddalena Archipelago, a national park of seven uninhabited islands with universal appeal.

Sassari & the northwest

Long before the Costa Smeralda was developed, the northwestern province of Sassari was the Italians' favourite Sardinian destination. It has all the trappings of the medieval mainland: a proud provincial capital, Sassari, with a corkscrew cobblestone centre and crumbling walls; the citadel of Castelsardo spilling over a rocky bluff, and a string of Romanesque churches frozen in time in the golden wheat fields of the Logudoro. But the region also possesses some curious cultural relics that could only be found in Sardinia. There's romantic Alghero, a piece of Iberia that sailed over to its seaside setting in Sardinia with the Catalan-Aragonese in the 13th century; Monte d'Accodi, a bewildering Neolithic monument resembling a Mesopotamian ziggurat, and Santu Antine, Sardinia's Sistine Chapel of Nuraghic engineering.

Lost between Europe and Africa and belonging to nowhere. Belonging to nowhere, never having belonged to anywhere.

DH Lawrence, Sea and Sardinia

Best of Sardinia

Top 20 things to see & do

❶ Castello
Duck into strangers' doorways as cars thread the needle-tight streets in Cagliari's classiest neighbourhood. Catch a sunset from the Bastione and don't miss the ancient *bronzetti* statues at the Museo Archeologico. See page 79.

❷ Nuraghi
Marvel at some of the 7,000 or more mysterious stone towers that dot the Sardinian landscape. You won't find them anywhere else on Earth. In their most complex form, they are true Bronze Age castles. The best are Santu Antine (Torralba; see page 246), Su Nuraxi (Barumini; see page 98), Losa (Abbasanta; see page 151), and Arrubiu (Orroli; see page 101).

❸ Giara di Gesturi
Admire the world's only species of miniature wild horse, which has survived high on the Gesturi plateau since Carthaginian times. As you hike the park on the look out for these endangered creatures, keep an eye peeled for orchids, nuraghi and shepherds' *pinnetta* huts. See page 100.

9 **Bosa.**

➍ Nora & Tharros
Wander among the colourful tiled mosaics and visit the theatre at Nora, Sardinia's earliest Phoenician settlement. Or, if you're in the west of the island, head to the key Punic-Roman trading post at Tharros, which faces the sea from a lonely peninsula. See pages 104 and 144.

➎ Carloforte
Bring your appetite and your bathing suit to the Genoese settlement of Carloforte on Isola di San Pietro. Part Cinque Terre, part North Africa, it's full of old-world colonial grace. Fish lovers will enjoy the tuna caught at Carloforte's annual *mattanza* fishing festival. See page 108.

➏ The Iglesiente
Pass the morning in the surprisingly sophisticated old mining town of Iglesias and the afternoon touring the abandoned mines of Sardinia's Wild West. Don a hard hat to visit the pit at Porto Flavia (Masua; see page 113), ride the train at Galleria Henry (Buggerru; see page 114) and admire sweeping views of the deserted southwestern coast. See page 110.

➐ Costa Verde
Explore Sardinia's wildest and least developed shoreline. You'll need a resilient car and an adventurous spirit to get there, but the green *macchia*, deep blue sea and sandy dunes of 'Italy's Sahara' are worth the effort. See page 114.

8 Santa Cristina.

10 A rock painting at Orgosolo.

➑ Santa Cristina
Marvel at the Bronze Age precision of Sardinia's most refined Nuraghic relic, the keyhole-shaped holy well at Santa Cristina. Scan the heavens from an opening at the bottom of the conical ceiling that early Sardinians cleverly aligned to track the moon's orbit. See page 150.

➒ Bosa
Watch women stitching lace, kayak the Temo river and try not to lose your footing or your breath as you ascend the medieval alleyways to the castle above beautiful Bosa. Beyond the town's Aragonese watchtower and beach, follow one of Sardinia's most scenic roads as it hugs a volcanic cliff along 42 km of undeveloped coastline towards Alghero. See page 152.

➓ The Barbagie
Experience some of Europe's most ancient traditions in Sardinia's unyielding centre. Take the time to admire Orgosolo's poignant murals, ascend the island's tallest peak, Punto La Marmora, and see Sardinia's traditional costumes paraded through the streets. See page 163.

12 Golfo di Orosei.

⑪ Hiking the Supramonte & Gola Gorroppu

Lace up your boots to hike in the bald Supramonte mountains. Descend through a sinkhole to discover the huts at Tiscali. Nearby in Ogliastra, trek down to Europe's deepest ravine, Gola Gorroppu. See page 169.

⑫ Golfo di Orosei

Explore this magnificent stretch of coastline which is also Sardinia's least accessible. For some 40 km, limestone cliffs dive dramatically into the emerald sea. There are no roads, so the only way to see them is to hop aboard a boat and cruise around for the day. See page 175.

⑬ Trenino Verde

Pack a copy of DH Lawrence's *Sea and Sardinia* and pierce Sardinia's mountainous backbone aboard Italy's most popular tourist train. For five hours, the antique carriages plunge, climb and twist through some of the island's least explored and most stunning landscapes. See page 185.

⑭ Costa Smeralda

Iron your Versace (or Levi's) shirt, wash your Lamborghini convertible (or Fiat) and head to the world-famous Costa Smeralda resort. This playboy playground isn't Sardinian but its faux-Arabian villas are certainly unique and its sparkling beaches are drop-dead gorgeous. What's more: you no longer need to be a millionaire to live it up here. See page 201.

⑮ La Maddalena Archipelago

Unlike the Costa Smeralda, these seven dazzling islands sprinkled off Sardinia's northeast coast remain largely uninhabited and off the radar for European celebrities, with the exception of Italy's most famous warhorse, Giuseppe Garibaldi. Spend a day puttering from island to island in your own boat – or someone else's. See page 208.

⑯ Alghero

Stroll the cobblestone lanes, try the spicy paella and whip out your Catalan dictionary in Sardinia's most attractive town. Four hundred years of Iberian rule have rendered this seaside settlement a virtual Spanish colony; its residents cling proudly to their ancient language and their newfound nickname, 'Little Barcelona'. See page 247.

⑰ Grotta di Nettuno

Marvel at the stalactites, stalagmites, columns and fanciful colours in one of the world's great caves. Half the fun is getting there: visitors must come by boat from Alghero or descend the 656-step Escala del Cabirol! See page 253.

⑱ Monte d'Accodi

Climb the ramp to one of Sardinia's anthropological mysteries and archaeological masterpieces: the western world's only Neolithic truncated pyramid temple. Monte d'Accodi is a cross between a Mesopotamian ziggurat and an Aztec temple. See page 242.

⑲ La Pelosa

Wade through Evian-clear water at one of Sardinia's most perfect (and popular) beaches. While you're tanning, peer across the strait at Asinara Island, named after the world's only species of albino donkey. See page 254.

⑳ Castelsardo

Blessed with a picture-perfect setting high above a rocky bluff, Castelsardo may be more gorgeous than functional these days. But thanks to its medieval castle, famous handicrafts and a killer sunset, you'll see why locals linger on despite the steep climbs. See page 255.

17 Grotta di Nettuno.

Month by month

A year in Sardinia

A young carnival member, Ottana.

January & February

Unpredictable weather and shorter days often lead the Sardi to retreat into social hibernation throughout the winter leaving revellers eager for spring. The island's mountainous centre is often blanketed in snow during these months just in time for Sardinia's greatest festival period (see page 46). February is usually Sardinia's rainiest month.

March & April

Spring rains awaken Sardinia in an aromatic rebirth of wildflowers, myrtle, heather and thyme *macchia*. Sardinia's bees pollinate the blooming flowers to produce the island's *millefiori*, *cardo* and *eucalipto* honey, while citrus harvests in Milis and Muravera yield the island's tastiest clementines and oranges. This is the best time of year to walk around the Supramonte, Gennargentu or Capo Testa countryside or drive along the Costa Verde. Some of the island's most colourful processions take place at Easter and many retain a Spanish influence (see page 47). By April the sea is usually warm enough for swimming, and the hotels and restaurants that shut up shop in winter re-open with much lower rates than in the summer months.

May

The month is marked by two of Sardinia's largest festivals, the Sant'Efisio parade through Cagliari to Nora and back (see page 47) and Sassari's Cavalcata Sarda (see page 48). Carloforte's annual tuna *mattanza* (see page 109) takes place between late May and early June and, although canned Carloforte tuna can be purchased year-round, the month following the catch sees the town's finest restaurants serving the fish at its freshest and best.

Windsurfing at Golfo Aranci.

June & July

Up to 11 hours of sunshine daily make June Sardinia's brightest month, while predictably hot weather and fewer crowds than August ensure that June and early July are the best times of year to swim at Sardinia's beaches and to try windsurfing, scuba diving, snorkelling or kite surfing. As more tourists arrive, you'll need to book well ahead at popular restaurants and at all hotels from mid-June to early September. If you're visiting in early July, don't miss the daring Ardia horse race in Sedilo (see page 48).

August

High summer can be suffocatingly hot and dry in Sardinia but the island's turquoise beaches never seem more enticing. This is far and away the most popular time to visit: restaurants and shops typically extend their hours to accommodate the tourist rush, and hotels significantly raise their prices. If possible, avoid visiting in August (especially around Ferragosto on the 15th), when it seems everyone in Italy takes a plane or boat to stretch out on Sardinia's beaches with the Sardi themselves. Accommodation is scarce, temperatures skyrocket and prices peak. To beat the heat and the crowds, head to the mountains. Sassari's Li Candaleri and Nuoro's Festa del Redentore festivals bring these two provincial capitals alive with costumes, music and lots of mouth-watering food (see page 49).

September & October

Autumn months bring warm days, cool nights and the return of the rains and northwesterly *maestrale* (mistral) winds that blow across Sardinia in the spring. Prices dip significantly from mid-September to October, although temperatures can remain bikini-friendly. October is a period of transition when Sardinia's social scene shifts from open-air beachside discos back to the confines of cosy bars, and many seasonal restaurants and hotels often close until Easter. Most nine-day *novenaria* rural religious celebrations take place in Autumn, including San Salvatore's famous *Corsa degli Scalzi* race in early September, (see page 49). Autumn is a wonderful time to head to the mountains around the Barbagie and Gallura to pick porcini mushrooms. It is also the start of the hunting season and is the best time to sample Sardinia's wild boar (*cinghiale*). In October, the chestnut and hazelnut harvest is celebrated in Aritzo (see page 49) and the *Vendemmia* (grape harvest) yields some of Sardinia's most delicious wines.

November & December

Hotel and airline prices are at their lowest from November to February (excluding Christmas) but many hotels close down for the season and accommodation in rural communities can be scarce. Sardinia's prized olive oil is at its most abundant and fragrant between November and February and this is the best time to taste and purchase it. Despite the cool and often wet weather, Cagliari's Poetto beach crowds with seafood-lovers from late October until late March, eager to taste the city's famous *ricci* (sea urchin) at the seaside kiosks. Christmas is less of a public affair than other holidays in Sardinia and is generally celebrated with family.

Screen & page

Sardinia in film & literature

Films

I Banditi a Orgosolo
Vittorio De Seta, 1960
This is Sardinia's version of *The Bicycle Thief* and a must-see for anyone travelling to the island's interior. Writer-director De Seta used amateur actors from the Barbagie to tell the tale of a peasant shepherd robbed of his flock by bandits.

Padre Padrone
Vittorio and Paolo Taviani, 1977
Based on the autobiographical book by Gavino Ledda, this film won the Palme d'Or at the Cannes Film Festival in 1977. A young shepherd tries to escape his overbearing father by learning Italian and attending university. The realities of Sardinia's pre-industrialized interior and pastoral lifestyle in the mid-20th century are poignantly authentic.

Tutto Torno
Enrico Pitzianti, 2008
Directed by Sardinia's top up-and-coming film-maker, the film follows an aspiring writer as he leaves his parents in rural Sardinia to study and live in the city. Shot exclusively in Cagliari's Marina and Castello districts, this is the first film that breaks from Sardinia's rustic image and displays its capital as a vibrant, cosmopolitan city.

On location

With sapphire-blue waters lapping its shores and a rugged interior, it's no surprise that Sardinia has been used as the backdrop for many films. In the 1960s and '70s San Salvatore's dusty square and squat Mexican-style homes set the scene for a string of Spaghetti Westerns, such as *Garter Colt* (1967) and *Trinity is Still my Name* (1972). In the 1977 Bond movie, *The Spy Who Loved Me*, Roger Moore and Anya Amasova stay at the Cala di Volpe Hotel in Porto Cervo and have enough time to do some diving before roaring through the Costa Smeralda in a high-speed car chase. The remake of the 1970s classic *Swept Away* (2002) features Madonna frolicking on the sands of Cala Cartoe near Cala Gonone, shot by then-hubby Guy Ritchie: terrible film, beautiful beach.

Fiction

After the Divorce (Dopo il Divorzio)
Grazia Deledda, 1902
No other book portrays so convincingly the fragile tension in Sardinian culture between individual goals and the constraints of tradition and custom.

Reeds in the Wind (Canne al Vento)
Grazia Deledda, 1913
The most famous novel by the island's Nobel laureate is Sardinia's equivalent of Sicily's The Leopard. The plot follows the decline of Sardinia's noble Pintor family and shows the strong pagan customs in Sardinia at the turn of the 19th century.

Cosima
Grazia Deledda, 1937
Deledda's autobiographical novel offers a sharp and heartbreaking look at the obstacles women had to overcome to gain literary acceptance in central Sardinia.

The Day of Judgement (Il Giorno del Giudizio)
Salvatore Satta, 1975
Satta's novel captures Sardinian culture on many levels: the yearning of younger generations to leave rural areas to work or study, the political tension that grips the island, and the ancient customs of all Sardi, regardless of class, that bind them together.

The Advocate
Marcello Fois, 2004
From one of Sardinia's top up-and-coming 'noir' novelists comes this tale of a Nuorese peasant wrongly accused of shooting a farmer dead. Fois masterfully tackles Sardinia's messy history of banditry, vendettas and honour.

Non-fiction

Sea and Sardinia
DH Lawrence, 1921
Inspired by his jaunt from Cagliari to Orosei, Lawrence returned home to Sicily to write what continues to be the quintessential armchair companion for anyone who has ever used public transport in Sardinia (see page 185).

The Bandit at the Billiard Table
Alan Ross, 1954
The former editor of the London Magazine journeyed to Sardinia some 30 years after Lawrence and wrote this entertaining, if impatient, treatise on the island in 1952.

La Civiltà Nuragica
Giovanni Lilliu, 1981
Nearly 700 pages long and only available in Italian, Lilliu's opus remains the base from which all scholars of Sardinia's mysterious nuraghi builders have constructed their theories. The book traces the history of the island from its first settlers through the Bronze Age.

Sweet Myrtle and Bitter Honey
Efisio Farris, 2007
A must-read for foodies. Sardinia's most famous chef takes readers on a culinary tour of his home with this beautiful cookbook, recipes included.

Alghero city walls.

Contents

About the island

History

Roccia dell'Elefante at Castelsardo.

Sardinia's strategic position at the crossroads of the Mediterranean sealed its fate as a pawn in the messy tug-of-war between Middle Eastern, African and European powers. As a result, the island has endured 1500 years of raids, rule and regulation by more than a dozen foreign occupiers. Yet, Sardinia's most distinctive characteristics didn't evolve under Punic, Roman or Spanish rule, but emerged long before anyone else was looking, when the Sardi were left to their own, independent devices.

Neolithic Sardinia

Primitive flint and quartz tools from as far back as 450,000 BC found near Perfugas attest to the presence of humans in Sardinia from the Paleolithic age, but Sardinia's past doesn't come into focus until the Neolithic age (6000-3500 BC). This prehistoric renaissance saw humans develop pottery, move from caves into outdoor settlements, and shift from hunter-gatherer subsistence lifestyles to agricultural and livestock farming. Of the world's Neolithic peoples, those in Sardinia were likely to be as wealthy as any thanks to the island's deposits of obsidian. This rare volcanic glass could be shaped into arrowheads, knives and other tools, rendering it more valuable than gold in the Neolithic world. From its discovery at Monte Arci in the eighth millennium BC, mined obsidian became prehistoric Sardinia's most important economic resource and was traded as far away as Tuscany and France.

As early Sardinians came into contact with the outside world, they exchanged not only goods, but also artistic techniques and religious theories, paving the way for the development of the Bonu Ighinu culture (4000-3500 BC). This period saw the production of the first stone statues of the chubby female Mother Goddess representing fertility, which became an icon of the island's earliest known religion. The Bonu Ighinu was a relatively peaceful matriarchal society, with women running domestic and village affairs while men often worked away in the fields.

Sardinia's Neolithic ingenuity peaked with the so-called Ozieri Culture (3500-2700 BC), named after artefacts retrieved from the San Michele cave near present-day Ozieri (see page 243). Sardinians started burying the dead in *domus de janas* ('fairy houses', see page 34), rock-cut tombs, ranging from single chambers to elaborate necropoli. Elongated stone menhirs (see page 35) were placed near burial sites to correspond to astrological cycles, and artists created pottery festooned with spirals and human figurines. The apotheosis of Ozieri engineering was the raised cult temple at Monte d'Accodi (see page 242), resembling nothing less than a Mesopotamian ziggurat pyramid.

The dawn of the Chalcolithic (or Copper) Age marked a distinct turning point in early Sardinia. Ozieri's craftsmen and their descendants were some of the earliest in the Mediterranean to develop metal tools, effectively marking the end of the peaceful farming society and the birth of competitive, warrior-driven clans. Artists began depicting menhirs as either female, with protruding breasts, or male, wielding a carved, double-edged dagger. The dominance of the male

Furat chi beit dae su mare
He who comes from the sea comes to rob.

Sardinian proverb

menhirs, coupled with the disappearance of the chubby female goddess statues, seems to suggest that, although Neolithic Sardinia may have developed as a matriarchal society, metals gave it a serious injection of testosterone. As social tensions rose with the Chalcolithic arms race, turreted walls were erected to defend villages and the first proto-nuraghi were developed. These were raised, rectangular stone platforms with galleries and staircases, topped by a wooden hut: the precursor to the great Nuraghic towers that were to come.

Nuraghic Sardinia & the Bronze Age

Most scholars identify the Nuraghic age (beginning 1800 BC) as the defining period in Sardinia's history, as individualized cultures developed into a distinct island-wide society characterized by architectural unity. In the absence of any evidence of a Nuraghic written language, historians have studied the thousands of visual clues that dot the island's landscape to shed light on a Bronze Age society that is finally gaining recognition as one of the Mediterranean's most advanced.

The Nuraghic period gets its name from its most identifiable monuments: stone towers known as a nuraghi (see page 35). Built between 1600 and 1000 BC, over 7,000 of these truncated, cone-shaped monuments remain, with countless others cannibalized over the years. Though they bear a resemblance to the underground tombs constructed by Sardinians' trading partners, the Mycenaeans, radiocarbon dating and archaeological evidence suggest that the construction and engineering ingenuity of these structures came from the Sardi themselves.

Nuraghe Santu Antine.

The earlier single-tower nuraghi were likely territorial markers between clans from which another nuraghe could almost always be seen, forming a communication chain. Between 1500 and 1200 BC, many mono-tower nuraghi developed into Bronze Age castles, rising up to 27 m and sprouting as many as 17 towers, as at Nuraghe Arrubiu (see page 101). These were likely palaces for a tribal chief, complete with connecting bastions, escape routes and courtyards designed to defend village settlements that increasingly sought their protection (Nuraghe Su Nuraxi is one of the best examples; see page 98.)

Nuraghic inhabitants enjoyed a surprisingly enlightened social structure. People lived in huts with circular, stone bases and thatched roofs, similar to the *pinnettas* still used by Sardinia's present-day shepherds. There were warriors, farmers, shepherds and artists, all of whom contributed to the building of nuraghi and paid a tax of grain or animal meat to the chief, which was distributed among the entire community. At the time of death (around 35 years' old) people were buried in vast communal *tombe di giganti* (giants' tombs; see page 35). The number of women and children found inside suggests an indiscriminate burial practice regardless of social hierarchy.

By 1200 BC local craftsmen were beginning to manufacture bronze objects, which would later evolve into intricate *bronzetti* (see page 35). These miniature statues were left as votive offerings at well temples (see page 35) as an integral part of Nuraghic religious practice and provide a window to the social strata that comprised the Nuraghic population, showing warriors, chiefs, hunters, wrestlers, women, animals, and imaginary beings.

Bronzetti production coincided with the decline of nuraghe building and the dawn of a new political and social structure. Many nuraghi were dismantled and incorporated into villages, and the community-orientated structures overseen by tribal chiefs were replaced by conclaves of landowners who nominated political representatives. More significantly, foreign merchants were tired of long-distance trading with the Sardi and were anxious to establish settlements on the island. Nuraghic villages coexisted for a time beside their new neighbours during the early Iron Age (900-750 BC), but the once-formidable island-wide society was on its last legs when the Punic invaders came knocking.

Phoenicians, Carthaginians & Romans

In about 1000 BC, Phoenician merchants began snooping around Sardinia's southwestern coasts, using the island's placid inlets to rest or repair their ships along their well-established trade route between present-day Lebanon and Spain. Lured by Sardinia's rich mineral deposits, these temporary moorings led to established settlements at Nora, Karalis (Cagliari), Sulci (Sant'Antioco), Bithia (Chia) and Tharros between the ninth and seventh centuries BC.

The Phoenicians arrival in Sardinia was largely peaceful, as the incomers generally remained on the coasts and integrated little with the inland inhabitants. However, they did import Etruscan and Greek pottery to the island and introduced Sardinia to urban design and writing: the defining characteristics of a unified civilisation that were never achieved by Nuraghic Sardinia's rival clans.

The happy coexistence turned sour in the seventh to sixth centuries BC, when the Phoenicians began expanding their settlements into Sardinia's interior, pushing indigenous villagers off their land and leading Nuraghic tribes to raid the Phoenicians' inland mining base at Monte Sirai. Fearful of a unified island uprising, the Phoenicians enlisted their powerful African colony, Carthage (present-day Tunisia), to help subdue the Sardi.

Sardinian tribes fought valiantly against their Punic invaders. Utilizing the maze-like corridors of nuraghi to conduct guerilla assaults, the Sardi humiliated Malchus – who had previously defeated the Greeks and conquered most of Sicily in a

Who were the Shardana?

"The unruly Shardana whom no one had ever known how to combat. They came boldly sailing in their warships from the midst of the sea, none being able to withstand them."
Pharaoh Rameses II, 13th century BC.

Most historians have rejected the outdated assumption that Sardinians were never a seafaring people. In fact, the latest theory posits that among Sardinia's earliest indigenous inhabitants were the Shardana, an enigmatic band of sea people born from the nuraghic society who boasted a naval and military prowess venerated throughout the ancient world. Once dismissed as fantasy, this hypothesis is now supported by many archaeologists and scholars who may succeed in re-writing Sardinia's history.

The prevailing theory is that at the height of the nuraghic period (14-13th centuries BC), Sardinia's population swelled to up to 600,000 and territory became increasingly scarce, causing islanders to venture elsewhere in search of resources. It is at this time that the first mention of the Shardana appear, courtesy of their contemporaries in Egypt, who depict them as ferocious warriors carrying elongated daggers, horned helmets and round shields with a raised nipple at its centre – identical images appear on hundreds of nuraghic *bronzetti*. The Shardana were so revered by the Egyptians that pharaoh Rameses II employed them as his personal bodyguards. During Rameses III's reign in 1278 BC, the Shardana took on the entire Egyptian Empire, occupying much of modern-day Palestine and bringing down the Hittite Empire (modern-day Syria and Turkey) in the 12th century BC.

The Shardana seem to have been on the move at the same time that nuraghic Sardinia developed bronze, a fusion of copper and tin. While Sardinia is rich in copper deposits, it is almost devoid of tin, a substance whose nearest sources outside the Middle East are Britain and Africa. Interestingly, a walk through Cagliari's Museo Archeologico (see page 82) shows a *bronzetto* statue of a musician playing the *launeddas*, the ancestor of the Scottish bagpipes, and many *bronzetti* depict monkeys, rhinos and antelopes from sub-Saharan Africa. On your way out of the museum, don't miss the first written mention of Sardinia on the Phoenicians' Nora Stone from the ninth or eighth centuries BC: it reads 'SHRDN'.

Ruins of Tharros.

matter of months – sending his troops packing in 540 BC. However, not before the invaders had introduced the malaria-carrying mosquitoes that would ravage Sardinia for the next 1,500 years.

It took another 30 years for Punic forces to take control of the island, with the exception of its forbidding mountainous interior. The Carthaginians expanded Phoenician settlements into profitable maritime cities and exploited Sardinia's agro-pastoral land and mines, enslaving much of the indigenous population while privatizing the island's natural resources. Local magistrates called *sufetes* governed cities and, for the first time, the island existed as part of a larger colony. Having stripped the Nuraghic culture of its ports, pastures and political influence, Carthage seemed poised to reign as the western Mediterranean's dominating force, until Rome flexed its muscles.

The First Punic War (264-241 BC) saw Rome sack Carthage's formidable navy, forcing it to surrender Sicily and agree to a strict peace treaty. To add insult to injury, many Punic soldiers returned to Sardinia to discover that their depleted empire could no longer afford to pay them! Outraged,

they revolted and pulled the ultimate about-face: they appealed to Rome. Recognizing a chaotic situation, the Romans violated their peace treaty in 238 BC and seized Sardinia's principal Punic cities without resistance. By 227 BC, a Roman governor controlled Sardinia and Corsica as Rome's second province.

Though they might not have realized it, the Romans had entered a very unstable situation in Sardinia. After 271 years of Carthaginian rule, much of the island was completely absorbed in Punic culture, and the remaining unruly *Sardi Pelliti* (hairy Sardinians), as the Romans called them, of the mountainous interior were not exactly known for rolling out the red carpet for outsiders. In 215 BC, during the Second Punic War (218-201 BC), Punic-Sardinian forces aligned under a Sardinian leader, Ampsicora, to revolt against the Roman occupiers in the name of *Bellum Sardum*. It took a fleet of 50 Roman ships to quell the insurgents but worse was yet to come. In 177 BC, Rome sent 30,000 soldiers and 5,200 horsemen to suppress indigenous uprisings around the Gennargentu mountains, killing 12,000 Sardi and enslaving or imprisoning another 80,000. Despite the slaughter, the Romans endured another 15 rebellions from the Gennargentu without ever fully subduing these mountain-dwelling mavericks. The Romans dubbed the area 'Barbarie' (present-day Barbagie) after the barbarian-like ferocity of its inhabitants.

Elsewhere, the Romans did much to modernize Sardinian infrastructure and laid the foundations for much of Sardinia's subsequent cultural development. Aside from the typical civic projects that accompany Roman *municipia* (theatres, forums, baths, temples, etc; see page 36), they introduced Latin (from which Sardinia's native language, Sardo, derives; see page 39), increased agriculture and mining production, spread Christianity and built a road network from Cagliari to Porto Torres that paved the way for today's SS131.

Vandals, Byzantines, Arabs & *giudicati*

The collapse of Rome created a power vacuum in Sardinia and the island's advantageous geographic position attracted numerous unwanted guests.

First came the Vandals, Germanic warriors who launched attacks on Sardinia from their colony in North Africa, occupying the island in AD 456. However, the scant records available from this period suggest that the Vandals' grip on the island was limited to a few coastal areas.

By 534, a reinvigorated Roman Empire based in Constantinople (Byzantium) was eager to reconquer the western half of its former glory. Led by Emperor Justinian, the Byzantines slashed their way through the Italian mainland before defeating the Vandals in North Africa. Following an island-wide insurrection in 533, Sardinia became one of Byzantium's seven African provinces.

The Byzantines ruled Sardinia for over 300 years. They built the island's first churches (see page 36) and established an advanced political structure that endured, in one way or another, throughout the Middle Ages. A military commander called a 'dux' was in charge of keeping an eye on the unyielding rebels from the Barbagie, and the island was divided into four provinces, each ruled by a judge called a *judex provinciae*. The districts were

The unruly *Sardi Pelliti* (hairy Sardinians), as the Romans called them, were not exactly known for rolling out the red carpet for outsiders.

further divided into *partes* (counties) overseen by a *curatore* (representative), with individual villages led by a *maiore* (mayor).

By the eighth century, Arab and Berber armies had succeeded in conquering much of Northern Africa and began pushing their way into Sardinia and Spain, posing a real threat to the Byzantine Empire. With its resources stretched thin, Constantinople seemed unable and unwilling to defend its distant colony. In 705 Arab raiders sailed away with 3,000 Sardi as prisoners. They even briefly occupied Karalis (Cagliari), threatening to conquer the island in 752.

While sporadic Arabic raids would be on the menu in Sardinia for the next 1000 years, the absence of sustained outside intervention permitted a nascent Sardinian independence to take shape. From the eighth century, the *judexes* created by the Byzantines gradually evolved into Sardinian-controlled *giudicati* (sovereign states or kingdoms) run by an elected *giudice*. The four *giudicati* were officially partitioned in 856: Torres, the most politically active, to the northwest; Arborea, the most unified, around Oristano; Gallura, the smallest, poorest, and most isolated, in the northeast; and Cagliari, the largest, wealthiest and most violent, in the south.

In 1015 the Arab emirate Mujahid launched a sea attack against the island, forcing the four *giudicati* to appeal to Pope Benedict VIII for assistance. Rival naval powers Genoa and Pisa intervened and the unified forces rid the island of its Arab invaders but this left the Sardi with another problem: their new allies had no intention of leaving.

About the island

Bastione di San Remy was built on Cagliari's old Spanish ramparts.

Pisa & Genoa, Aragon & Spain

By the 11th century, the four *giudicati* had developed into independent states, each frequently clashing with its neighbours in a continuing tug-of-war over land, wealth and power. Recognizing the economic opportunity offered by the island's political instability, the Pisans and Genoese established alliances with Sardinia's rival factions, which shifted with the winds for the next 300 years.

On the surface, the *giudicati* seemed to have entered into a healthy marriage with their mainland *maestri*: the Pisans and Genoese generated a period of island-wide progress, bringing with them the modern trappings of medieval Europe. International trade boomed, irrigation techniques improved, and salt and mining extraction increased. Sardinia's strengthened international alliances also enticed monastic orders to the island from Provence and Pisa to spread Christianity and work with local artists to create a series of stunning Romanesque churches. But Pisa and Genoa had not come to make friends and, as their involvement in the island's internal affairs increased, so did their control of its economy and government.

By the 12th century the *giudicati* had begun ceding large swathes of land to Pisa and Genoa's noble families: Malaspina in Bosa, della Gherardesca in the Iglesiente, Doria in Sassari, and Visconti throughout the island. In calculated moves, these wealthy barons began marrying their way into power and, after 1250, three of the *giudicati* passed into Pisan or Genoese control, leaving only Arborea to carry the torch of Sardinian independence.

While Italian powers were fast dividing up Sardinia for themselves, bigger sharks began circling the Mediterranean. After snatching power from Charles of Anjou and his Sicilian territories in 1282, the Barcelona-based Aragonese seemed poised for a full-scale invasion. Anxious to maintain his ecclesial sway in Sicily, Pope Bonifacio VIII created the 'Kingdom of Sardinia and Corsica' and offered it to the King Jaume II of Aragon in 1297 in lieu of Sicily. As a competing maritime power of both Genoa and Pisa, Jaume was all too eager to accept the Pope's open invitation to invade.

Quattro mori

Sardinia's flag is baffling: four severed black heads, sometimes looking to the left, sometimes to the right or, sometimes, nowhere at all, as they're blindfolded. Ask the locals and they'll probably tell you it symbolizes the expulsion of Arabs by Sardinia's four independent *giudicati* but, in fact, the image was originally the war flag of the Aragonese. It was introduced to the island at the infamous Battle of Sanluri as a replacement for Arborea's flag, which depicted a green tree.

After establishing an alliance with their Genoese rivals, the Aragonese finally made good on Bonifacio's offer in 1323 and sent 11,000 troops to Sardinia. Aligned with independent Arborea and with the Genoese Malaspina and Doria families, the Catalan-Aragonese forces quickly took control of Iglesias, Cagliari and the rest of Pisa's holdings. However, Arborea soon realized that the Aragonese were only using them as a pawn to gain control of the island and rebelled against their former allies in a series of revolts beginning in 1353.

The fight for the independent *Repubblica Sardistica* was championed by Arborea's Mariano IV. Known as Sardinia's greatest *giudice*, Mariano crushed an Aragonese insurgence in Oristano in 1368. Better remembered, however, is Mariano's daughter, Eleonora d'Arborea, who became *giudicessa* in 1383 and created the *Carta de Logu*, an exhaustive 198-chapter code of progressive laws written in Sardo and including concepts such as female suffrage, joint property ownership, the liberty to divorce following sexual assault, and the recognition of servants as citizens, a first in Italy. Amended only slightly over the years, the Carta formed the legal core of a nascent Sardinian nation and remained the law of the island until 1817.

Sardinia's struggle for independence started to unravel following Eleonora's untimely death in 1404. In the Battle of Sanluri in 1409 half of the island's volunteer army of 20,000 men were killed by the Aragonese, leading to a last-stand revolt in the Battle of Macomer in 1478.

After more than 100 years of struggle with their subjects, the Aragonese were ready to wring what reward they could from Sardinia. Their rule was marked by feudalism and taxes designed to fund the Iberians' expansionist dreams. Sardinia's new landlords did their best to ethnically cleanse the island by replacing Sardo with Catalan as the official language and banishing the indigenous inhabitants from their fortified settlements.

The marriage of Isabella and Ferdinand in 1476 brought Spain's confederation of states into a unified monarchy and did little to help Sardinia's cause. While many Cagliaritani merchants and artists benefited from the profitable Spanish trade, political opponents were imprisoned and tortured, and elsewhere on the island, the neglected coast suffered from malaria outbreaks and Arab raids. As their empire declined in the 16th and 17th centuries, the Spaniards constructed hundreds of pirate watchtowers along the Sardinian shoreline but could rarely be bothered to come to the island's aid.

Austrians, Savoyards & Italian Unification

When the last Spanish Hapsburg, Charles II, died in 1700 without heirs, the Spanish Empire died along with him, leaving Sardinia for the taking once again. Like much of Europe, Sardinia divided its loyalties between Spain's two competing successors, the French and the Austrians, until an

About the island

Austrian-British alliance disembarked in Cagliari in 1708. Expanding their grip over much of Sardinia, the Austrians thwarted two French invasions until the Treaty of Utrecht officially placed the island under the control of the Austrio-Hungarian Empire in 1713.

Austrian rule over Sardinia lasted all of five years, after which it was passed to the growing independent state of Savoy based in Turin. The Dukes of Savoy were a power-hungry bunch who lacked a crown. Eager to claim a kingdom, they revitalized Pope Bonifacio VIII's long-forgotten Kingdom of Sardinia (see page 30) and sent a series of viceroys to rule in Cagliari. However, the Savoyards ultimately showed as little interest in their new kingdom as previous rulers, and Sardinia remained a neglected and impoverished colony.

The French Revolution brought more trouble. Lacking any Savoyard support, the Sardinians were forced to field a militia and fight off French attacks. In 1793, Sardinian forces succeeded in repelling a young Napoleon Bonaparte from the Maddalena islands. Following their heroic stand, Sardinians sought the same autonomous rights their neighbours enjoyed in Corsica but the Savoyard King Vittorio Amedeo III refused the request for constitutional reform, causing fiery uprisings to erupt throughout the island from 1794 to 1796, killing several royal administrators.

In the 19th century, two Savoyard kings finally showed more interest in the island: Carlo Felice (Happy Charlie: 1821-1831) built Sardinia's modern Cagliari–Porto Torres SS131 highway, and his successor, Carlo Alberto, sought to abolish Sardinia'a crippling feudalism in the 1830s and '40s. However, the existing Enclosure Act of 1823 privatized public land once harvested by Sardinia's peasants and economic reforms resulted in heavy taxation. In Sardinia's poorest regions, frustration often led to banditry. In 1847, Carlo Alberto merged the Kingdom of Sardinia with Piedmont, which gave Piedmontese lumberjacks a green light to deforest much of Sardinia for their own gain.

Despite its impoverished status, Sardinia played a central role in Italian unification in 1861. The island not only hosted the leader of the Risorgimento, Giuseppe Garibaldi who built his home on Caprera (see page 210), but also provided Italy's first king, Carlo Emanuele, when Italians voted to be annexed into the Kingdom of Sardinia, technically making Italy a part of Sardinia! Things began looking up for Sardinia in the late 19th century: the railway was completed in 1874, overseas trade re-emerged, educational funding increased and banks appeared, giving the Sardi access to credit for the first time.

20th century

The First World War saw Sardinians emerge as heroes of the young Italian nation, as the Brigata Sassari, an all-Sardinian brigade, fought valiantly on some of the war's most dangerous fronts (see page 235). When they returned home, many brigade members played critical roles in forming the Partito Sardo d'Azione, whose central goal was greater control for the Sardi over their own affairs.

Mussolini promoted various agricultural schemes, designed to turn Sardinia's malarial wastelands into profitable pastures and although 75% of Cagliari suffered bombing damage during World War Two, the rest of Sardinia escaped largely unscathed. The island was finally granted a degree of autonomy in 1948, when it was given its own Regional Council and President. More importantly, the US-funded Rockefeller Foundation provided the DDT needed to eliminate malaria from the coastal regions in 1951, thus opening up areas that had been largely inaccessible and unproductive since Carthaginian times. The 1950s also saw Sardinia selected as one of Italy's underdeveloped zones in need of funding by the Cassa del Mezzogiorno, an ambitious, $2 billion programme designed to lift southern Italy from its economic inertia. Recently drained swamps that had formerly been malarial

Making a statement in Nuoro.

breeding grounds were given to peasants in 15-acre plots, and millions of dollars were targeted at creating artificial lakes to bolster the island's electricity generation and irrigation capacities.

However, despite these occasional government handouts, in many ways Sardinia remained a neglected, backwater colony for much of the late 20th century, receiving as few favours from Rome as it had under its previous rulers. A series of unproductive industrial schemes in the 1960-70s littered the island with sprawling petrochemical plants owned by outside interests that still funnel most of the profits off the island. Similarly, the Costa Smeralda, which was developed by the Aga Khan in 1962 (see page 201) may have put Sardinia on the worldwide map, but the coast's profits headed offshore. With more NATO bases per square kilometre than anywhere else on Earth, parts of the island resemble a remote dumping ground for the industrial and military ventures that Italy depends on but doesn't want to look at.

But there's hope on the horizon. As the island slowly awakens to its own natural beauty, tourism has grown steadily since mainland Italians first started coming in the 1950s and is helping to drag Sardinia out of its economic hibernation. A lack of industry caused 45% of Sardinia's population to move to larger cities or off the island between 1955 and '75 but emigration has since slowed and unemployment dipped under 10% in 2007 for the first time in the island's history. As this once remote colony drifts closer and closer to its neighbours, only time will tell whether the Sardi can manage to foster a future of economic sustainability without sacrificing their ancient, cultural roots (see page 39).

Art & architecture

Nuraghe, Su Nuraxi.

Sardinia's most inspired architectural period was during the late Stone Age and early Bronze Age: proof that its residents were capable of monumental feats long before visitors came knocking. Since then, Sardinia's cultural history has been defined more by the artistic contributions of occupying cultures than by the creations of Sardinians themselves. While the island's tangled history of foreign rule has done much to cripple the local population's economic and political development, the mix of cultures has undoubtedly left Sardinia with a fascinating artistic heritage.

Neolithic & Nuraghic

Domus de Janas

These 'fairies' houses' are actually Neolithic tombs dug into the rock by the Ozieri culture (3500-2700 BC). There are more than 2,000 in Sardinia and they exist throughout the island except in Gallura. The tombs range from simple single rooms to elaborate multi-chambered necropoli. The more advanced examples have architectural elements, such as beams, vaults and pillars, representing the home of the living. Others show a bull's head carved into the outside of the chamber as a symbol of fertility. Alghero's **Anghelu Ruju** site preserves 37 stylized 'fairies' houses.' (see page 251).

Dolmen

Contemporaneous with the *domus de janas*, dolmen are single-chamber megalithic tombs made by sticking four rock slabs into the ground vertically and covering them with a fifth horizontal slab, like a table. **Luras** has several examples (see page 215).

Menhir

These 'long stones' are Neolithic religious monuments found throughout Europe, Africa and Asia. However, only those in Sardinia show etched figurative reliefs distinguishing the menhirs as male or female. Male menhirs are engraved with an upside down trident motif above and a double-edged dagger below, while female menhirs have protruding breasts. Many are clustered in groups and align with the sun or moon's astrological rotation. Goni's **Pranu Mutteddu** park (see page 95) and Laconi's museum (see page 95) are the best places to find them.

Nuraghe

Sardinia's most intriguing architectural monument has become synonymous with the island itself. In its simplest form, a nuraghe is a stone tower made without mortar by aligning heavy blocks in circles of diminishing circumference so that they form a truncated dome (*tholos*) that supports its own weight. A circular terrace supported by stone corbels originally capped the tower, though none of these survive. Less commonly, a central tower with a spiral staircase rises up to three stories and is connected to as many as five other towers by an enclosing wall.

The nuraghi are the world's first example of a circular tower and above-ground cupola. Like the Egyptian pyramids, the Sardi used ropes, wooden ramps, and a series of balances and weights to build these structures. **Su Nuraxi** (page 98), **Torralba** (page 246), **Arrubiu** (page 101) and **Losa** (page 151) are the most famous examples.

Bronzetti

Beginning around the 10th century BC the nuraghi builders' descendants started making elaborate miniature bronze statues. Artists modelled the figure in wax and then covered it with a clay mould that had a hole drilled in the top. When molten metal was poured on the object, the wax melted and the metal took the form of the figure. Many *bronzetti* have been retrieved near well temples, leading archaeologists to believe they were used as votive offerings. Cagliari's **Museo Archeologico** displays Sardinia's largest *bronzetti* collection (see page 82).

Tombe di Giganti

These Bronze Age graves date from roughly 1500 BC and derive from dolmen. They are characterized by a vast, rectangular chamber behind which bodies were buried, fronted by a semi-circular court (*exedra*). The name ('giants' tombs') most likely derives from their sheer size; some held more than 200 bodies. The most distinctive feature is the façade, which consists of vertically placed, smooth stone slabs that rise towards the centre stele, which is often elliptical. At the base of the stele is a small, symbolic entrance where relatives would offer gifts to the departed. The archaeological sites around **Arzachena** preserve the island's most impressive examples (see page 205).

Well temples

The nuraghi builders constructed these monuments to honour the sacred cult of spring water during the Final Bronze Age (1200-900 BC). Most temples are located near a nuraghe, have a stairwell shaped like a keyhole leading down to the water, and are enclosed by a *tholos* dome. **Santa Vittoria** near Serri (see page 100) and **Santa Cristina** outside Paulilatino (see page 150) are Sardinia's best preserved examples.

About the island

Punic & Roman

The Phoenicians and Carthaginians brought an artistic sensibility strongly influenced by their Egyptian and Greek trading partners: gold filigree jewellery, sinister masks used to repel evil spirits, and *tophet* steles with engraved columns flanking images of pharaohs.

The Romans created a system of roads and infrastructure typical of any proper Roman settlement. Theatres were built, bridges designed, aqueducts constructed, thermal baths dug and basalt roads laid. They constructed opulent country villas with mosaic floors and built monumental temples.

The **archaeological museums** in Cagliari (see page 82) and Sassari (see page 236) are full of Punic and Roman relics. **Nora** (see page 104), **Tharros** (see page 144) and **Sant'Antioco** (see page 107) are the best places to find Punic tophets. Roman ruins are still visible at **Fordongianus** (see page 150), **Nora**, **Tharros** and **Porto Torres** (see page 240), though for the best preserved Roman structure, head to Cagliari's **amphitheatre** (see page 83).

Byzantine & Romanesque

The Byzantines erected Sardinia's first three Christian churches at Cagliari, Sant'Antioco and San Giovanni. The fifth-century structures were designed on a Greek cross plan with a dome over the centre. The Middle Ages saw a burst of creativity in Sardinia as the independent *giudicati* (sovereign states) facilitated a collaboration between Benedictine monks, local artists and craftsmen from Iberia, Provence and Pisa to create over 100 Romanesque churches; a cluster can be found in the **Logudoro** region (see page 243). **Santissima Trinità di Saccargia** in Codrongianos (see page 244) and **Nostra Signora di Regnos Altos** in Bosa (see page 153) are good examples.

Catalan-Gothic & Sardinia's Stampace School

Aragonese rule in the 14th century essentially ended the creative collaboration between the Sardi and Pisans and ushered in a phase of Catalan-Gothic church building until the 17th century. Cagliari's **Basilica di Nostra Signora di Bonaria** (see page 89) was the first and remains one of the most famous.

Local artists found a particular niche creating Catalan-derived retables or altarpieces, many of which can be seen in Cagliari's **Pinacoteca Nazionale** (see page 83). Iberian artists, such as Joan Mates, Rafael Thomas and Joan Figuera, inspired local artists, including the enigmatic Maestro di Castelsardo, who is named after his *Madonna con gli Angeli* retable in **Castelsardo** (see page 255), and Giovanni Muru, known for his contribution to Ardara's **Chiesa di Santa Maria del Regno** (see page 244). Their work laid the foundations for the creation of Cagliari's Stampace School, which nurtured the talent of Pietro Cavaro, painter of *Santi Pietro e Paolo* (now in the Pinacoteca Nazionale), and the Maestro di Ozieri, who created the *Madonna di Loreto* retable (see page 243). The 18th century saw a fusion of Gothic and Baroque architecture in Sardinia. The most significant examples are **San Michele** in Cagliari (see page 85), **San Nicola** in Sassari (see page 238) and **Santa Maria Assunta** in Oristano (see page 138).

Modernity & *murales*

Following unification, Italy experienced a period of neoclassical urban planning focusing on the principles of proportion and symmetry.

Contemporary art became increasingly popular in Sardinia in the early 20th century. Artistic expression shifted away from the stylized techniques imported or absorbed from elsewhere, and moved towards subjects and themes particular to the island's nascent regional identity.

A mural in Muravera presents an ironic view of the changing face of rural Sardinia.

The island produced a remarkable group of talented painters at this time, the most famous being painter Giuseppe Biasi and sculptor Francesco Ciusa. Biasi was a non-conformist who started drawing as a cartoon illustrator in his native Sassari before collaborating with Grazia Deledda to create her book covers. Much of his work is characterized by dark oil paintings of everyday rural Sardinian life that reflect the overwhelming poverty of the region. Biasi's friend, Ciusa, received international acclaim after winning the grand prize at Venice's Biennale art festival in 1907 for his poignant sculpture *Mother of the Murdered*, which depicted a peasant mother grieving in silent anguish. (It is now displayed at Cagliari's **Galleria Comunale d'Arte**, see page 87.)

After the Second World War, many sculptors found inspiration in Ciusa's work, adding their own twists. One was Costantino Nivola, a former stonemason who fled the Fascist regime in 1939 with his Jewish wife and emigrated to New York. The museum in his hometown of Orani houses many of his architectural sculptures.

Nuoro's **MAN** museum (see page 167) houses Sardinia's most complete collection of modern art, while the 20th-century heavyweights like Biasi and Ciusa are displayed at Cagliari's **Galleria Comunale d'Arte** (see page 87).

The most visible artistic development in recent years is the Sardinian *murales* movement, derived from Latin America, which was adopted by the residents of Orgosolo in 1975 to celebrate the 30th anniversary of the fall of Fascism. The trend has since spread from town to town, wall to wall, with an estimated 3000 murals currently lining the streets in Sardinia. The themes of many murals are heartbreaking and depict the pain and suffering the Sardi have endured from a history of poverty, isolation and foreign domination. Others are almost triumphant and are meant to renew a sense of *Sardità* or regional pride. The *murales* capital, **Orgosolo** is known for its politically charged, abstract designs (see page 170), while **Fonni** (see page 180) and **San Sperate** employ *trompe l'oeil* techniques. For a visual sneak preview, check out muralesinsardegna.net.

Sardinia today

Pelosa beach.

Sardità

The sea and the mountains have been formative factors in the shaping of the Sardinian identity. In different ways, they have contributed to the islanders' isolation, both from the outside world and from each other, causing many towns to develop independently from their neighbours. However, isolation has also helped preserve the island's ancient traditions – no other Italian region remains as attached to its folk roots as Sardinia – and what binds all Sardinians is an unwavering

pride in their identity and heritage, something the Sardi call 'Sardità'.

History has forced the Sardi to rely on themselves and their island for survival, producing an introspective culture that is bound to the land and initially wary of outsiders. As a result, Sardinians are probably the most socially conservative Italians you'll meet, and visitors, whether from a different commune or country, will inevitably receive some lingering stares on the

Sardigna non est Italia

- Sardinia is the only region in Italy whose native inhabitants are recognized as ethnically distinct from the rest of the country by constitutional law.

- Sardinia is one of five special-status areas in Italy granted a degree of legislative autonomy; it also has its own president.

- Sardinians speak Sardo. Italian and Sardo are the official languages of the Sardinian government.

- Sardinians usually identify themselves as Sardo first and Italian second, often referring to the mainland as 'il continente'.

- Sardistas continue to dream of Sardinian independence and almost every town on the island has a variation of the graffiti tag 'Sardigna non est Italia!' (Sardinia isn't Italy!).

street. Even in the cosmopolitan capital, the Cagliaritani are careful never to say the first and last name of someone they're talking about in public, and they would never approach someone of the opposite sex at a bar without first being introduced. At the same time, Sardinians are famous throughout Italy for their hospitality. Visitors who show interest in the local customs and culture may find themselves whisked around on an impromptu tour of the village, treated to drinks or invited home for dinner.

To Italians, the Sardi are a brawny, backwater bunch who raise sheep and live in huts, sensitive about their reputation and fiercely proud of their island. It's no wonder, then, that in the Italian TV version of *The Simpsons*, Groundskeeper Willy, the resolutely independent Scot who lives in a shack, speaks with a dubbed Sardinian accent.

Delve beyond the stereotypes and you'll find that the Sardi are protectors of their home-grown cuisine and, on average, live longer than anywhere else on Earth except Okinawa, Japan. They produce talented poets, politicians, jockeys, debaters and storytellers. While Italians tend to marginalize Sardinians' lack of urban sophistication, the Sardi prove that you can still make a *bella figura* in dignity, sincerity and simplicity.

Sardo

Unlike other regions, Sardinia doesn't have a divergent Italian dialect but an entirely different language, Sardo. Sardo is the largest minority language in Italy and the backbone of *Sardità*. Distinctly fragmented dialects of Sardo are spoken in different parts of the island, so to understand the local jargon is to understand something of Sardinia's history of upheaval.

Sociolinguists agree that Sardo is the closest living form to Latin.

Like French, Spanish or Italian, Sardo is a Romance language rooted in Latin which was introduced to the island during the 700-odd years of Roman rule. Sardinia's subsequent invaders peppered Sardo with a few words from their own tongues but the long power vacuum that followed the fall of Rome enabled Sardinians to preserve the language's ancient roots. Today, sociolinguists agree that Sardo is the closest living form to Latin; its grammar and over 500 words are nearly identical to that used during the Roman Empire: eg *domus* (house), *janna* (door), etc. There are also more distant words, stemming from Sardinia's earliest indigenous people, that often refer to geological formations or animals, such as *giara* (plateau), *marxani* (fox) and *nuraghe*.

There are two main groups of Sardo: Lugodorese, the purest form, is spoken in the north, while Campidanese, which retains more influences from Pisan invaders, is spoken in the south. Within these, there are so many deviating subgroups – from western Oristanese to Nuoro's

When people lose their language, they lose their identity.

Gavino Ledda, Padre Padrone.

Barbaricina and Cagliari's Cagliaritano – that, in reality, every Sardinian town speaks a different version that is seldom well understood by other communities. To make matters more complicated still, there are also pockets of Sardinia where the local language has nothing to do with Sardo at all. In Alghero residents still cling to a medieval form of Catalan introduced by the Aragonese. Carloforte's residents speak Tabarkino, a mixture of old-time Ligurian mixed with North African, and the northeastern Gallurese dialect has been shaped by a history of Corsican immigration.

Speaking Sardo

Speak Italian to a Sardinian and they'll respond; speak Sardo to a Sardinian and they'll smile. Here are a few common expressions that are sure to be well received:

Ajò (pronounced 'i-yo') or
 Andausu (an-dahu-zu) – let's go!
Eja (a-ya) – yes
Boh (bowh) – I don't know.
A si biri! (ah zi beer ee) – see you soon.
Adiosu (ah-dee-o-su) – goodbye.

Alghero.

Trying to make sense of a language that changes within a 10-minute drive has long impeded the island's unity and has encouraged many younger Sardinians to speak Italian. Today, the island's greatest writers have all abandoned Sardo, opting for wider audiences over localized heritage, and, with the exception of a nightly news broadcast in both Italian and Sardo on the regional Videolina channel, the island's TV is produced exclusively in Italian.

However, Sardinia's regional government is now trying to reverse the trend. A study, which showed that the percentage of Sardinians identifying themselves as fluent in Sardo had dropped from 80% in 1990 to 68% in 2006, prompted the creation of a government committee charged with finding common attributes between the hundreds of Sardo dialects to form a single hybrid language. Surprisingly, it seems to have worked. Nearly 93% percent of the population seems to understand this version of Sardo and it was adopted as the official legislative language of the island alongside Italian in 2007.

Cultural crossroads

Modern Sardinia is searching for a middle ground between preserving the unique qualities that lure tourists to the island, and trying to build its way out of a history of economic inertia by promoting its tourist industry.

There are pockets of Sardinia where the local language has nothing to do with Sardo at all.

The historical lack of industry that drew DH Lawrence to Sardinia has kept its economy non-competitive and the island's natural beauty is offset by its man-made lack of opportunity. Sardinians are hemmed in by some of the lowest median wages in Western Europe, hovering at roughly €1,050 a month. Couple that with a 35% unemployment rate for those under 35, and it's not surprising that many young Sardinians have moved to the island's cities and to the mainland in search of work. Today, nearly half of the population lives in or around Cagliari and Sassari, and Sardinia's small

The loss of traditional agriculture is likely to have serious consequences for the island.

towns, where the island's proud heritage is at its strongest, are shrinking. To help combat the rampant depopulation, in 2008 several villages in the Barbagie started offering couples upwards of €1,000 for every child they bore.

Instead of spending money to combat the lack of infrastructure and industry around the region's endangered rural areas, Sardinia is funnelling its capital into tourism. At first glance, this seems like an encouraging development: the island's tourist industry has grown steadily since 1995, RyanAir opened two hubs in Sardinia in spring 2009 and Cagliari is awaiting a world-class €30-million art centre designed by Zaha Hadid, due in 2012. However, the tourist expansion comes at the expense of Sardinia's shepherds, the guardians of the island's pastoral traditions.

In 1988, Sardinia's government started offering generous subsidies to shepherds to help curb emigration but, in 2006, the EU determined that the loans were illegal and forced the shepherds to repay them with interest. Many haven't been able to pay back these substantial debts and up to 5,000 farms have been affected, with many auctioned off by the court in late 2007, despite desperate pleas and hunger strikes from their beleaguered owners.

As the Costa Smeralda proved in the 1960s, coastal pastures represent valuable real estate for development vultures. Although pecorino cheese may not drive the economy like beachside resorts, the loss of traditional agriculture is likely to have serious environmental and social consequences for the island. In November 2008, the island's Decreto Soru law, which prohibited any development within 2 km of Sardinia's coast in an effort to

A shepherd from the Marmilla.

preserve its natural beauty and restore vitality to the interior, was not renewed. Upon hearing the Regional Council's vote, Sardinia's then-President Renato Soru addressed his colleagues: "To not recognize the ecological and cultural effects of what you've just done is a serious mistake," he said, and then resigned.

Nature & environment

Sardinia is the second-largest island in the Mediterranean at 24,090 sq km, barely smaller than Sicily but with only a third as many people (1.65 million) and an overwhelming sense of space. Its diverse landscapes are as unpredictable as the winds that shape its shores. You can pass from the snow-capped peaks of the Gennargentu, to the desert dunes of the Costa Verde, to lagoons where flamingos nest around the Sinis or Cagliari within a day. You'll often hear the Sardi say, Sardinia is more than an island; it's a continent.

Geologically, Sardinia predates Italy and is one of the oldest places in Europe. Sandstone deposits formed the Sulcis-Iglesiente during the early Cambrian period and volcanoes later spewed out enough trachyte, basalt and obsidian to make the island's geology as tumultuous as its history. Undulating *mammelle* hills flatten to tabletop *giare* (plateaus) or tilt into mountain massifs without any rhyme or reason, rendering only 14 per cent of the island flat. Yet, compared to its next-door neighbour Corsica, Sardinia's mountains aren't especially high, peaking at **Punto Lamarmora** (1,834 m) outside Fonni. The granite **Gennargentu** and limestone **Supramonte** are the largest mountain areas on the island and cover much of Nuoro and Ogliastra provinces in Sardinia's centre and east. Time and weather have eroded a labyrinth of sinkholes and caves in the island's core, leaving it with more caves than anywhere else in Italy and Europe's deepest ravine, **Gola Gorroppu.**

Page opposite: Capo d'Orso. Above: Tree frog.

Sardinia is more than an island; it's a continent.

The Piedmontese deforested much of Sardinia's interior in the 19th century, when they mined for coal and downed trees to build Italy's railroads, but there are still shady swathes of holm oak, cork oak, pine and protected juniper trees around Sardinia's mountainous slopes that shelter a variety of fox, mouflon (horned wild sheep), vulture, raven and the rare golden eagle. The areas around **Pattada** and **Monte Limbara** are especially wooded, as are southern Sardinia's basalt plateaus and the **Sette Fratelli** park. Outside Cagliari, the 3,600-ha **Monte Arcosu** reserve is the largest forest in the Mediterranean.

Much more common than forest, however, is the prickly green Mediterranean *macchia* that dominates Sardinia's rolling countryside. These dense patches of heather, lentisk, thyme, myrtle, rosemary and arbutus erupt in an organic perfume and sprout a sea of wild flowers each spring. Sardinians will tell you that the most valuable of these varieties is undoubtedly the myrtle plant, whose violet berries are used to make the island's beloved *digestivo, mirto*. Where the thick *macchia* permits, pockets of violets and periwinkles also bloom, and many of the island's plateaus shelter rare species of orchid. Green prickly pears and rainbow-coloured oleander flowers add a splash of variety to the golden wheat fields of Sardinia's only extensive valley, the southern **Campidano**, which extends from Cagliari north toward Oristano. Like Sardinians themselves, many of the island's indigenous animals tend to be slightly smaller than those of continental Europe. Among them are the

cinghiale sardo (Sardinian wild boar), which lives throughout the island's woods, and the elusive *cervo sardo* (Sardinian deer), which was nearly poached to extinction in the 1970s but has been recovering steadily in numbers since its reintroduction around Monte Arcosu and southern Sardinia. In addition, the world's only species of miniature albino donkeys is found on **Asiniara island,** and squat, wild *cavallini* horses roam the **Giara di Gesturi.** Other residents include wild cats, rabbits, martens and weasels, as well as the Sardinian skink (lizard).

The island's three main rivers are the **Coghinas** in the north, the **Flumendosa** in the east, and the longest and most important, the **Tirso** in the west. This last is fed by the snow and rainfall from the Gennargentu mountains and, in turn, nourishes eucalyptus trees and citrus groves east of Oristano. Sardinia only has one natural lake (**Baratz**, near Alghero) but, during the 20th century, many of Sardinia's rivers were dammed to form artificial lakes in an effort to stabilize the island's water supply and irrigation. Among them is Italy's largest artificial lake, **Omodeo.** Sardinia's rivers also feed into an extensive network of saltpans, lagoons and wetlands that buffer its coasts, creating an ideal habitat for migratory birds. The largest concentration of these marshes is around Cagliari

Top: The skink twists its way through the Sardinian landscape. Above: A mouflon (wild sheep).

A young local eyes up a cormorant.

and Oristano, where more than 200 species of migratory birds, including herons, harriers, coots, cranes, cormorants, stilts and ducks, come to ruffle their feathers between September and June. The most popular seasonal resident is undoubtedly the pink flamingo, which has been nesting in Sardinia since 1993. The **Stagno di Cabras** in the west is the largest marsh in Europe and teems with bass, mullet and eel, among other fishy finds.

Sardinia's rivers feed into a network of saltpans, lagoons and wetlands, creating an ideal habitat for migratory birds.

The 1,849 km of seashore that frames Sardinia constitutes roughly one quarter of Italy's entire coastline and is far and away the country's most pristine: at the last count, 97% was deemed suitable for bathing. Nature remains hard at work sculpting Sardinia's beaches with near-constant winds: the western *ponente* (poniente) piles Europe's tallest dunes at **Piscinas**, the northern *maestrale* (mistral) carves bizarre granite formations and deep bays in the **Gallura**, and the southeastern *scirocco* (sirocco) dusts Cagliari's cars and beaches with sand from the Sahara after rainstorms.

Look out for turtles who lay their eggs along the **Costa Verde**; dolphins who swim around **La Maddalena** islands and **Capo Caccia**; griffon vultures who nest between **Bosa** and **Capo Caccia**, and peregrine falcons who hover above the limestone cliffs of the **Golfo di Orosei** and the **Riviera del Corallo**, when not migrating to Madagascar each November. Prawns, lobsters and sea urchins are found all around the island's rocky shores (and in its numerous seafood restaurants), and barracuda have shown increasing interest in the island's warm seas. Divers will have a field day exploring Sardinia's many karstic underwater grottoes, including **Nereo** near Alghero, which is the biggest underwater cave in the Mediterranean.

Festivals & events

La Sartiglia Festival in Oristano.

More than 1,000 festivals take place in Sardinia every year (more than in any other Italian region), with many drenched in the influences of the island's past. Some traditions, such as the rural novenaria celebrations, hark back to the Bronze Age and are rooted in Pagan rites. Others are steeped in Punic, Roman, Byzantine and, above all, Spanish customs. Sagre (harvest festivals) still mark the passage from one season to another, and each town always honours its patron saint.

Most festivals, whether they be literary competitions, feasts or parades, are celebrated with traditional songs, dances and costumes. Rather than spectacles for tourists' cameras, these celebrations are genuinely local affirmations of Sardinian pride and identity: the essence of *Sardità*. Never turn down an invitation from a local to attend a festival: from town-wide processions to small gatherings in the woods, the Sardi are famous for indulging their guests and making them feel at home.

Festa di Sant'Antonio Abate (16-17th)

This celebration harks back to Pagan rites marking the winter solstice. Dorgali, Bosa, Desulo, Orosei and other towns pray to Saint Antonio for miracles and then light a giant bonfire in their squares. In Mamoiada, the *Mamuthones* awaken, while Ottana sees the *Merdules e Boes* parade through the streets in otherworldly, animalistic masks.

Merdules e Boes parade in Ottana.

February

Carnevale (the week before Ash Wednesday)

The central Barbagie continues its ghoulish parades, particularly in Gavoi, Ollolai and Orotelli, and daredevil horsemen race in Oristano's Sartiglia (see page 139) and Santu Lussurgiu's Carrela 'e Nanti (see page 148). For more on Carnival in the Barbagie, see page 171.

March/April

Settimana Santa (Easter week)

Holy Week is marked by mock-funerals and silent processions throughout Sardinia, many of which still show the influence of the island's former Spanish rulers. Some that stand out are the Passion of the Christ procession in Alghero, where confraternity members don Spanish-influenced robes, and the Good Friday procession in Iglesias (see page 126). Also recommended are the S'Incontru parade at Oliena, the Su Concordu Gregorian chants in Santu Lussurgiu and the Lunissanti feast in Castelsardo.

Sagra del Torrone (Easter Monday)

Tonara, Sardinia's *torrone* (nougat) capital, hosts a festival with plenty of samples and demonstrations showing how the sweet is made.

April/May

Sa Festa Manna (15 days after Easter)

The oldest festival in Sardinia takes place on the island of Sant'Antioco and celebrates the African immigrant credited with bringing Christianity to the island. Folk groups parade the streets and women make the island's famous *coccoisi* bread.

May

Sant'Efisio (1st-4th)

Sardinia's most famous festival pays tribute to Cagliari's patron saint who rid the island of the plague in the 17th century. Thousands of people parade through the streets on ox-pulled carriages before trekking to Nora and back with a statue of the saint (see page 85).

Sagra degli Agrumi (first week)

Like a scaled-down version of Sant'Efisio, revellers parade through Muravera in costume to celebrate the citrus harvest, followed by music and dancing.

About the island

Carrela 'e Nanti in Santu Lussurgui.

Novena di San Francesco d'Assisi (1st-9th)
Pilgrims arrive in Lula on foot from throughout Monte Albo, congregating at a Baroque church.

Cavalcata Sarda (penultimate Sunday)
Sardinians throughout the island descend on Sassari, where participants parade through the streets. The procession culminates with dancing. A horse race takes place the afternoon before.

June

Madonna dei Martiri (Monday after first Sunday)
Fonni's faithful carry a statue of the Virgin from their basilica through the town.

Girotonno (late May-early June)
To honour Carloforte's *mattanza* tuna catch (see page 109), the town puts on a food festival.

July

Ardia (6th-7th)
Sardinia's bareback Palio-style horserace in Sedilo is dedicated to San Costantino. Spectators watch jockeys fly around a sanctuary dedicated to the local martyr as gunshots are fired (see page 152).

Sagra delle Pesche (17th)
Little San Sperate marks its peach harvest by celebrating in its mural-decorated streets.

August

Is Fassonis (last Sunday of July to first Sunday of August)
Fishermen from around the Sinis Peninsula race through the Santa Giusta lagoon on handmade *fassonis* rafts that have changed little since Phoenician times.

Arresojas (late July-early August)
Each summer since 1994, the abandoned mining compound of Montevecchio holds a fair displaying some of the finest, largest and oldest handmade knives from the Gusipini and Arbus region.

Sagra del Vino (4th)
Things can get messy at this generous wine-tasting gala in Jerzu, one of Sardinia's Cannonau capitals. Come well fed.

Time in Jazz (9th-15th)
Sardinia's resident jazz maestro, Paolo Fresu, returns to his hometown of Berchidda with an eclectic gang of world-class musicians to jam in the woods, on stages and in country villas.

Li Candaleri (14th)
One of the island's most colourful festivals sees nine enormous candle towers paraded through the streets of Sassari (see page 239).

Madonna Assunta (15th)
Introduced by the Byzantines, the cult of the 'Risen Madonna' is celebrated throughout Sardinia when women in traditional costume carry a statue of the sleeping Virgin around town. The largest processions are in Cagliari, Orgosolo and Domusnovas.

Festa del Redentore (29th)
Nuoro hosts roughly 100,000 spectators for its lively procession in traditional costume up to Monte Ortobene in honour of Christ the Redeemer.

Cabudanne de sos Poetas (end of the month)
A literary festival in Seneghe, with poetry competitions as well as music, food and dancing.

Corsa degli Scalzi (first weekend)
On the Sinis Peninsula, thousands of local men don white mantles and run barefoot from Cabras to the rural sanctuary at San Salvatore, 7 km away, to hide a statue of the Madonna, just as they did hundreds of years ago (see page 143).

Premio Biennale (third Saturday)
Ozieri hosts Sardinia's most important poetry competition in honour of Antonio Cubeddu, the local man who first organized the island's *poesia a bolu* competitions.

Autunno in Barbagie (September to December)
This is an open-house invitation to see the traditions kept alive in the rural communities of the Barbagie. A different town hosts the event each weekend (see page 191).

Rassegna del Vino Novello (early October)
Milis celebrates the production of the season's new wines with one helluva party in its town square (see page 147).

Sagra delle Castagne e Nocciole (fourth Sunday)
You can smell the roasting chestnuts and hazelnuts from nearby Belvì at this harvest celebration in Aritzo. Folk groups sing and dance at night.

Festa della Madonna dello Schiavo (15th)
Carloforte honours its patron saint by parading a statue of the black Virgin through town. The statue is said to have watched over kidnapped residents of Carloforte who saw it washed up on shore in Tunisia while working as slaves in 1800.

Christmas (24th and 25th)
Many churches display elaborate nativity scenes and devout Sardi attend midnight mass. The day is usually spent with family.

Cap d'Any (31st)
Alghero puts on a festive New Year celebration with fireworks above the medieval bastions. Other popular celebrations take place in Cagliari, Sassari, Olbia, and Castelsardo.

Sleeping

Camping on the beach.

Accommodation in Sardinia is varied enough to suit billionaire and backpacker alike. As the island has slowly awakened to its potential as a tourist destination, the range and overall quality of accommodation has greatly improved. Since the boom of the Costa Smeralda in the 1960s, copycat luxury resorts have sprouted throughout Sardinia, allowing upmarket visitors more opportunity to explore the island without sacrificing comfort. The latest trend in Sardinia's cities and towns is to faithfully restore antique palazzi and transform them into modestly priced B&Bs with old-world elegance. For those seeking something more adventurous and unquestionably Sardinian, no trip to the island is complete without spending at least one night in an *agriturismo* (farmhouse B&B).

From ritzy resorts to casual campsites, there are a few constants that apply to all accommodation on the island:

- Lodgings closer to the coast are generally more expensive than those found inland.
- Accommodation prices rise during the high season (July to September) and peak in the two weeks around Ferragosto (15th August).
- During July and August hotels throughout Sardinia fill quickly, so if you plan to visit during this period, book months ahead.
- Hotels and resorts that are popular often require a minimum stay of several days during their peak season; others may insist on half- or full-board.
- Those visiting out of season should note that many facilities shut down between late October and Easter.
- All accommodation requires guests to check in with a valid picture ID card; a passport is preferred to a driver's licence.

Resorts

Sardinia is home to some of the Mediterranean's most stylish and expensive resorts. From the Costa Smeralda and its five-star neighbours to the swathe of luxury getaways hidden around Santa Margherita, Palau and Villasimius, the vast majority of these pamper-palaces are built with real architectural flair and good taste. Just don't think about checking in unless you have a very full wallet: you may spend anything between €500 and €2,000 a night for a double in the summer!

Inevitably, the vast majority of Sardinia's resorts are built on or near the coast and come with private beaches. Most offer enough activities, such as sailing trips, diving excursions and windsurfing instruction, to ensure that their guests never feel the need to leave the resort's confines. A variety of restaurants is usually on hand, as are spas, pools and babysitting services.

Multiple options are usually available. Several resorts offer luxury hotel stays (Villasimius' Timi Ama and most complexes around Porto Rotondo and Baia Sardinia); others offer detached suite apartments (such as throughout the Costa Smeralda), and several offer guests the choice of both (Santa Margherita's Forte Village).

Hotels

In general, hotels in Sardinia are disappointing. Before the 1950s, the island's lack of tourists meant that there were very few hotels around. Most that you see today were built faily recently and suffer from the same lack of imagination that has plagued post-war architecture throughout Italy. While you will rarely encounter a hotel without air conditioning or private bathrooms, many seem outdated. If you do chance upon a hotel that combines character, class and comfort, it is likely to come with a resort price tag.

In Sardinia's cities and larger towns (Cagliari, Sassari, Oristano), hotels tend to cater to the business crowd. The closer to the coast you travel, the more hotels tend to resemble full-on resorts. Those located in popular tourist destinations are often affiliated with excursion outfitters and can organize day trips for you. A good resource for Sardinia's better hotels and villas is paridisola.com.

Tip...

In October 2008, Sardinia became the first Italian region to switch from cable to digital television. As part of the change, residents must buy a converter box or purchase new TVs that fit the updated format. While most facilities advertise that they have televisions in each room, some groups have been slow to make the change. If a working TV is important to you, determine whether the hotel's TVs are digitally equipped before booking.

About the island

B&Bs

Where Sardinia's hotels are often modern, impersonal affairs, the island has a burgeoning selection of stylishly restored B&Bs that brim with character at a fraction of the price of larger hotels. Many B&Bs are tucked into the residential historic districts of larger towns or cities, providing an unbeatable location and an open-door invitation to live like a local for a few days.

Double rooms usually cost between €50 and €70 a night, come with their own bathroom, modern comforts and an invaluable asset: your host. B&B owners are almost always local, knowledgeable and keen to make sure you enjoy your stay in their town. It's rare to find a host who speaks polished English but with maps, a dictionary and a little patience, you may well find that they are a more valuable source of information than the local tourist board. Check out sardegnabb.it for a list of B&Bs around the island.

Agriturismi

You won't find accommodation that is more faithful to the spirit of Sardinia than the *agriturismo*. An *agriturismo* is a working farm that takes paying guests. Visitors book *agriturismi* because they offer an unparalleled glimpse into the island's authentic rural heritage. With very reasonable prices and plenty of opportunities to get your hands dirty on the farm, a good farm stay can be the highlight of a Sardinian holiday.

You won't find accommodation that is more faithful to the spirit of Sardinia than the *agriturismo*.

There are nearly 600 *agriturismi* in rural Sardinia, with most clustered around Gallura, Oristano and Nuoro. Accommodation varies but most are more functional than fancy. In some cases, guests live like a member of the family, stay in the guest bedroom and eat meals at the family table. More commonly, guests stay in ranch-style detached apartments clustered around a central building where meals are served. Rooms almost always have their own bathrooms and, increasingly, air conditioning, but if you want luxury, this style of accommodation is probably not for you.

Agriturismi are famous for their four- or five-course meals, so book a dinner when you book your room. The owners often raise sheep, chickens, horses, goats and pigs by day, and serve them to you as part of the evening meal at night, so you never have to worry about the freshness. Following most meals, the chef or owner usually makes the rounds to ask guests how they enjoyed the food. The website agriturismodisardegna.it is a good resource.

A healthy hotel breakfast.

Campsites

There are roughly 100 campsites in Sardinia and most are by a beach. A basic tent space with use of the showers and parking costs between €10 and €20. Some sites also have hotel-priced bungalows and mini villas with their own showers and kitchenettes. Campsites generally have a pizzeria, restaurant, playground and, often, a pool and are practical ways to enjoy Sardinia's famous coastline without paying exorbitant prices. Most are only open between May and October and fill quickly in high season, so book ahead.

Campsites are practical ways to enjoy Sardinia's famous coastline without paying exorbitant prices.

Both campeggievillaggi.it/en/camping-Sardegna.html and campeggi.com are useful links for campers.

Hostels

There are very few hostels in Sardinia and those that exist aren't usually found in key tourist destinations. Compared to others throughout Europe, Sardinian hostels aren't cheap (between €12 and €35 a night). Some hostels have an evening curfew starting as early as 2200. Search ostellionline.org for a complete list.

Sheep at the *agriturismo* Su Costiolu, north of Nuoro.

Eating & drinking

Piglets roasting on an open fire…

Sardinia's isolation and poverty have combined to preserve the most distinct regional cuisine in Italy. Until fairly recently, most Sardi couldn't afford to import foods from across the sea so their tables did not feature Italian favourites. Instead, they depended on combining their own simple, home-grown ingredients. The result is a diverse regional menu whose highlights are not found anywhere else: paper-thin 'music sheet' bread, saffron-hinted dumplings, suckling pig wrapped in aromatic leaves and slow-roasted in makeshift underground ovens, and a digestive liqueur made from myrtle berries, to name a few.

Although surrounded by water, most of Sardinia's signature dishes are meat-based. However, as invaders, immigrants and tourists have come and gone, the island has absorbed outside culinary influences and has awakened to the mouth-watering potential of its marine resources, such as spicy Catalan lobster, mullet roe grated over clams and mussels, and some of the world's most sought-after tuna. Seafood restaurants have proliferated, especially around the coasts.

So, while you can certainly find pizza, lasagne, ethnic restaurants and Irish pubs in Sardinia's principal cities, if you're smart and just a little adventurous, you'll sample the local specialities.

Antipasti

Sardinian antipasti are designed to be a lighter preview of what is to come but as the portions are large, they can comprise a full meal. The most common starters are *verdure miste* (mixed vegetables) and *antipasto di terra*, in which salted sausage, *salame* and *prosciutto* are displayed alongside Sardinia's breads and cheeses (see below), often on a tray of cork bark.

Sardinia's most famous seafood ingredient, Cabras' *bottarga* (mullet roe; see page 142), is served thinly sliced and drizzled with oil on bread. You'll also find *buccinis* (molluscs) or *arselle* (clams), served in a broth with parsley and lemon. Around Cagliari, *ricci* (sea urchin) and *burrida* (dogfish stew with hazelnuts) are also popular.

Bread

No Sardinian meal would be complete without bread and there are hundreds of different varieties. Each village traditionally has its own version, with additional loaves baked for special occasions.

The most famous variety is the *pane carasau*, often called *carta da musica* (music sheet) bread because it's paper-thin and cannot exceed three millimeters in depth. Dipped in olive oil and dashed with salt, *pane carasau* becomes *pane guttiau*. A thicker, rectangular and slightly harder version is *pane pistoccu*, a traditional shepherds' treat from the Sarrabus and Ogliastra.

Pane civraxiu ('chee-vrah-shew') is one of the island's most popular breads, thanks to its circular shape and dark, thick crust, which make it perfect for scooping leftovers from your plate! Around Ozieri and Gallura, *pane spianada* is a light circular loaf that was once decorated and served for feasts but is now eaten daily.

How to eat like a local

Sardinians have adopted the mainland-style breakfast, which is a quick, sugar-infused wake-up call doused with caffeine. Most hotels, B&Bs and *agriturismi* will offer a variety of meats and cheeses to accommodate their guests' diets, though locals do not consume such filling fare before noon. Instead, Sardi head to a bar or café, where they typically order a *pasta* (pastry) or *cornetto* (croissant) and down it with a cappuccino (strictly a breakfast drink).

Sardi generally sit down for *pranzo* (lunch) between 1300 and 1400, and linger at the table during their generous afternoon siesta. When lunching out, locals may order a main dish, a *contorno* (side dish) or *insalata* and a drink, totalling €15 to €25. *Cena* (dinner) is eaten between 2000 and 2200 and is a multiple-course, belt-loosening affair, consisting of mixed antipasti with bread and cheese, a *primo* of pasta or seafood, a *secondo* of meat or fish, and a *contorno* or *dolce*. It will cost €30 to €50, depending on how many courses you order. Most Sardi would never mix seafood with meat, though no one will bat an eyelid if you do. Top it all off with a *digestivo* and a toast ("*Cin-cin*") – looking your partner in the eye as you clink glasses – and get ready for the *passeggiata*.

Typical home-made Sardinian biscuits.

About the island

Cheese

Sardinia is to pecorino what Naples is to pizza and Parma is to *prosciutto*. Sardinia produces 80% of all Italian pecorino and the island boasts three DOP (*Denominazione d'origine protetta*) varieties. *Fiore sardo* is the most famous and has been produced by shepherds since long before they learned to make nuraghi. It consists of whole sheep's milk aged for four to six months in a damp place and often smoked over herbs. *Pecorino sardo* comes in two distinct varieties: *dolce* (sweet), which can be eaten a month after production, and *maturo* (mature), which should be aged for two to 12 months. Finally, there's *pecorino romano*, which originated in Lazio but is now primarily made in Sardinia.

Ricotta is one of Sardinia's best known (and healthiest) creamy cheeses and can come from goat, sheep or cow's milk. The three most common varieties are *gentile*, which is sweet and never aged, *salata* (salted) and *mustìa*, which is dry and smoked.

Pasta & first courses

The secret ingredient in many of Sardinia's distinct *primi piatti* is saffron, which is cultivated around San Gavino Monreale in the southern Campidano. The aromatic spice finds its way into Sardinia's two most typical first courses: *malloreddus*, which are dumplings rolled by thumb around a ridged surface and typically served *alla campidanese* (with sausage, tomato sauce and grated pecorino), and *fregola* (or *fregula*), which are small, circular grains of bran similar to couscous, best eaten covered in a sauce with mussels or clams.

Culurgiones are oblong ravioli rolled by hand. Around Ogliastra they come stuffed with potatoes and mint; in the south they're packed with cheese, laced with olive oil and sprinkled with crushed walnuts; and around Gallura they're made with sugar and traces of lemon inside a ricotta filling.

Maccarones de busa are common around Nuoro and are formed by piercing semolina dough with metal wire so that it absorbs the ricotta, garlic and tomato sauce that usually accompanies it.

Tip...

Always buy pecorino cheeses whole rather than grated to retain the flavour.

Pecorino cheese.

Still hungry?

Sardinians have never wasted a potential meal when times were tough. During the Second World War, residents in Cagliari's suburb, Quartu, resorted to eating cats and dogs to avoid starvation. While those days are long gone, the Sardi have always had a knack for turning stomach-churning ingredients into à la mode delicacies. Daring diners should seek out these island favourites:

Casu marzu Health officials have deemed it illegal to sell this rural speciality but shepherds continue to make it for themselves. A roll of pecorino cheese is aged for months until flies lay eggs in it. The larvae produce enzymes that break down the cheese into a tangy goo, which gives it a tasty, spicy kick. Swallowing the wriggling larvae is all part of the experience.

Cordula Lamb intestines stuffed with peas, tied into a braid and spit-roasted.

Granelli Fried ox testicles.

Sanguinaccio A black pudding made from pig's blood sweetened with sugar, raisins and walnuts.

Other mainstays are the Spanish-introduced *panadas* (fried patties) filled with beef, pork, boar or eel, which are popular around Gallura, and *cascà*, a Ligurian and North African-infused couscous variation served in Calasetta and Carloforte. Also good is Gallura's *zuppa gallurese* (or *suppa cuata*), made by baking a piece of bread with fennel, parsley, mint, basil and pecorino in sheep's broth.

Meat

Meat dominates the Sardinian menu. The island's most famous dish is also one of its best: *porcheddu*. A suckling pig is spit-roasted over ilex embers with a glistening of lard. In rural hamlets, traditionalists still dig a makeshift oven in the ground and wrap the piglet in leaves and myrtle berries to cook it, just as fugitive bandits once did.

Agnello (lamb) and *capretto* (goat) are often roasted with garlic, parsley and herbs, or made into *stufato,* a winter casserole with saffron, artichokes,

eggs and red wine. If you're visiting Montiferru, try the local *bue rosso* braised steaks, which are some of the tastiest varieties in the Mediterranean. You'll also come across *bistecca di cavallo/asino* (horse or donkey steak) topped with oil and parsley. *Cinghiale* (wild boar) is commonly found in meat *ragù* sauces and at its freshest during the autumn and winter hunting seasons.

Fish & seafood

The best seafood is found around Cagliari, Alghero, Carloforte and the Sinis Peninsula. From March to August, *aragosta* (spiny rock lobster) is a common delicacy around Alghero, where it is served *alla catalana* with olive oil, tomatoes, lemon and a dash of spicy herbs. The Sinis is famous for its smoked *muggine* or *cefalo* (mullet), which produces *bottarga* (see page 142), while the Cagliaritani, dine on *burrida* (see above) and *ricci* (sea urchin) pulp at Poetto beach each winter. Carloforte is one of the Mediterranean's principal tuna (*tonno*) capitals and serves its prized catch in a myriad of varieties (best in early summer).

Desserts

Instead of packing head-splitting amounts of sugar into their desserts like other Italians, the Sardi have fine tuned a simple mixture of eggs, honey, almonds, fruit and ricotta to form the basis of hundreds of treats. The most common restaurant dessert is *sebadas* (or *seadas*), made by frying a pastry filled with ricotta cheese and lacing it with honey. *Pardulas* are puffy cakes made from a fresh ricotta base into which saffron and orange peel are blended. *Amaretti* are sweet almond biscuits made from eggs and sugar, while *gueffus* are a mixture of almonds, eggs and lemon peel rolled into balls. *Torrone* (Sardinian nougat) hails from Tonara and is commonly sold at festivals. For detailed descriptions and pictures of Sardinian desserts, consult durke.com.

In the wine cellar of the Hotel Lucrezia, near Oristano.

Wine

Sardinia's wines have long had a reputation for knocking out unsuspecting visitors. Italian poet Gabrielle D'Annunzio scribbled a lyrical rapture to his Sardinian drinking bender, and wine critic, Hugh Johnson, declared them to be "for the supermen [who built the nuraghi]". However, since the 1990s, Sardinian vineyards have started combining local grape varietals, diluting their notoriously high alcohol content and softening their sharp edges to produce sophisticated blends garnering some of Italy's top honours.

The following is a list of the island's best varieties, with a few suggestions for affordable bottles that are available at most supermarkets.

Red wines

Cannonau This strong ruby red is Sardinia's most famous red wine. Introduced by the Spanish in the 13th century, its full body matches well with meat and cheeses. The Nepente di Oliena is a wonderful choice, as are the Turriga and Costera varieties from Sardinia's top up-and-coming label, Argiolas.

Monica A drier red that turns purple as it ages. It was introduced by Spanish monks and goes well with fruit. Try the Karel cantina.

Carignano From the Sulcis, this is a sweeter choice in both red and rosé varieties. The Grotta Rossa and Nur labels are both excellent.

White wines

Vermintino Sardinia's only DOCG (*Denominazione d'origine controllata e garantita*) wine is this crisp, dry white produced around Gallura. It goes perfectly with seafood and is best from Sardinia's most famous bottler, Sella & Mosca. The Argiolas version is also excellent.

Nuragus This fruity blend has largely been replaced by Vermentino but Argiolas makes a quality version.

Dessert wines

Vernaccia A strong, sherry-like wine that goes well with *bottarga*. It is made around San Vero Milis in the west of the island. Josto Puddu has received recent acclaim for its varieties.

Moscato Made from Muscat grapes, this often fizzy and always-sweet wine is usually enjoyed alone or with fruit. Zaccagnini's Plaisir is pleasant

Malvasia Introduced by the Byzantines and produced around Bosa, this strong, sweet wine hides a hint of almond. It's best by itself or with shellfish. Go with Malvasia di Bosa.

Beer & spirits

On average, Sardinians consume more beer than any other Italian region. The local brew of choice is Ichnusa, a pale lager that locals enjoy for reasons of pride as much as taste. For something with a bit more body, try Jennas, also bottled by Ichnusa.

The most famous after-dinner drink is *mirto*, a deep purple liqueur made by blending myrtle berries, alcohol and sugar to form what tastes like a delicious alcoholic cough syrup. It's best served straight-up but chilled. The island's potent *filu 'e ferru grappa* (literally 'iron wine') is made from grape skins and gets its name from the piece of iron that distillers used to stick in the ground when burying their hooch in the early 20th century to avoid paying taxes.

Menu reader

General

affumicato smoked
al sangue rare
alla griglia grilled
antipasto starter/appetizer
arrosto roasted
ben cotto well done
bollito boiled
caldo hot
contorni side dishes
coppa/cono cup/cone
cotto cooked
cottura media medium
crudo raw
degustazione tasting menu of several dishes
dolce dessert
fatto in casa homemade
forno a legna wood-fired oven
freddo cold
fresco fresh
fritto fried
piccante spicy
primo first course
ripieno stuffed
secondo second course

Drinks (bevande)

acqua naturale/gassata/frizzante still/sparkling water
birra beer
birra (alla spina) beer (draught)
bottiglia bottle
caffè coffee (ie espresso)
caffè macchiato/ristretto espresso with a dash of foamed milk/strong
spremuta freshly squeezed fruit juice
succo juice
vino bianco/rosato/rosso white/rosé/red wine
vin santo a dark, sweet, fortified wine

Fruit (frutta) & vegetables (verdure)

agrumi citrus fruits
anguria watermelon
arance oranges
carciofio globe artichoke
castagne chestnuts
ciliegie cherries
cipolle onions
fagioli white beans
fichi figs
finocchio fennel
fragole strawberries
funghi mushrooms
lamponi raspberries
legumi pulses
lenticchie lentils
mandorla almond
melagrana pomegranate
melanzana eggplant/aubergine
melone melon
mele apples
noci walnuts
nocciole hazelnuts
patate potatoes, which can be *arroste* (roast), *fritte* (fried), *novelle* (new), *pure' di* (mashed)
peperoncino chilli pepper
peperone peppers
pesche peaches
pinoli pine nuts
piselli peas
pomodori tomatoes
rucola rocket
spinaci spinach
tartufi truffles
zucca pumpkin

Meat (carne)

affettati misti mixed cured meat
agnello lamb
bistecca beef steak
carpaccio finely sliced raw meat (usually beef)
cinghiale wild boar
coda alla vaccinara oxtail
coniglio rabbit
involtini thinly sliced meat, rolled and stuffed
lepre hare
manzo beef
pollo chicken
polpette meatballs
polpettone meat loaf
porchetta roasted, stuffed suckling pig
prosciutto ham – *cotto* cooked, *crudo* cured
salsicce pork sausage
salumi misti cured meats
speck a type of cured, smoked ham
spiedini meat pieces grilled on a skewer
stufato meat stew
trippa tripe
vitello veal

Fish (*pesce*) & seafood (*frutti di mare*)
acciughe anchovies
anguilla eel
aragosta lobster
baccalà salt cod
bottarga mullet-roe
branzino sea bass
calamari squid
cozze mussels
frittura di mare/frittura di paranza small fish, squid and
  shellfish lightly covered with flour and fried
frutti di mare seafood
gamberi shrimps/prawns
grigliata mista di pesce mixed grilled fish
orata gilt-head/sea bream
ostriche oysters
pesce spada swordfish
polpo octopus
sarde, sardine sardines
seppia cuttlefish
sogliola sole
spigola bass
stoccafisso stockfish
tonno tuna
triglia red mullet
trota trout
vongole clams

Dessert (*dolce*)
cornetto sweet croissant
crema custard
dolce dessert
gelato ice cream
granita flavoured crushed ice
macedonia (di frutta) fruit salad
panettone type of fruit bread eaten at Christmas
semifreddo a partially frozen dessert
sorbetto sorbet
tiramisù rich dessert with cake, cream,
  coffee and chocolate
torta cake
tozzetti sweet, crunchy almond biscuits
zabaglione whipped egg yolks flavoured with
  Marsala wine
zuppa inglese trifle

Useful words & phrases
aperitivo a pre-dinner drink,
  often served with free snacks
posso avere il conto? can I have the bill please?
coperto cover charge
bicchiere glass
c'è un menù? is there a menu?
aperto/chiuso open/closed
prenotazione reservation
conto the bill
cameriere/cameriera waiter/waitress
che cosa mi consegna? what do you recommend?
cos'è questo? what's this?
dov'è il bagno? where's the toilet?

Other
aceto balsamico balsamic vinegar, always from Modena
arborio type of rice used to make risotto
burro butter
calzone folded pizza
formaggi misti mixed cheese plate
formaggio cheese
frittata omelette
insalata salad
insalata Caprese tomatoes, mozzarella and basil
latte milk
miele honey
olio oil
polenta cornmeal
pane bread
pane-integrale brown bread
panzanella bread and tomato salad
provola smoked cheese
ragù a meaty sauce or ragout
riso rice
salsa sauce
sugo sauce or gravy
strangozzi/strozzapreti a thick, Umbrian sort of spaghetti
umbricelli thick spaghetti
zuppa soup

Entertainment

Detail from a traditional Sardinian costume.

string of film festivals throughout the island, the most popular of which is the biennial Sardinia International Ethnographic Film Festival held in Nuoro in September.

Dance

No Sardinian festival would be complete without a group of people linking arms in Sardinia's native dance, *su ballu sardu*. Recently, it has seen something of a resurgence and is customarily performed at weddings, feasts or other large-scale social gatherings by groups in traditional dress.

The two most common styles are *su ballu tundu* or *seriu* (the 'round' or 'serious' dance), and *ballu alligru* ('lighthearted dance'). In the first, couples lock together in a circle and move clockwise with a quick series of foot passes and formations. The livelier second style sees individuals or couples perform fast-paced solos involving tricks, such as being held upside down between two dancers, or dancing while balancing a shot of wine on their heads without spilling it.

Gay & lesbian

There is no openly gay scene in Sardinia outside Cagliari and Sassari. Sardinians have been slow to accept homosexuality, and public displays of affection between two members of the same sex are likely to draw unfavourable attention. For a list of gay-friendly bars, discos, beaches and

Cinema

As in mainland Italy, all foreign films in Sardinia are dubbed into Italian and shown without subtitles, which makes cinema-going a struggle for visitors who are not fluent in Italian. A growing interest in documentaries and international films has led to a associations, visit geocities.com/gaysardinia (in Italian). Or contact the **Associazione ARC** (via Leopardi 3, T347-291 9800, associazionearc.eu) in Cagliari and the **Movimento Omosessuale Sardo** (via Rockfeller 16/c, T079-219024, movimentomosessualesardo.org) in Sassari.

Music

The island's most famous instrument is Europe's oldest. *Launeddas* consist of three pipes made from reed shoots of different lengths held together with beeswax and string. The longest reed, *sa tumbu*, bellows the deepest of the polyphonic sounds, *sa mancosa manna* supplies accompanying notes and the *sa mancosedda* produces the bubbly melody that characterizes the wind instrument. A *bronzetto* statue in Cagliari's archaeological museum proves the instrument has been around at least since the eighth century BC.

Sardinia is also known for its male vocal quartets who sing *canto a tenore*, a call-and-response chorus that sounds unimaginably old. The *boche* sings lead in a tenor tone, soulfully rhyming melodramatic poetry as the *contra*, *mesa'oche* and *bassu* accompany him by vibrating their vocal chords in a guttural drone of syllables and sharp intonation jumps that are rooted in shepherds' calls. The most popular groups hail from the interior Barbagie region. The Tenores di Bitti are Sardinia's most famous musical group, having toured throughout the world, performed for the Pope, and recorded with Peter Gabriel.

I first discovered Sardinian music in 1988 and was astonished by what I heard.

Frank Zappa

Nightlife

You won't find much action in Sardinia's small towns and rural interior but the coast and the provincial capitals have some fantastic bars and clubs. Nightlife is seasonal: between October and May the action takes place in indoor bars; from June to September the Sardi prefer outdoor clubs on the beach. Expect a lull during transition months (April and October). People typically head to bars after 2200, stay there for a few hours and then move on to a nightclub which will stay open until 0330 or 0400, an hour after bars close. Many bars have regular live music sessions at weekends, with *ragazzi* strumming crowd-pleasing Italian or Sardo folk. In the clubs, house and electronic music is hugely popular, as is 'revival' (popular Italian jams from the '70s).

Theatre & performance

Experimental theatre has been slow to take hold in Sardinia but major towns each have professional venues that attract international plays, operas and ballets. More interesting are the lyrical performances that take place in Sardinia's interior and showcase the island's rich oral history of poetry and storytelling. Since the 1890s, shepherd bards called *cantadores* have come together on feast or holy days to take part in *poesia a bolu* competitions, in which poets are given a theme by the audience and invent a lighthearted satirical rhyme on the spot. If a *cantadore* deviates from the mandatory rhyming scheme of eight verses with eleven syllables each, they are disqualified. The competitions were banned by the Fascist authorities in the 1930s but today, hundreds of rural towns sponsor *poesia a bolu* festivals. The most famous are Ozieri's Premio Biennale (see page 49) and Seneghe's Cabudanne de sos Poetas (see page 49).

Shopping

S ardinia's traditional arts and crafts are an integral part of its social fabric and are not produced solely for the tourist market. Instead, they are objects that would be found (and used) in the houses of Sardi themselves. Craft techniques have changed little over the centuries and remain distinctly indigenous in style. Most towns have at least one store advertising '*Prodotti Tipici Sardi*' and the more popular tourist destinations are filled with them. These shops usually carry a wide variety of souvenirs from across the island, so you won't need to travel to a distant town to purchase its famous rugs or ceramics.

Like all stores in Sardinia, those selling souvenirs generally open early, close for a long lunch, and reopen at around 1630. Although typical Sardinia food and drink can be purchased at many independent gastronomy stores, supermarkets are usually found in even the smallest of towns and are often cheaper. However, if you find yourself in a town known for producing specific handicrafts, you'll often find a greater variety available at the area's many independent retailers than you would at a larger chain, though you may pay a bit more.

Left: Strolling past the designer shops of Iglesias.
Page opposite: Creating coral jewellery.

If you plan on purchasing a large souvenir in Sardinia, leave space in your carry-on luggage or suitcase to store the item when you depart. Both the Italian post and Italian-based express carriers are notoriously unreliable, slow and expensive, especially for shipping outside the EU. For example, a handmade knife weighing between five and 11 ounces will cost roughly €35 to send to London and €55 to send to New York by standard delivery.

Ceramics

Sardinian ceramics are limited to objects of practical, everyday use – mixing bowls, water jugs, vases and plates – and cost anywhere from €30 to €300. These are typically hand-thrown in clay and coloured by glazing or by dying natural soils with grains or local spices. Many objects incorporate images of birds, particularly peacocks or doves, rendered in light blue or yellow. Oristano, Sassari and Siniscola all have a history of ceramic-making.

Cork

Sardinia is Italy's cork capital and second only to Portugal in worldwide production. The trade is centred in Gallura but cork products can be found in most souvenir shops on the island. The most common souvenir is an unworked piece of curved bark stripped from a cork tree and used as a serving tray for meat and cheese appetizers (under €40). Other objects are heated and moulded into water jugs, satchels or model nuraghi.

Food & drink

You may not be able to cook like a Sardinian, but you can still savour the island's mouth-watering delicacies back home. *Fregola* and *malloreddus* pasta are sold in all supermarkets for under €1 and are easy to transport. Most countries will also allow you to bring home small amounts of regional meat and cheese without declaring them at Customs. However, if you're carrying wine, be sure to pack the bottles tightly in your suitcase, as airlines prohibit liquids in carry-on luggage.

Jewellery

Sardinian jewellery is most visibly displayed on the traditional costumes that Sardi wear for religious festivals. The most famous adornment is the golden filigree featured on necklaces, rings, earrings, cufflinks and buttons, which can be bought in ISOLA shops in Cagliari, Oristano and Alghero for €100 to €400. Santa Teresa and Alghero are famous for their blood-red coral, which is a highly prized commodity; see pages 227 and 265 for recommended outlets.

Knives

Sardinia is renowned for its handmade pocket knives. Traditionally used by shepherds, these fine pieces of art have become collectors' items, and talented blacksmiths can now fetch serious prices for their creations (€100 to €750). All artisans use a mouflon or ram horn to craft the knife's handle but each village is known for the distinct design of its blades. Arbus, Gusipini and Santu Lussurgiu each produce high-quality knives but, as any good Sardo will tell you, the ultimate in craftsmanship is a knife from Pattada (see page 241). Note: Airport restrictions prohibit passengers from placing knives in carry-on luggage, so make sure you check them in your suitcase.

Lace & embroidery

In Oliena, women have historically used silk to embroider bright colours on their black shawls, while, in Bosa there is a school where experienced artisans teach girls the town's lace-making techniques. Al Vecchio Mulino in Bosa sells small pieces starting at €20 (see page 160).

Weaving

It's no coincidence that an island of shepherds has a rich history of wool tapestry and rug production. These items are woven on horizontal or oblique looms, with each village's distinct design serving as a sort of signature. The two ends are adorned with intricate geometric patterns, called *mustras*, while the centre is woven with a variety of symbols representing Sardinia's rural origins: warriors, dancers, deer or floral reliefs. The various dyes used in the design are produced from berries and herbs that are soaked in a cauldron of cold water for a month. Many villages around Nuoro keep up the practice, but the Mecca of the industry is undoubtedly Aggius (see page 214). Rugs and tapestries usually range from 60 x 120 cm to 200 x 300 cm and start at €100 for single-colour designs, topping €500 for multi-coloured motifs.

It's no coincidence that an island of shepherds has a rich history of wool tapestry and rug production.

The art of basket weaving is also firmly rooted in ancient Sardinia. In Castelsardo, it is not uncommon to see women weaving baskets from dwarf palm leaves, rushes and asphodel as they have for generations. Decorative baskets incorporate geometric shapes, similar to those found on rugs, and can be bought for between €25 and €100. Outside Castelsardo, San Vero Milis and Ottana also have rich basket-weaving traditions.

Wood

The most famous wooden souvenirs are the hand-carved masks worn in the Barbagie during Carnival. Most depict either a man with exaggerated facial features or an animal (oxen, deer and pigs are common) and are made from an aged piece of wild pear or alder wood. For the best selection, head to Mamoiada or Ottana (see page 192). Expect to pay between €40 and €150.

Activities & tours

What Sardinia may lack in infrastructure, it more than makes up for in adventure. At 68 people per sq km, the island has one of the lowest population densities in Italy, and its varied landscapes not only provide a beautiful backdrop but also serve as a playground for a wide range of outdoor pursuits.

Cultural

The best way to absorb Sardinia's unique culture is to taste its culinary specialities, observe its festivals and wander through its towns. Many provincial capitals and larger tourist destinations offer walking tours (either by audio guide or English-speaking professionals) and the best place to enquire about them is at the local tourist office. With advance notice, popular archaeological sites and museums can also often arrange English-language guides to accompany visitors.

Cycling

Sardinia's tumultuous topography can be challenging for recreational cyclists but well-maintained roads and stretches of low-lying terrain mean there are still quality cycling routes for riders of all abilities. Beyond the large towns, the island's roads are rarely busy, allowing riders to focus on the breathtaking panoramas all around them. Those in search of a leisurely pedal should head to the low-lying Sinis Peninsula or the Nurra; more hardened cyclists should push inland, especially to the Gennargentu and Supramonte mountains.

You need not necessarily bring your own wheels to explore Sardinia by bike. Dozens of operators rent bikes by the day or week, especially around popular destinations (just be sure you get one with easy-to-use low gears). Guided bicycle tours of the island, including accommodation and meals, are provided by a number of operators, including dolcevitabiketours.it, ichnusabike.it, gallurabiketours.it and sardiniahikeandbike.com.

Page opposite: Divers explore underwater caves.
Above: The Golfo di Orosei's Cala Mariolu beach is stunning.

Diving & snorkelling

Many of Sardinia's prime attractions lie under the crystal-clear seas that surround its nearly 2000 km of coastline. Major coastal resorts and high-end hotels tend to be affiliated with scuba and snorkelling outfitters. These offer daily or weekly lessons to gain certification, one-time excursions, rental equipment and, occasionally, accommodation in a lodge along with other underwater enthusiasts. The popular dive centres are Asinara Island, Gallura, Tavolara Island, Alghero and Capo Caccia, the Golfo di Orosei, Cagliari, Pula and Villasimius. For further information, consult scubatravel.co.uk/italy/sardop.html.

About the island

Food & wine

Sardinia doesn't boast the wide range of cooking courses and culinary tours that are available in other Italian regions, although **Motus in Sardinia** (motus.sardinia.it) and **Ciao Laura** (ciaolaura. com/1sardinia.html) do provide a limited selection, and the people at foodwineandculture.com will customize a foodie tour of the island for you. Some language schools, such as Cactus Language in Cagliari (cactuslanguage.com) and Tricolore (tricolore.eu) in Alghero, also offer Sardinian cookery classes. Many small *panefici* (bakeries), *mercati* (markets) and *artigianati* (speciality food shops) are quick to share their products' ingredients and occasionally offer samples to curious customers.

Most of the island's wineries open their doors to visitors on guided tours (book ahead to ensure availability), allowing tourists to see the bottling process first-hand. Check the links below for a list of Sardinia's most famous wine producers: cantine-argiolas.it (in Serdiana, north of Cagliari); sellaemosca.com (outside Alghero); cantinapuddu. it (in San Vero Milis); cantinadisantadi.it (in Santadi, in the Iglesiente); jerzuantichipoderi.it (in Jerzu).

Hiking

Sardinia's varied landscape makes trekking a highlight whatever your ability or location. However, the rugged terrain, limited number of marked trails and lack of available water mean that you should hire a knowledgeable guide before venturing far. The best time for hiking in Sardinia is undoubtedly the spring when the air is ripe with the perfume of budding wild flowers. Avoid the dead of summer when scorching temperatures can be brutal. To download a free map of some of Sardinia's prime hiking routes, go to sardiniahikeandbike.com.

Those seeking a gentle ramble should consider the easy trails between Santa Teresa di Gallura and Capo Testa (see page 212), the coastal route along the Sinis Peninsula's quartz beaches (see page 142), or the paths criss-crossing the Giara di Gesturi (see page 100). Mildly fit walkers can tackle trails around the Supramonte and Gennargentu, such as Tiscali (see page 173) and the Gola Gorroppu (see page 182) as well as those around the Montiferru mountains (see page 147). Experienced hikers can explore the peaks of Monte Limbara (see page 216) and Punto Lamarmora (see page 43), the *tacchi* of

Surfing Sardinia.

Ulassai (see page 185) or the trail between Baunei and Cala Goloritzè (see page 183).

Watersports

The blustery winds whipping Sardinia from every direction make for some of the most ideal surfing, windsurfing and kitesurfing conditions in the Mediterranean. Buggerru, the Sinis Peninsula and Fluminimaggiore are popular surfing spots, while Cagliari, Porto Pollo, Chia and San Teodoro are renowned for kite and windsurfing. Browse ciaosardinia.com/eng/what-to-do/windsurf-kitesurf and discover-sardinia.com/activities/windsurfing.htm for a detailed list of prime destinations and companies offering lessons.

Kayakers and canoers can paddle around Bosa on Sardinia's only navigable river, the Temo, or venture south on the narrow Coghinas river starting from Valledoria. Otherwise, you can rent sea kayaks at the island's coastal resorts; exploring the limestone cliffs of the Golfo di Orosei is especially sublime.

Well-being

Since Roman times, Sardinia's natural springs have been utilized to alleviate aches and illnesses. In recent years, many of their sources have been expanded to form full-on spas and wellness centres, with Fordongianus (see page 150) and Sardara (see page 97) being the most famous.

In addition to the island's natural baths, luxury spas can be found in the island's high-class resorts, providing a wealth of mud, massage, cleansing and muscle-relaxing options designed to rejuvenate your body in style. Check justsardinia.co.uk/spa.aspx to find out more.

Trekking the coast.

The beach at Poetto.

Contents

Cagliari & the south

Introduction

Set at the head of the Gulf of Cagliari, Sardinia's capital looks out towards the Mediterranean from atop a natural amphitheatre. The south's placid inlets, fertile farmland and rich mineral deposits have historically made it the foreigners' favourite stomping ground on the island. From the Punic settlements at Nora and Sulci, to the dozens of coastal Spanish towers and the island's indigenous Bronze Age fortresses, southern Sardinia is littered with reminders of its tangled past.

The capital and largest city, Cagliari, is an urbane beacon on a traditionally provincial island, boasting Sardinia's most vibrant nightlife and progressive mentality. It also has the most fascinating relics of the island's mysterious Nuraghic forefathers – the *bronzetti* statues – in its archaeological museum. Beyond the capital, the south reveals a palette of colours that make it Sardinia's most varied region: there are the dusty golden wheat fields of the Campidano, the green *macchia*-covered hills throughout the Sarrabus and Gerrei, and the rusty abandoned mining towns of the Iglesiente – all of which are flanked by crescent-shaped pristine beaches stretching from the Costa Verde to the Costa Rei.

What to see in...

...one day
Wander through **Cagliari's** medieval kernel, **Castello**, stopping in at the **Museo Archeologico** and take in the views from the **Bastione**. Venture to **Poetto** for the beach then return to the city for the *passeggiata* and to dine in the **Marina** district.

...a weekend or more
After a day in the capital, customize a day trip according to your interests. Beach lovers should take the coastal route from **Cagliari** to **Villasimius**; archaeology enthusiasts should head to **Su Nuraxi** or **Nora**, and nature seekers should explore the **Giara di Gesturi**.

Explore the far-flung islands of **San Pietro** and **Sant'Antioco**, delve into the **Iglesiente's** abandoned mines, hike the **Parco dei Sette Fratelli** and splash around in the waters of the **Costa del Sud**.

Left: Piazza Yenne, Cagliari.

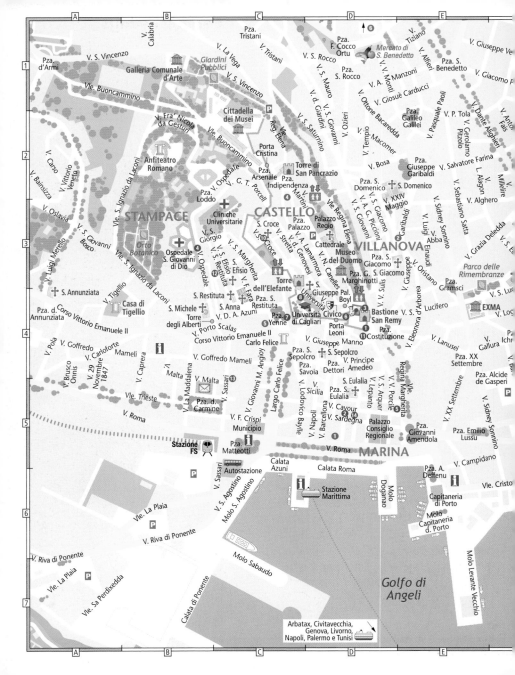

Cagliari listings

❶ Sleeping

1 A&R Bundes Jack *via Roma 75*, **D5**
2 B&B Garibaldi *via Garibaldi 120*, **E3**
3 Calamosca *viale Calamosca 50*, **H5**
4 Kastrum *via Cannelles 78*, **C2**
5 Le Suite Sul Corso *corso Vittorio Emanuele 8*, **C4**
6 T Hotel *via dei Giudicati 66*, **D1**

❶ Eating & drinking

1 Antico Caffè *piazza Costituzione 10*, **D4**
2 Antica Hostaria *via Cavour 60*, **D5**
3 Caffè degli Spiriti *Bastione Saint Remy*, **D4**
4 Chez Victor *via Ospedale 42*, **B3**
5 Dal Corsaro *viale Regina Margherita 28*, **E5**
6 De Candia Wine & Spirits Café *via de Candia 3*, **D4**
7 Isola del Gelato *piazza Yenne 35*, **C4**
8 Karel Café *via Università 37*, **C4**
9 La Paillote *viale Calamosca*, **H5**
10 Libarium Caffé Nostrum *via Santa Croce 35*, **C3**
11 Orso Bianco *piazza Martiri d'Italia 1*, **D4**
12 Per Bacco *via Santa Restituita 72*, **C3**
13 Sa Domu Sarda *via Sassari 51*, **C4**
14 Trattoria Lillicu *via Sardegna 78*, **D5**

Cagliari & around

Tucked between two lagoons teeming with wildlife, a fertile plain to the north and a strategically placed natural harbour to the south, Cagliari (pronounced cal-ya-ree) has long enticed visitors. The island's windswept capital has also historically been its front door, allowing Sardinians access to ancient Mediterranean trade routes and acting as a gateway to foreign invaders keen to exploit the surrounding region. Like Rome, the city is spread across seven hills but, with its founding attributed to the Phoenicians in 814 BC (who called it Karalis, literally 'white rock'), Cagliari actually predates the Eternal City. The tides have brought Cagliari one distant ruler after the next; their influence has been absorbed and has evolved into a distinct cultural cocktail. Inside the cement sprawl of its suburbs, the four historic districts of the city still radiate laidback sophistication.

Bastione San Remy.

The Castle district is the city's most alluring neighbourhood. Standing guard over the port and city from high on a limestone bluff, its natural defensive importance has led to a complicated history of foreign control which mirrors the island itself. Today, many of Cagliari's landmarks are tucked inside its prominent medieval walls and even its name in Sardo, 'Casteddu', is used to define the entire city and surrounding province.

The Phoenicians, Carthaginians and Romans all settled this white outcrop but it wasn't until the Republic of Pisa took control in 1216 that the neighbourhood – which never had an actual castle – took its present shape. The Pisans built a series of eight defensive towers and an imposing wall around Castello, limiting access from other neighbourhoods to three doors: San Pancrazio, connecting Villanova; Elefante, connecting Stampace; and Aquila, connecting Marina.

For centuries, Castello was the city's political, economical and religious centre, inhabited by Pisan, Aragonese and, finally, Spanish nobles. The Sardi were only allowed to enter Castello to sell goods during the day.

Castello's regal importance waned as the city expanded under the House of Savoy and into the 20th century, and it suffered from the heavy bombing that decimated parts of the city in 1943. Yet, in recent years, various reconstruction projects have sought to restore the grandeur of the neighbourhood. Sardinian artisans have reclaimed the district's narrow alleyways, exhibiting traditional handicrafts and artwork and turning Castello into a virtual gallery of Sardità by those who were once kept outside it.

Cars without special permits will be fined if they enter Castello between midnight and 0900. Drivers should use the underground car park on viale Regina Elena and ascend to piazzetta Mercede Mundula in one of the city's three outdoor elevators: there are two on viale Regina Elena and one up the hill from piazza Yenne, to the left of Santa Chiara church.

Essentials

❶ Getting around Cagliari is a relatively compact city with chaotic drivers. If you plan on staying in the city, you won't need a car, as most sights are within walking distance and the bus service is surprisingly efficient. You can buy bus tickets at most newsstands and some cafés (€1 single, €2.50 all-day pass). Useful routes include bus 7, which climbs from via Roma up to Castello every 30 mins, and buses PF, PQ, 3P and 9P, which run from the city centre to Poetto beach. If you want to explore greater Cagliari and southern Sardinia, hiring a car is highly recommended as public transport is unreliable and dishearteningly slow.

❷ Bus station Stazione Autolinee, (inside McDonald's) piazza Matteotti, Marina, T070-409 8324, for both ARST and FdS bus tickets.

❸ Train station Stazione Ferroviaria, piazza Matteotti, Marina, T070-67941, trenitalia.it, 0600-2200.

❹ ATM piazza Matteotti (outside the bus station); **Banca Nazionale del Lavoro**, Carlo Felice 11, T070-60021; **Banca di Roma**, piazza Yenne 5, Stampace, T070-678331.

❺ Hospital Ospedale Civile, via Ospedale 46, Stampace, T070-663237.

❻ Pharmacy Farmacia Maffiola, piazza Yenne 8, Stampace, T070-656691, Mon-Sat 0900-1230 and 1630-1900.

❼ Post office Poste Italiane, piazza del Carmine 25, Stampace, T070-60541, Mon-Fri 0800-1300 and 1500-1850, Sat 0800-1315.

❽ Tourist information Ufficio Turistico, piazza Matteotti, Marina, T070-669255, Mon-Fri 0830-1330 and 1400-2000, Sat-Sun 0800-2000.

And suddenly there is Cagliari: a naked town rising steep, steep, golden-looking … It is strange and rather wonderful, not a bit like Italy.

DH Lawrence, Sea and Sardinia

Exploring Castello

The view of Castello from Stampace.

Take the elevator from via Regina Elena to the top of Cagliari's most recognizable landmark, the **Bastione di San Remy**. Built between 1899-1903, its neoclassic promenades carved into the side of the rock sit as a two-tiered balcony overlooking the city below. Named after the first Savoyard viceroy, the Bastione was built over the old Spanish ramparts to better link Castello with Cagliari's surrounding districts. These days, its function is more recreational: with magnificent views of the Capoterra mountains, Cagliari and the Golfo degli Angeli, the Bastione is the city's best place to catch a sunset. On summer nights, two open-air bars pump house music as Cagliari's finest sip Mojitos in hammocks or flop down on outdoor beds (see page 123).

Tip...

The best time to visit Castello is in the late afternoon when the setting sun illuminates the Golfo degli Angeli from the Bastione in magnificent cobalt hues.

As you walk down the steps from the side of the Bastione leading to via De Candia, the pink-hued **Palazzo Boyl** rises to the right. It was built in 1840 by Count Carlo Boyl who hoped to construct the most striking palace in the city and incorporates the base of the Pisan **Torre dell'Aquila**. Though it was never finished, the tower was used as a prison during the Spanish reign. Above the palace's four marble statues representing the seasons, there are three cannon balls fixed into the building's façade in memory of the bombing raids the city endured in the 18th century: 1708 by the Dutch, 1717 by the Spanish and 1793 by the French.

Just past the palace on the right, the recently restored **Teatro Civico** in Castello (via De Candia, T070-677 7660, comune.cagliari.it, daily 1000-1300 and 1700-2000, see page 127) is one of Cagliari's oldest theatres, dating back to 1775. Continue straight on, along via Università past the University of Cagliari. The 42-m limestone **Torre dell'Elefante** (piazza San Giuseppe 5, Tue-Sun 0900-1300, 1530-1930, €4, €2.50 concessions) looms in the background and gets its name from the small marble elephant facing via Università. Built by Giovanni Capula in 1307, the tower, like its twin, San Pancrazio, was erected by the Pisans as a military fortress; its fourth wall, facing into Castello was left open to communicate to the population inside. The tower's two sets of spiked gates were slammed shut each night and still hover over passers-by as they walk below. Under the Aragonese and Spanish, the fourth wall was enclosed and the tower was used as a torture chamber for political deviants. Decapitations were common; the heads were either displayed outside the tower in iron cages or thrown onto the cobblestone piazza below. The tower marks one of the windiest points in the city and legend has it that at night you can still hear the prisoners crying out for help.

If you veer left onto via Santa Croce the **Bastioni Spagnoli** terrace offers fantastic views of the Stampace district below. Below the Torre dell'Elefante, piazza San Giuseppe leads to **via dei Genovesi** where the rubble and skeletons of two apartment complexes have remained since the 1943 bombing. A right turn down the street will bring you to Porta Castello and the beginning of **via Lamarmora**, Castello's backbone. This is where the most important Pisan nobles lived in the 13th century and where succeeding Catalan merchants left a Gothic influence in many of the street's palaces. A right turn past the statue of St Francis in piazza Carlo Alberto takes you to via Cannelles, named after the man who introduced the printing press to Sardinia. His former home is at No 65 marked by a first-floor plaque.

Continue up to piazza Palazzo and you'll see the limestone **Cattedrale di Santa Maria** (see page 82). The accompanying museum is to the right on via Fossario. Piazza Palazzo is also home to **Palazzo Regio** (T070-409 2000, daily 0800-2000, free), from where the viceroys of the House of Savoy ruled from the 1700s to 1850. Its regal council and ballrooms are used today for political conferences. Where Palazzo Regio meets via Martini, there's a small piazzetta dedicated to the Sardinian poet Mercede Mundula. It affords fantastic views across the Villanova neighbourhood, past Cagliari's salt marshes and up into the Monte dei Sette Fratelli.

As you reach piazza dell'Independenza, notice the Mussolini slogan still visible on the façade of the building separating via Cannelles and via Martini. More interesting, however, is the 36-m limestone **Torre di San Pancrazio** at No 7 (Tue-Sun 0900-1300 and 1530-1930, €4, €2.50 concessions). Built two years before the Elephant Tower as a Pisan lookout point, it rises 129 m above sea level and is the highest point in Cagliari. Following the construction of a new entrance into Castello to the right of the tower in 1563, the Aragonese had little use for the outdated defensive fortress and turned it into a prison. Spanish viceroys would pardon three inmates a year on Good Friday, while those less fortunate were executed to entertain the nobility in piazza Carlo Alberto.

Watch out for the traffic in busy piazza Arsenale as cars shoot out of Porta Cristina to the left and S'Avanzada to the right. Straight ahead, an imposing door flanked by four Doric columns marks the entrance to the **Cittadella dei Musei**, a city within the city. Comprising the old military arsenal used by the Pisans, Aragonese and Savoyards, the site now houses three permanent museums (see pages 82-83): choose between archaeology, art or Siamese artefacts – or visit all three! The Cittadella is a fascinating place to pass a rainy day or to cool a sunburn.

Cattedrale di Santa Maria (Duomo)

Piazza Palazzo, T070-663837, duomodicagliari.it.
Apr-Oct daily 0900-1200 and 1700-1900,
Nov-Mar daily 0900-1230 and 1600-1800, free
Map: Cagliari, D4, p76.

Built in the 1250s by the Pisans, the cathedral's restorations showcase many influences that have come and gone in Cagliari. The original Gothic-Roman façade was replaced by a Genoese Baroque version in 1702, only to be torn down in an attempt to recreate the original in 1931. Today, the bell tower, transept wings, architrave and internal façade are all that remain of the 13th-century building.

Inside, a beautifully detailed ambo with scenes from the life of Jesus was built by Maestro Guglielmo in 1162 and was intended for the cathedral in Pisa. It was split in two and placed at the back of the church during restoration in the 18th century. The four lions at the ambo's base now sit at the sides of the high altar. The chapel to the left of the altar was elaborately wrought in silver by the Catalan-Aragonese, while the chapel to the right pays tribute to Martino II, whose Aragonese troops killed 10,000 Sardinians at the Battle of Sanluri (see page 31). This melting pot continues under the altar where the remains of 179 martyred Cagliaritani are buried, including Marie Louise, wife of Louis XVIII from the Savoyard reign.

To make sense of it, follow the signs outside the church to the right towards the **Museo del Duomo** (via Fossario 5, T070-652498, museoduomodicagliari.it, Tue-Sun 1000-1300 and 1630-1930, €4, €2.50 concessions) for tours in Italian.

Museo Archeologico Nazionale

Cittadella dei Musei, T070-684000.
Tue-Sun 0900-2000, €4, €2 concessions, free
children and over-65s.
Map: Cagliari, D2, p76.

Spread out on four floors is a display of archaeological artefacts found throughout the island, dating from the Neolithic era (6000-3500 BC) up to the Byzantine period (AD 535-800).

The first floor presents a chronological summary of Sardinian history, from the primitive early Neolithic ceramics found in the Grotta Corbeddu cave to coins used by the Byzantines in the high Middle Ages. Don't miss the clay statuettes of the chubby female goddess from the Bonu Ighinu culture (see page 25), as well as a collection of obsidian tools, arrowheads and a recreation of a Punic *tophet* burial site for newborns (see page 107). There are also complex prototypes of nuraghi, *domus de janas* and *tombe di gigante* structures (see page 34). But the stars of the museum are undoubtedly the intricately-detailed *bronzetti* statues from the late Nuraghic era (16th to seventh centuries BC). The small bronze figurines depict warriors holding spears, hunters aiming bows and boats decorated with deer antlers carrying animals. Look for the cloaked tribal rulers, the man playing the *launeddas* (see page 63) and a mother grieving over her fallen son. With no written record from this period, these statues provide the most fascinating look into life in Nuraghic Sardinia.

Tip...

The museum's layout can be quite confusing, so follow the numbers above the display cases as a chronological guide.

The second floor highlights relics retrieved from the Sarrabus-Gerrei and Marmilla-Trexenta regions, with particular focus on the towered Nuraghic fortress Su Nuraxi (see page 98) and the Punic necropolis, Tuvixeddu, in Cagliari (currently undergoing restoration).

The third floor focuses on the central Campidano region east to the Iglesiente. Particularly interesting are the prehistoric finds from Monte Arcosu, including the largest Bronze Age statue of a tribal chief ever found. The fourth floor is occupied by relics found underwater in Oristano province.

Pinacoteca Nazionale

Cittadella dei Musei, T070-684000.
Tue-Sun 0900-2000, €2, €1 concessions, free children and over-65s.
Map: Cagliari, D2, p76.

The three-floored art gallery wraps around the former arsenal's defensive walls, which were built in the mid 1500s. The pieces on display come from churches throughout the island, many of which, like San Francesco in Cagliari, are no longer in existence. Especially significant are the pieces by Catalan artists Joan Figuera, Rafael Thomas and Joan Mates on the first floor. Aside from displaying Spanish-Flemish and mainland Italian painters, the museum also showcases Pietro Cavaro from Cagliari's acclaimed Stampace School.

Museo d'Arte Siamese 'Stefano Cardu'

Cittadella dei Musei, T070-651888.
Tue-Sun 0900-1300 and 1600-2000, €4, €2 concessions, €7 including ticket to Galleria Comunale d'Arte.
Map: Cagliari, D2, p76.

The museum's 1300 pieces constitute the largest collection of Siamese art in Europe. Most of it was donated in 1917 by Stefano Cardu who served at the King's court in Siam. Among the exhibits are religious works of art, coins, weapons and some porcelains from the Ming dynasty.

Above: A glimpse of Castello. Left: Lions at Cattedrale di Santa Maria.

Stampace

Porta Cristina marks the boundary of Castello and the beginning of the Stampace neighbourhood. From viale Buoncammino, the district spreads down the hill as far as the city's port.

Anfiteatro Romano

Via San Ignazio da Laconi (entrance opposite Convento Cappuccini), T070-652956).
Apr-Oct Tue-Sat 0930-1330, Sun 0930-1330 and 1530-1730; Nov-Mar Tue-Sat 0930-1300, Sun 1000-1300. €4.30, €2.60 concessions, free under-6s. Call ahead for guided tours in English.
Map: Cagliari, C3, p76.

Dating back to the second century AD, the amphitheatre is the most important Roman relic in Sardinia but for years it served as the island's largest communal dump; it took architect Vincenzo Crespi and his crew nine years to dig out the trash that had accumulated over the centuries. When they finished in 1871, they were left with the remains of a structure that could hold 10,000 people – the entire population of the Roman *municipum*, then known as Carales. While the original enclosing wall has since toppled, much of the ringed seating of the three-storey structure remains dug into the limestone, as do the more interesting underground passageways.

In its heyday, the amphitheatre played host to all-day spectacles ranging from prisoner executions to gladiators battling lions. These days you can pay to hear some of Italy's finest musicians here, when the amphitheatre comes alive for the annual summer concert series. If you can't get a ticket or don't want to stump up the cash, the sound and views are just as good from via Laconi.

Casa di Tigellio

Via Giovanni Antonio Carbonazzi, T331-473 1394.
Tue-Sun 0900-1300 and 1600-2000, €3, €1.90 concessions, free under-6s. Call ahead for guided tours in English.
Map: Cagliari, B4, p76.

Two Roman columns sprouting from a large excavated lot signal Cagliari's most misleading landmark. The site was said to be the home of Tigellius Ermogene, a singer and poet from the first century BC, who was allegedly born into slavery but freed by his master on account of his voice. He then climbed the Roman social ladder to befriend the imperial elite, including Caesar and Cleopatra.

However, excavations have revealed that this site was, in fact, constructed roughly a century after Tigellius' funeral in 40 BC. What's more, it's not a villa at all but rather the remains of three large second-century Roman dwellings on one side and thermal baths on the other – a sort of Beverly Hills for the *municipum*'s elite. The first house has a golden stucco design on the floor, while the second has a black-and-white mosaic. The third dwelling is in the worst state of repair but retains the outline of its atrium.

Orto Botanico

Via Laconi 11, T070-675 3516.
Apr-Oct Mon-Sat 0830-1930, Sun 0830-1330, Nov-Mar 0900-1600 Sun 0830-1330; closed 1 Jan, 1 May, 15 Aug, 25 and 26 Dec. €3, free under-6s, students and over-65s. Free guided tours on the 2nd and 4th Sun of the month at 1100.
Map: Cagliari, C4, p76.

Cagliari's Stampace district as seen from Castello.

Cagliari's main public garden is spread over five hectares and boasts more than 500 species of plants from every continent except Antarctica, making it one of Italy's largest and most varied botanical collections. Look for 200-year-old ficus trees, the palm garden, a 15-m cave and a Roman cistern dating back to AD 140.

Chiesa di San Michele

Via Ospedale 2, T070-658626.
Mon-Sat 0800-1100 and 1800-2100, Sun and hols 0730-1200 and 1900-2100, free.
Map: Cagliari, C4, p76.

Continuing down via Laconi, you'll pass under the city's oldest Pisan tower, the late 13th-century **Torre degli Alberti**, on your way to the church of St Michael. Underneath the scaffolding of the church's never-ending restoration project is the most impressive example of Baroque architecture on the island. The building dates back to the Byzantine era but underwent a series of makeovers by the Jesuits in the 16th and 18th centuries. The façade is topped by a statue of St Michael sculpted from a block of marble found at Tigellio's villa. A vaulted atrium houses a pulpit from which the Holy Roman Emperor Charles V spoke at a mass before setting sail on his expedition against Tunisia in 1535. Inside, the church's eight chapels are opulently decorated with frescoes and sculpted marble statues. The sacristy to the left of the high altar holds paintings from the seventh and eighth centuries, as well as ornate wooden carvings depicting the Passion of the Christ.

Chiesa di Sant'Efisio

Piazzetta Sant'Efisio, T070-677 6400.
Tue-Sun 0900-1300 and 1600-1900, free.
Map: Cagliari, D4, p76.

This small 18th-century church was built above the crypt where the third-century martyr Sant'Efisio was imprisoned (see box, right). The ring to which he was chained is still visible.

Sant'Efisio, Sardinia's unofficial patron saint

Born in Jerusalem in AD 250, Efisio spent his formative years in the Roman army exterminating Christians and beating back those pesky rebels from Sardinia's Barbagie. It may not sound like a recipe for Sardinian martyrdom but in an ironic twist, the largest and longest Christian festival in the world is now dedicated to the island's most beloved son.

After hearing the voice of God and seeing crosses imprinted on his hands, Efisio converted to Christianity, moved to Sardinia to spread the Gospel and even wrote to the Roman emperor Julio in an attempt to convert him. Julio didn't take kindly to Efisio's suggestion and imprisoned him in a cave where he was tortured with burning embers and beaten. Despite pleas from his mother, Efisio refused to renounce his Christianity and was beheaded on the beach in Nora – but not before praying for the city of Cagliari and for the protection of Sardinians against invaders.

Efisio's prayers seemed to fall on deaf ears, as Sardinia became a virtual Mediterranean youth hostel for foreign invaders for well over a thousand years. It wasn't until 1652, when Cagliari was devastated by the plague, that the martyr made good on his promise to guard the city. With half of its population dead, the municipality begged the saint for help and promised that it would honour him with a procession if he rid the city of the disease. The city was spared and Efisio became known as the unofficial patron saint of Sardinia.

Since 1659, 6,000 Sardi from across the island have converged on the capital on 1 May every year in recognition and thanksgiving, parading in traditional clothes and singing atop ox-drawn carriages. The climax comes when a statue of Saint Efisio is brought from his church (see page 47) and carried by men through the capital to the site of the martyr's beheading in Nora and back, a gruelling 80-km pilgrimage that lasts four days, concluding with the intimate and moving return to the city on the evening of 4 May.

Tip…

Head down largo Carlo Felice towards the port to see the capital's Catalan-Gothic-meets-art nouveau municipal building. Rebuilt after the bombing raids of 1943, its towers rise above the rest of the neo-Gothic palaces along via Roma.

Top: Cagliari's impressive Orto Botanico.
Above: Piazza Yenne.

Cripta di Santa Restituta

Via Sant'Efisio 14, T070-640 2115.
Tue-Sun 1000-1300, free.
Map: Cagliari, D4, p76.

This church and crypt are dedicated to the African martyr Santa Restituta. A flight of steps leads down from the church's interior to a large natural cave with dug-out tunnels and cisterns dating back to the Nuraghic age. The Romans housed African refugees here in the fifth century AD and the Byzantines used it as a dwelling for monks. Legend has it that Santa Restituta's remains were brought to Cagliari from present-day Tunisia and were discovered in the cave inside a terracotta urn in 1614. Look for the scribbled signatures of Cagliari's Second World War refugees who sought sanctuary in the cave during the 1943 air raids.

Piazza Yenne

Map: Cagliari, D4, p76.

This lively piazza marks the boundary between the Stampace and Marina neighbourhoods and is the social hub of the lower city. Café tables spill out into the square which is shaded by palm trees and makeshift canopies. At night, the piazza pulsates with life as modish locals and tourists stop for a drink or a gelato, making it the city's best place for people watching. A bronze statue of the Savoyard King Carlo Felice is found just south of the piazza and marks the official beginning of the muddled highway that runs between Cagliari and Porto Torres. To the left, piazza Yenne connects to **corso Vittorio Emanuele**, whose winding, bar-lined alley is your best bet for a late drink.

Tip…

Note the plaque at via Sant'Efisio 18 paying homage to Cagliari's "defenceless crowd" who were "massacred" by American forces in bombing raids in 1943.

The Marina

The Marina district around the port has always served as Cagliari's front steps. Today, the road from the airport converges at the city's ferry, train and bus stations in piazza Matteotti, so chances are that it will be your welcome mat to the capital as well.

To reach the Marina from piazza Matteotti, follow the marbled walkway under vaulted arcades along via Roma and across largo Carlo Felice. Or, just follow your nose. The smallest of Cagliari's four districts is packed with the city's best restaurants. Ambling along the one-lane streets (little changed since Roman times) each evening is an aromatic experience: the wafting scents of exotic blends mix with parsley-sprinkled on locally caught seafood. Restaurants abound from via Roma to Cagliari's most attractive square, the compact piazza Savoia. However, your best bet is via Sardegna, a narrow strip of unpretentious real estate whose kitchens merge Sardinian specialities with mainland favourites.

Chiesa di Sant'Eulalia & Museo del Tesoro di Sant'Eulalia

Piazza Sant'Eulalia and Vico del Collegio 2, T070-663724, http://web.tiscali.it/mutseu
Church: Daily 0800-1045 and 1700-2000, free.
Museum: Tue-Sun 1000-1300 and 1700-2000, €4.
Map: Cagliari, E5, p76.

The Aragonese bequeathed the Marina its parish church but dedicated it to their patron saint in Barcelona. Like most of the city's churches, the Catalan-Gothic style has undergone many facelifts since its original 1371 construction. A 19th-century replica of Leonardo da Vinci's *Last Supper* hangs under the cupola but the church's real gem lies underground. In 1990, humidity problems led to the excavation of the church's foundations where the remains of Roman road, water cistern and pagan temple dating back to the Punic age were unearthed. See the discoveries at the adjacent museum, along with a collection of artefacts.

Villanova

The newest of Cagliari's four historic quarters, Villanova and the vias Sidney Sonnino and Dante Alighieri comprise the city's modern business centre, but the district also holds an ancient surprise: Sardinia's oldest church.

Giardini Pubblici & Galleria Comunale d'Arte

Largo Dessi, T070-490727, collezioneingrao.it.
Gallery: Jun-Sep Wed-Mon 0900-1300 and 1700-2100, Wed-Mon Sep-Jun 0900-1300 and 1530-1930, €6, €2.60 concessions, €7 including admission to Stefano Cardu museum.
Map: Cagliari, C2, p76.

At the top of viale Regina Elena, the former Savoyard kings' private playground has been turned into Cagliari's public gardens. The city's most scenic jogging path rings a massive ficus tree, fountains and mimosa trees whose dramatic flowers are in bloom from April to early July.

The old Savoyard Royal Powder Room at the end of the gardens is now an art gallery and houses two permanent exhibits: a smaller collection by 20th-century Sardinian artists, with haunting sculptures by Francesco Ciusa, and the Ingrao Collection, named after the man who donated the museum's 500-piece exhibit.

EXMÀ

Via San Lucifero 71, T070-666399.
Jun-Sep Tue-Sun 1000-1400 and 1700-2400, Oct-May Tue-Sun 0900-2000. Admission varies.
Map: Cagliari, F4, p76.

The marble bull's head at the entrance to EXMÀ is a reminder that this cultural centre was once Cagliari's slaughterhouse. The open atrium where the animals were kept was designed on a slope to allow the detritus to flow into a series of outdoor drains. The last slaughter took place in 1966 and the site underwent a glossy makeover. It now hosts temporary art exhibitions and festivals.

Basilica di San Saturnino

Piazza San Cosimo, T070-659869.
Mon-Sat 0900-1300, free.
Map: Cagliari, G4, p76.

Just up the street from EXMÀ, what appears to be a mosque is actually Sardinia's oldest Christian church, dating from the fifth century AD. Its Greek

The evening *passeggiata*... and Cagliari's best shops

Via Roma's parade of shiny display cases may be tempting but most of them cater to cruise ship day-trippers. Instead, join the Cagliaritani as they take the evening *passeggiata* along the city's best shopping route. Starting from the bottom of the pedestrian-only via Manno in the Marina, dip into clothing boutiques as you climb the Spanish-influenced street towards piazza Costituzione (stopping for a gelato at Orso Bianco, see page 123). Then cross into the Villanova quarter where the window-shopping continues – as does the chaotic walking pattern – along via Garibaldi with its fashion emporia. You can continue straight on until the street hits piazza Garibaldi, or follow the city's glitterati on to via Alghero for Cagliari's highest-end retail outlets.

Spiaggia del Poetto

Bus PQ or PF from piazza Matteotti.

It's hard to imagine a finer city beach than Poetto, located just a 15-minute bus ride east of the city centre. The 11-km shoreline constitutes the longest city beach in Italy and, whenever the summer *maestrale* wind calms to a whisper, as many as 50,000 people stretch out along the sand. Out of season, locals flock to the many kiosks that line the beach for an afternoon aperitif or for the freshly caught *ricci* (sea urchins); these are best from October to March.

Those in the know divide the beach according to bus stops: the best area is the first, hugging the quaint **Marina Piccola** tourist port and the dramatic **Sella del Diavolo** ('Devil's Saddle') cape. Legend has it that Lucifer expelled God's angels from Cagliari until Gabriel's slashing sword sent him packing, leaving only the devil's saddle high atop the curved ridge overlooking the *Golfo degli Angeli* (Gulf of the Angels). The outcrop separates Poetto from Cagliari's smaller secondary beach, **Calamosca** (take bus 5 or 5/11 from via Roma).

cross plan is divided by three barrel vaults and topped by a tiled dome. The church is dedicated to a local martyr who is said to have been beheaded at the site in 303 but recent findings suggest the church's origins can be traced to another St Saturn from Africa. A Roman necropolis, dating from the second century AD is visible under the church.

Around Cagliari

Various efforts to jumpstart Cagliari's stagnant economy in the 19th century and, again, after the Second World War have left the capital with industrial eyesores and messy residential development on its outskirts. The ride into town from the airport reveals a landscape dotted with refinery plants along the Santa Gilla lagoon, while the east end of the city wraps around the Molentargius marsh and connects to Cagliari's commuter satellite, Quartu Sant'Elena, which has grown to become the island's third most populated city. If you don't mind travelling through the modern sprawl to get to them, greater Cagliari has a few diamonds in the rough.

Stagno di Molentargius

Bus PQ or PF from piazza Matteotti.

Cagliari is bordered by two brackish lagoons, Santa Gilla to the west and Molentargius to the east. Covering over 4000 hectares, the two low-lying basins form one of Europe's largest marshlands and are home to over 200 species of migratory birds (roughly one-third of the population for the entire continent), 49 of which are endangered.

Molentargius Regional Park, located next to Poetto, is the smaller of the two lagoons but is more accessible. Its extinct salt pans radiate a purplish hue and were once panned by prisoners. The lagoon's name derives from the practice of packing the salt onto donkeys ("*su molenti*" in Sardo) to haul back to town.

For the best view of widgeons, cormorants and flamingos, come between March and August and park on the side of the road running along

Poetto (especially across from the Ippodromo racetrack), then follow the narrow dirt paths which separate the lagoon's shallow pools. Alternatively, take your binoculars up viale Europa to the top of **Monte Urpinu** (which, coincidentally, has an impressive population of peacocks and swans) for a long-distance panorama.

Castello di San Michele

Colle di San Michele, T070-500656.
Jun-early Sep Tue-Sun 1000-1300 and 1700-2100, mid Sep-June Tue-Sun 0900-1300 and 1600-2200. €5, €2-3 concessions.
Bus 5 from via Roma.

This 10th-century Byzantine fortress high on a hill northwest of the city centre is the only real castle in Cagliari. It was built to defend the Giudicato of Cagliari and was later used as a hospital during the plague of the 1650s. Temporary art exhibits now fill the complex's three towers and surrounding walls.

Basilica di Nostra Signora di Bonaria

Piazza Bonaria 2, T070-301747, bonaria.eu.
Basilica & sanctuary: daily 0630-1130 and 1730-1930, free.
Museum: daily 0900-1130 and 1700-1830, donation requested.

Basilica di Nostra Signora di Bonaria.

The name Bonaria (literally 'good wind') stems from the church's position high on the Montixeddu hill. Built in 1325 by the Aragonese as they plotted to overtake the city, it is the only church in Cagliari with a radio station (104.6 FM). Its importance, however, has spread far beyond its wavelength and lured Pope Benedict XVI to visit in 2008.

According to legend, Catalan sailors, in the midst of a terrible storm in 1370, threw all of their cargo overboard, including a wooden statue of the Virgin. The statue calmed the rough seas and floated to the port below the church. As a result, the Virgin of Bonaria became a revered protector of all sailors – so much so that Pedro de Mendoza prayed to Bonaria for her fair winds before his expedition to South America in 1536 and, when he

and his men established their colony in present-day Argentina, they named it Buenos Aires.

The wooden Virgin is still displayed by the high altar inside the sanctuary. To the right is a larger, modern basilica in Gothic Catalan style. Note the votive boat dangling from the ceiling and the columns flanking the wide single nave. The sanctuary museum in the church's cloister displays the statue's wooden crate that floated to shore, as well as six mummified corpses of the Catalan Alagon family who succumbed to the plague.

Beach-hopping along the southeastern coast

Had Prince Aga Khan ever driven along the southeastern coast's Litoranea Panoramica, he might have built the Costa Smeralda in Cagliari's backyard. Fortunately, when Khan was busy mapping out his coastal resort in 1961, the only way to travel from Cagliari to Villasimius was by boat. These days, a winding two-lane rollercoaster passes along some of the island's most pristine coastline, making for a day-trip from the capital that shouldn't be missed.

At the end of **Poetto**, follow signs towards Villasimius. After passing signs for Nuraghe Diana in Quartu, the road climbs, hugging the coast and offering breathtaking views of the entire Golfo degli Angeli. **Cala Regina** is the first in a series of hidden coves but the fairest of them all is **Mari Pintau**. A true Cagliaritano retreat, this beach is discernable by the number of boats anchored in its azure bay, as well as by the long line of cars parked along the hard shoulder. A small brown sign indicates the dirt path leading down to the pebbled beach.

After a swim, apply more sunscreen before continuing towards Villasimius. As you approach the vacation homes at **Geremeas** and **Solanas,** look for the 16th- and 17th-century Spanish lookout towers built to defend against pirate raids. After coiling up another *macchia*-covered mountain, the road shoots down towards grazing goats to the left and **Piscadeddus** and **Campus** beaches to the right.

Once you get to Villasimius' main drag, take the fork in the road to the right at the bottom of via del Mare, past rows of oleander bushes and a golf course. Don't drive too fast or you'll miss the left-hand turn at the Porto Turistico for southeastern Sardinia's finest beach, **Porto Giunco**.

Take the same road back, following signs for Poetto as you reach Cagliari. Heading into the city, take the exit towards **Calamosca** on viale Poetto and turn right. At the beach's entrance, veer to the left at Hotel Calamosca and continue until you reach the gated entrance to **La Paillote** (see page 123), a bar with its own beach. Cap off the day sitting in the terraced garden overlooking Cala Fighera.

Note: Avoid this itinerary on summer weekends – it takes two hours in traffic to return to Cagliari from Villasimius.

The Sarrabus & Gerrei

Sardinia's southeastern corner is a mixture of surf and turf. The coastal Sarrabus region's emerald waters are framed by the mountain ranges of its inland neighbour, the Gerrei, which are blanketed in *macchia* and myrtle berries. Between these contrasting regions, the rugged peaks of the Parco dei Sette Fratelli provide a natural buffer. The SS387 is the Gerrei's mountain artery, whose sweeping views justify risking its hairpin turns.

Capo Carbonara.

Parco dei Sette Fratelli

Off the SS125, Km 30, T070-27991.
Daily 0800-1700, free.

The Seven Brothers Park takes its name from a chain of seven granite peaks that dominate this 4,000-ha forest. In the 19th century, coal miners created eight hiking paths, ranging from three to 24 km in length, which dissect the park's thick Mediterranean brush and stripped cork trees. Bring binoculars to catch a glimpse of wild boar, mouflon, golden eagles and the endangered Sardinian deer, which is best seen (or at least heard) during rutting season each September. The park has dedicated a museum to its antlered star: **Museo del Cervo Sardo** (T335-809 1112, Tue-Sun by appointment only).

To reach the park, take the old SS125 from Cagliari to Muravera. At Km 30, the road forks at the Arcu e Tidu mountain pass with a sign marking the park's entrance to the right.

Tip...

A left turn at Arcu e Tidu will take you to Sardinia's cherry capital, **Burcei**, whose delicious spring-time harvests can make for a scenic picnic when eaten in the surrounding countryside.

Parco dei Sette Fratelli.

Villasimius & Capo Carbonara

Once a quiet town of farmers and granite miners, Villasimius' tourist economy got a jumpstart with the arrival of electricity and telephones in the 1950s. By the 1960s, Sardinia's southeastern tip had become a haven for European artists, including German writer Ernst Jünger, who wrote about the town in his collection *Terra Sarda*. Today, Villasimius' stuccoed homes have become a fashionably affordable summer getaway for Italians seeking vintage Sardinia rather than vogue Smeralda.

The area's popularity is partly due to the 9,000-ha **Carbonara Cape Marine Park**, which, stretches from Capo Boi north to Punta Porceddus and ensures that Villasimius' 15 pristine beaches stay that way. Much of the park is off-limits but various charter companies offer trips from the tourist port to spot dolphin migrations and red coral reefs; your best bet is aboard the *Matilda* (see page 130).

Just offshore, **Isola di Serpentara** and the oddly named **Isola dei Cavoli** ('Cabbage Island') remain uninhabited, in part due to African pirate raids, which continued well into the 19th century. Their rocky sea beds have created a nautical graveyard and a divers' paradise over the centuries, with shipwrecks dating from Roman times to the Second World War. Learn about it all at the **Museo Archeologico di Villasimius** (via Frau 5, T070-793 0290, Tue-Sun 1000-1300 and 2100-2400, €3, €1.50 concessions, free under-6s.)

Costa Rei

Heading north from Villasimius, veer left at the sign for Hotel Oleandro, taking the dirt path under the bridge to reach **Punto Molentis**, where two granite formations are connected by a narrow sandy isthmus. Just up the road is the crescent shaped **Cala Pira**, whose turquoise cove is even more attractive (and less crowded) than the area's main draw, **Costa Rei**. Stretching for 8 km north to the lighthouse at Capo Ferrato, this golden shoreline, with its refreshing breezes, draws hordes of northern Italian, German and Dutch tourists to its many resorts each summer.

Isola dei Cavoli.

Muravera

Found in a low-lying plain at the mouth of the river Flumendosa, the town of Muravera bakes in Sardinia's hottest average temperature. Yet, the town's surroundings are shaded by citrus groves which produce the most abundant and best oranges in Sardinia. They can be bought at **Agrumicola Sarrabus** (Km 62.7, SS125, T070-993 0465, Mon-Fri 0900-1200 and 1500-1800). Every Easter, Muravera hosts the three-day **Sagra degli Agrumi** festival to celebrate the orange harvest as well as to show off the costumes and traditions of the Sarrabus-Gerrei region. If you can't make it for Easter, the town puts on a scaled-down summer encore every Tuesday and Thursday night from 15 July to 30 September along its main drag, via Roma. The town is also awash with murals depicting local traditions.

Close by is the **Stagno di Colostrai**, whose expansive lagoon is one of southern Sardinia's best places to spot egrets, herons and flamingos from April to October.

San Vito

Neighbouring San Vito is believed to be the original home of the *launeddas* – the three-cane reed precursor of the bagpipe, which produces Sardinia's mellifluous pastoral soundtrack. It's also home to Sardinia's most famous musician, Luigi Lai. "*Il Maestro*", as he is affectionately called, has converted his home at via Spano 26 into the island's only official school for aspiring *launeddas* players; it's a good place to check for impromptu performances. For the real deal, come back for the town's **Sagra delle Launeddas** in early August.

The SS387 travels inland from the coast towards a mountain range resembling a human face, known locally as 'La Sfinge' (the Sphynx), and the lonely Gerrei region.

Armungia

After winding your way up 300 m, you'll come to Armungia, whose stone houses and surrounding schist walls make it the most picturesque village in the area. A nuraghe from 1400-1500 BC stands guard in the centre of the town; it is the only place in Sardinia that preserves the Bronze Age tradition of a village settlement around a nuraghic tower. Entrance is at the **Museo Storico Etnografico** (Thu-Sun 0900-1300 and 1600-2000, €3.50, €2.50 concessions, free under 6, €1 nuraghe only).

Pranu Muttedu Archeological Park

Località Pranu Muttedu, T070-982059, pranumuttedu.com.
Daily 0830-1800, guided tours every hour; €4, €2 concessions.

A left-hand turn on the SP23 takes you towards Goni and southeastern Sardinia's most important Neolithic site. Excavations in 1986 uncovered a prehistoric cult attributed to the Ozieri culture from roughly 3200 BC, complete with mass grave tombs chiselled out of sandstone and roughly 60 menhirs (the highest concentration in Sardinia) aligned to mark the sun and moon's position during the equinoxes over 5000 years ago.

Menhirs and graves at Pranu Muttedu Archaeological Park.

Central Campidano

The SS131 highway shoots north of Cagliari towards Sardinia's central Campidano, a 25-km wide low-lying basin separating the mountains of the Iglesiente and Gerrei. To the north, the Campidano gives way to a landscape of bumpy, conical hills, dubbed the 'Marmilla' by ancient Sardinians who thought that these seductive rolling mounds resembled breasts (*mammella* in Latin).

The Campidano's fertile cereal fields and accessibility from Cagliari have always attracted outside attention and exploitation: the Carthaginians ensured that their wheat fields stayed in full sunlight by threatening to kill anyone who planted a single tree, while the Romans' strict feudal laws, designed to exploit the land and indigenous population in this area, gave Sardinia the nickname Rome's 'granary'. In fact, from the third to the first century BC, the Campidano's seven inhabitants per square kilometre produced one third as much grain as the whole of Sicily. The area's landlocked sea of vast golden stalks can seem suffocatingly dusty in the summer but where its small towns fall short on stimulation (or nightlife), they make up for in antiquity and geological wonder and are a must-see for history buffs. A detour to this sensuous plain will allow you to explore the Bronze Age fortresses of Nuraghe Arrubiu, Genna Maria and Su Nuraxi; discover the world's only miniature wild horses roaming the Giara di Gesturi, and marvel at medieval castles perched high on Sardinia's swelling bosom.

Sanluri

Sanluri's 14th-century **Castello Giudicale** is the only one of Sardinia's original 88 castles that doesn't lie in ruins and remains completely inhabitable. After housing Eleonora d'Arborea for five years until 1387, the four-towered fortress served as the backdrop for the Battle of Sanluri in 1409. These days, the castle is home to the **Museo Risorgimentale Duca d'Aosta** (via Gen. Nino Villa Santa 1, T070-864 5867, Tue, Wed, Fri, Sat 1100-1300 and 1730-2000, Sun 0945-1300 and 1730-2000, €6), which displays antique military curios collected by the palace's former owner, Count Nino Villa Santa (long-serving secretary to the Duke of Aosta). The Count's spry, 80-something son is your guide. He single-handedly rebuilt the castle's first floor and talks you through two hours of weapons, maps and letters dating from the First World War up to Italy's failed conquest of Ethiopia in the Second World War. The castle's upper floors hold a surprise: 343 wax figurines – the largest private collection in Europe.

Sardara

Cobbled streets, arched doorways and bougainvillea-clad stone houses give Sardara an elegantly weathered historic atmosphere. In the middle of it all is the **Chiesa di San Gregorio**, a sixth-century Romanesque church with a narrow Gothic façade. The 16th-century Gothic bell tower of the **Chiesa Parrocchiale Beata Vergine Assunta** (piazza Parrocchia, T070-938 7048, Sun 0800-1200 or by appointment) looms high above the town. Nearby, the old municipal building has recently been converted into the **Civico Museo Archeologico Villa Abbas** (piazza della Liberta' 7, T070-938 6183, coopvillabbas.sardegna.it, daily 0900-1300 and 1700-2000, €2.60, €4.50 including entrance to Sant'Anastasia), which beautifully presents a concise history of Sardinia and displays recreated tombs found at Sardara's Terr'e Cresica necropolis and several *bronzetti* archers from the

eighth century BC. The museum also shows relics found just down the street at the nuraghic temple well of **Sant'Anastasia** (vico Sant'Anastasia, T070-938 6183, €2.60, €4.50 including entrance to archaeological museum). The site preserves the ruins of a village built between the ninth and eighth centuries BC enclosing a sacred well from a nearby spring; you can descend the 12 steps to its source. Known as *'De is Dolus'* (pain reliever) by locals, the spring water was used for medicinal purposes by the nuraghic population.

Genna Maria

Nr Villanovaforru, 8 km northeast of Sardara, T070-930 0050.
Oct-Mar Tue-Sun 0930-1300 and 1530-1800, Apr-Sep 0930-1300 and 1530-1900. €2.50 or €5 with Villanovaforru archaeological museum.

This nuraghic complex is one of southern Sardinia's most important Bronze Age sites. The fortress preserves an original central tower from the 15th century BC around which multiple side towers were later built, connected by a rampart. As the site lost its defensive function in the Iron Age, a village of beehive huts for up to 70 people sprang up around the old fortress. The original nuraghic inhabitants abandoned the complex in the eighth century BC, possibly due to a devastating fire. For more information, visit the **Museo Archeologico** (piazza Costituzione 4, Oct-Mar Tue-Sun 0930-1300 and 1530-1800, Apr-Sep 0930-1300 and 1530-1900, €3.50 or €5 with nuraghic complex).

Genna Maria.

Around the island

Las Plassas

As you enter Las Plassas driving towards Barumini on the SS197, you can't miss the skeleton of the ruined 12th-century **Castello di las Plassas**. Built by the Giudicato of Arborea as a southern outpost against its troublesome neighbour, the Giudicato of Cagliari, it sits perched atop a cone-shaped mound that epitomizes Marmilla's curvaceous landscape and clearly resembles one of Madonna's bras from the early 1990s.

Nuraghe Su Nuraxi

Off the SS197, 500 m west of Barumini towards Tuili, T070-936 8128.
Daily 0900-1930 guided tour only, €7, €5 under 18s, €10/€8 including admission to Casa Zapata.

Declared a UNESCO World Heritage site, 'Sardinia's Stonehenge' is the island's most famous nuraghic monument. Ironically, Su Nuraxi was rediscovered completely by accident. For roughly a thousand years the site lay buried under a mound of dirt that blended in so perfectly with the Marmilla's rolling grain fields that no one knew it was there. When a chance flood eroded the soil in 1949, a circular stone wall was revealed. Sardinia's most famous archaeologist, Giovanni Lilliu from Barumini, assembled a team of workers in 1951 and started digging, not knowing that it would take five years of non-stop labour to excavate the site fully.

When the digging finally finished in 1956, Lilliu's crew had uncovered the remnants of an entire nuraghic village built around a Bronze Age castle whose central tower dates back to the 15th century BC. Considering the period, some 200 years before the founding of Athens, the quality of engineering is unbelievable. Despite understandable deterioration over the past 3500 years, its overall structure remains remarkably well preserved and retains a striking grandeur. The castle's 11 towers were built by shaping enormous basalt rocks into square blocks and somehow transporting the one-tonne stones from their

Su Nuraxi – the jewel of the nuraghic fortresses.

Inside Su Nuraxi.

Tip...

The best way to get to Su Nuraxi is by car; buses from Cagliari to Barumini take one hour 40 minutes and require an additional 30-minute walk from the bus stop. Visitors must be accompanied by a guide who leads bi-lingual tours every 30 minutes (call ahead to ensure English availability). The site gets busy in the summer and waits are possible, so bring plenty of water and your own shade.

source at the Giara di Gesturi 5 km away (see page 100). The original three-storey nuraghe once rose 20 m (but has since crumbled to just over 14 m) and formed the centrepiece for the rest of the complex, which was constructed in three phases.

Following the collapse of the complex's third wall after the 13th century BC, its inhabitants entered the castle by scaling an 8-m wall, probably by rope, which could then be retracted in case of attack. Today, visitors need only climb a scaffolded stairway to reach the narrow tunnel that descends steeply into the inner courtyard (whose 20-m well still has water in it!). The courtyard surrounds the central tower and is protected by a bastion with four two-storey towers facing each cardinal point, which were built between the 14th and 12th centuries BC. The hidden gem of the castle's inner core is its north tower. A needle-tight passage wraps around the central tower and opens into a virtual refrigerator of soil and stone insulation cleverly used by the nuraghic population to store food. Enclosing this bastion is a hexagonal defensive fortress rising 7 m and pierced with slits just large enough to shoot arrows through.

More than 200 huts surround the castle and all preserve their stone bases in extraordinary detail. The oldest huts were built in the 13th century BC. As the castle's towers collapsed, its fallen stones were cannibalized to make successive rectangular huts by the Carthaginians and Romans up until the seventh century AD when the site was finally abandoned. Wandering this confused warren of alleys reveals modern-looking fireplaces, wells, atriums, arched entranceways and even a canal system.

A cumulative ticket to the Su Nuraxi archaeological site includes admission to **Casa Zapata** (viale San Francesco 16, T070-936 8476, daily 0900-1930 , €7, €5 for under-18s, €10/€8 including admission to Su Nuraxi) in nearby Barumini. This ethnographic museum displays the agricultural tools of the area and demonstrates the craftsmanship of the *launeddas* players in creating their own reed instruments. Another building contains various artefacts from the Su Nuraxi site. Below Casa Zapata are the visible remains of **Nurax' e' Cresia**: a nuraghe from the 12th century BC discovered during restoration work in 1990.

Around the island

Giara di Gesturi

5 km north of Barumini, T349-075 8602.
Daily 0900-1900, €3.

Gesturi is the next town up the road from Barumini, a 1300-person hamlet dominated by the late Gothic Chiesa di Santa Teresa d'Avila. Just past the church on the left is a single-track road that

coils up to one of Sardinia's most famous geological oddities, a 43-sq-km basalt plateau (*giara* in Sardo) that rises 500-600 m above the surrounding plain like a perfectly flat table.

This suspended highland's isolation fosters a virtual climatic biodome that is home to 56 species of flowers (including 15 varieties of orchid), dense cork forests and the undomesticated *cavallino sardo*. Probably introduced by the Carthaginians, these miniature dark brown horses stand roughly 120-cm tall and once roamed all of Sardinia. However, as a result of centuries of hunting, there are only 600 left and the only place to spot them is the *giara*, usually near the plateau's seasonal lagoons, known as *paulis*.

The plateau also preserves 26 nuraghi, including **Broncu é Madili**, the oldest 'proto-nuraghe' in Sardinia, built in the 18th century BC on the western side of the plateau. In much better shape are the thatched *pinnettas* scattered throughout the park, which have been used as shelters by passing shepherds for thousands of years and perfectly resemble nuraghic-age huts.

Santuario Nuragico di Santa Vittoria

Serri, 20 km east of Barumini, T388-049 2451.
May-mid Sep daily 0900-1900, mid Sep-Apr daily 0900-1700, €4, €2 children.

East of Barumini, a narrow road winds back towards the province of Cagliari and into Serri, a downright ugly cinderblock town in the remote Sarcidano region. Scattered across a three-hectare site nearby are the remains of a nuraghic settlement constructed between the 13th and eighth centuries BC to honour the god of water. Over 20 buildings have been excavated, including a small collection of village huts (which pale in comparison with the nearby chief and priest's huts) and an assembly room. The ringed seating here is where the town's elders conducted civic and religious rituals, often culminating in the sacrifice of a goat or a wild boar.

Gesturi.

The site's crowning feature is a 3-m deep sacred well which drew pilgrims to participate in pagan rites that lasted many days. The pilgrims were housed in the large, elliptical 'feasts' enclosure', a porticoed communal dormitory where guests feasted on sheep, beef and clams with the locals before passing out for the night. Some 3000 years later, many rural Sardinian churches still continue this tradition of providing room and board in small dwellings called *cumbessiàs* to guests who are attending prolonged rites.

The site gets its name from the stone church, originally built by the Byzantines on top of a nuraghe in the sixth century AD but rebuilt by the Vittorini monks in the 11th century (hence, Santa Vittoria). The monks began the custom of serving an outdoor lunch following mass on 11 September each year, a tradition that is maintained by the residents of Serri to this day.

Nuraghe Arrubiu

15 km east of Serri, T0782-847269, nuraghearrubiu.it.
Mar-Oct daily 0930-1300 and 1500-2030,
Nov-Feb 0930-1700. €4, €2 children.

Five kilometres southeast of Orroli is Sardinia's largest nuraghic complex. Though the site lacks Su Nuraxi's accompanying village, its red-tinted blocks (*arrubiu* is red in Sardo) paint a prettier picture than Barumini's more famous fortress. The nuraghe's 14-m central tower has crumbled from its original lofty 27 m but is surrounded by the island's only example of a five-towered fortress. A narrow courtyard separates the fortress from a rampart, once connected to 12 further towers. Remarkably, the whole structure was built at the same time (in the 14th century BC) and was dated when the oldest ceramic Mycenaean vase in Sardinia was recovered under the central courtyard.

The Sulcis

Sardinia's southwestern corner was the Phoenicians' favourite. The ancient Lebanese traders developed Sardinia's first foreign settlement, Nora, on a lonely peninsula; settled on the golden sands of Bitia (at modern-day Chia) and built one of the largest cities in the Mediterranean, Sulci (after which the entire area is named), on an offshore island. In recent times, wealthy entrepreneurs have started buying large swathes of coast around Santa Margherita and developing it with glitzy resorts reminiscent of the Costa Smeralda. However, the more stunning Costa del Sud, with its rows of juniper trees and placid inlets, remains relatively undeveloped and is one of Sardinia's most gorgeous drives. Continuing clockwise around the coast you'll pass the islands of Sant'Antioco and San Pietro. Sant'Antioco is the site of the Mediterranean's largest Punic necropolis, while San Pietro retains more than a hint of Liguria in its only town, far-flung Carloforte.

The coast at Nora.

Riserva di Monte Arcosu

20 km west of Cagliari, T070-968714, wwf.it.
Sep-May Sat-Sun 0900-1800, Jun-Aug Sat-Sun
0800-1900 (open daily to groups by
appointment), guided visits Sun 1100 and 1500.

You'll see Monte Arcosu before you come across
the signs that tell you how to get there: turn off the
SS195 12 km west of Cagliari, go past the Chiesa di
Santa Lucia and follow signs to the reserve.
Covering 3,600 ha of rocky peaks and ravines,
Monte Arcosu is the largest natural reserve in Italy
and the largest forest in the whole Mediterranean.
It is criss-crossed by over a dozen hiking paths
covering 80 km, allowing you to discover streams,
sweeping mountains, 100 species of flowers, plus
wild boar, foxes, mountain cats and rare native
deer. The whole area used to belong to a real
estate company who couldn't get a return on the
property, so the World Wildlife Federation snapped
it up in 1985 to thwart poachers from killing off the
last of Sardinia's native deer. The investment has
paid off, as the deer population has soared from 80
in 1985 to over 1,000 today. Along with the Parco
dei Sette Fratelli (see page 93), the reserve offers
one of the last wild refuges for this elusive animal.

Above: A rare Sardinian deer.
Below: Wild boar.

Nora

Località Nora, T070-920 9138, norascavi.it.
Daily 0900-2030, guided tours every hour (1100
in English). €5.50 including admission to
archeological museum, €2.50 under-14s.
Shuttle buses run between piazza Municipio in
Pula and Nora, 9 daily, €2.

Driving south through the modern beach town of
Pula, you'll see the 12th-century Romanesque
Chiesa di Sant'Efisio (T340-485 1860, Sat
1000-1200, Sun 1000-1200 and 1630-1930) standing
just off the crescent-shaped Spiaggia di Nora. Every
3 May, pilgrims arrive at the site from Cagliari to
honour the city's patron saint who was allegedly
martyred here (see page 85). The road continues to
the end of the cape where scattered Roman
columns mark the once great city of Nora.

Founded by Phoenicians travelling from Iberia
in the ninth to eighth centuries BC, Nora was the
first foreign colony in Sardinia. Phoenician sailors

Above: The columns and mosaics attest to Nora's former glory.

Tip...

The archeological site has precious little shade and can be a sweltering place in the summer, so come at dusk when spotlights illuminate the former city's splendour.

Above: A lone column.
Right: Detail from the mosaic.

used the isthmus' three natural harbours to repair their vessels and later built storehouses to trade with the indigenous population. The site became a wealthy city under the Carthaginians who took it over in the sixth century BC and transformed Nora into an important maritime trading post: ivory from Africa, copper from Cyprus and gold from the Sahara have all been found here. However, aside from the ruined temple dedicated to the Carthaginian fertility goddess, Tanit, and a *tophet* necropolis containing 200 urns of cremated newborn babies, little remains of the settlement.

Instead, nearly everything visible was built by the Romans who conveniently knocked down their predecessors' work to construct wide roads, a sewer system, stately *domus* houses and temples.

Under the Romans, Nora was Sardinia's most important city and remains the island's best preserved *municipum*. A falcate-shaped marble theatre (the only one in Sardinia) was built to hold political meetings and plays and is still used each summer for poetry recitals. Four deep thermal baths were constructed next to the sea in a complex that was large enough to hold both an indoor library and a medley of prostitutes (a real one-stop shop for all your needs). The site's opulence is best revealed in the various mosaics made from black, white and ochre *tesserae* that once adorned the floors. In fact, thanks to the African-inspired mosaic designs, the *opus africanum* style of the condominium dwellings (which use small stones joined by mud combined with square pillars) and the tight alleys, the city was far more reminiscent of northern Africa than Rome and logically so, considering its close proximity.

Various artefacts excavated from the site are displayed at Pula's **Museo Archeologico di Patroni** (corso Vittorio Emanuele 67, T070-920 9610, hours and prices as above). If you fancy treasure hunting for yourself, rising tides and storm erosion left much of Nora's original settlement submerged and littered the whole coastline with underwater relics, so bring your snorkel! The best place to explore is in the shallow **Laguna di Nora** (see page 130), though the **Spiaggia di Nora** reveals part of the original port structure. A 12-year-old boy discovered a Roman anchor while snorkelling here in August, 2008!

The Porto Campana beach in Chia.

Tip...

You'd never guess it from the road but the 14-km stretch of coast between Pula and Chia, known as Santa Margherita, is full of private beach resorts hidden by dense pinewoods. The beaches here pale in comparison to those at Chia and Teulada, but, if you're intent on sharing towel space with VIPs, turn left at the arrow for 'La Pineta'.

Chia & the Costa del Sud

Turning off the SS195 towards Chia, a dazzling 26-km road hugs the coast, winding past some of Sardinia's most picturesque and unspoiled beaches, known as the Costa del Sud.

A brown sign in Chia indicates the turn-off for the Torre di Chia (access from Su Portu beach, mid Jul-mid Sep daily 0930-1230 and 1530-1900, €1), one of only three Spanish watchtowers on the island that you can still enter. The tower offers extraordinary views of Chia's five other beaches and marks the focal point of the ancient Phoenician settlement of Bitia. This colony from the eighth century BC now lies underwater but a handful of Punic and Roman coins dating from the third century BC are on display inside the tower.

With emerald water lapping fine powdery sand set among juniper trees, there are any number of good places to drop your towel in Chia. The granite outcrops in the natural bay at Cala Cipolla (Onion Cove) form a great picture but nothing tops the golden dunes and nesting flamingos in the nearby Capo Spartivento lagoon around Su Giudeu beach. (Bring your snorkel and lay out your towel just in front of the offshore islands.)

Leaving Chia, a twisting road climbs towards Teulada with sweeping ocean views. After a hairpin turn, Capo Tuerredda's half-moon bay and cerulean-coloured water will appear out of nowhere. (Use the official car park, as cars left on the hard shoulder will be fined.) After the sign for Malfitano, pull off to the left at Capo Malfitano for another great photo-op and a scenic hike to a Spanish watchtower at the end of the cape.

Monte Sirai

4 km northwest of Carbonia, T0781-62665. Wed-Sun 1000-2000, €6.

Northwest of the run-down former mining town of Carbonia, signs on the SS126 indicate the turn-off for the ancient Punic military base at Monte Sirai. In 650 BC, Phoenicians from Sulci (present-day Sant'Antioco) settled the 190-m plateau to control access to the region's rich mineral deposits. They were replaced by the Carthaginians in 510 BC who built a *tophet*, defensive tower and necropolis, a few of which can still be entered. The site's preservation leaves a bit to be desired but its elevated position does make for a fantastic sunset... as long as you look away from Portovesme. A small collection of finds from the site are displayed in Carbonia at Villa Sulcis (via Napoli 4, T0781-63512, Apr-Oct Tue-Sun 0900-1300 and 1600-2000, Nov-Mar Tue-Sun 0900-1300 and 1500-1900, €6).

Tip…

Although it's overlooked by the kilometre-long aluminium plant at Portovesme – a glaring industrial eye-sore on the otherwise undeveloped coastline – Portoscuso has an attractive tourist port and a fantastic restaurant (see page 124), making it a pleasant place to wait for the ferry to Carloforte.

Sant'Antioco

The Phoenicians built Sulci, their largest Sardinian settlement, on the northeast coast of this island, beneath present-day Sant'Antioco town. It would be Italy's fourth largest island – after Sicily, Sardinia and Elba – if it hadn't been for the Romans, who constructed a causeway across the 4-km Golfo di Palmas in the third century BC. (The causeway can be seen on the right as you drive across the modern jetty). The Romans named Sant'Antioco 'Plumbea' (lead town), after its most precious resource, and, unlike its swaggering resort neighbour, San Pietro, the island limps along unpretentiously in the shadow of its glorious past, welcoming visitors with a salty, purposeful air.

Sant'Antioco town & Sulci

Sant'Antioco (the larger of the two towns on the island) is built on the ruins of Phoenician Sulci. Stroll under the charming tree-lined avenue of corso Vittorio Emanuele and climb away from the sea towards the **Chiesa di Sant'Antioco** (piazza Parrocchia, T0781-800455, Mon-Fri 0900-1200, 1500-1800 and 1900-2000, Sat-Sun 1030-1115, 1500-1800 and 1900-2000. Guided tours of the catacombs €2.50, €2 children). Inside its sixth-century red Baroque façade, the elegant stone interior houses the remains of St Antioco. According to legend, his Mauritanian countrymen sentenced him to die at sea alone on a boat for refusing to renounce his faith but winds blew him to Sant'Antioco where he established Sardinia's first Christian colony. To the right of the transept you

The *tophet*

Of all the Punic religious relics scattered throughout the Mediterranean, none are as eerie or controversial as the *tophet*, whose best preserved example is at Sant'Antioco. According to ancient Graeco-Roman scholars like Diodorus, these open-air necropolises ("tophet" literally means "roasters" in Hebrew) were where the first-born children of wealthy families were gruesomely burned alive as a sacrifice to bring prosperity to the village. This claim carried weight until the 21st century when careful studies of *tophet* sites revealed that 80 per cent of those cremated were miscarried foetuses, while the others had died shortly after birth.

Today, most scholars agree that the *tophet* was a sacred site to honour the fertility gods Tanit and Baal in an era (eighth to the first centuries BC) when seven out of ten infants died within the first year of life. The infants' remains were cremated and placed inside a clay vase with the bones of sacrificed animals, while the grieving parents prayed for another child. During Carthaginian times, if the mother became pregnant again, the parents returned to the *tophet* site and placed intricately carved stele tombstones (the earliest depicting fascinating pharaoh-inspired deities) to thank the gods.

More than 4,000 urns and 2,000 steles have been found in Sant'Antioco's *tophet* site, the best of which are preserved inside the adjacent **Museo Archeologico** (end of via Karalis, T0781-841089, Mon 0900-2400, Tue-Sun 0900-2000, €2.50, €6 for archaeology museum and *tophet*, €13 for archaeology museum, *tophet*, caves, ethnography museum and castle), which also displays local jewellery, vases and masks from the Phoenician, Carthaginian and Roman eras.

can descend with a guide into a series of second-century catacombs where a few faded frescoes have been preserved.

Beneath modern Sant'Antioco is the Mediterranean's largest Punic necropolis, covering six hectares and encompassing over 1500 tombs. Reconstruction and Italian bureaucracy have rendered much of the necropolis inaccessible to tourists since 1997, leaving exposed only the excavated **Villaggio Ipogeo** (via Necropoli,

Around the island

T0781-841089, archeotur.it, Mon 0900-2400, Tue-Sun 0900-2000, €2.50, €6 with museum and castle, €13 with museum, castle, *tophet* and archeological museum). These 40 hand-dug caves were used as burial chambers from the sixth century BC through Roman occupation and were then used as homes by Sant'Antioco's working class from the 1600s until (get ready…) the 1950s. Children slept on straw mats and the lack of water or electricity kept the rent down. Sant'Antioco's commune eventually displaced the cave dwellers.

Nearby, the **Museo Etnografico** (via Necropoli 24, T0781-841089, Mon 0900-2400, Tue-Sun 0900-2000, €2.50, €6 with caves and castle, €13 with caves, castle, *tophet* and archeological museum) is a converted farmhouse with a collection of agricultural tools, handicrafts and domestic items once used on the island.

The Savoyard fort, **Su Pisu** (T0781-841089, Mon 0900-2400, Tue-Sun 0900-2000, €2.50, €6 with caves and museum, €13 with caves, museum, *tophet* and archaeological museum) guards the town from its highest point. Built in 1812 to defend against pirate attacks, the citadel couldn't prevent Saracens from raiding the town three years later and seizing nearly 150 of Sant'Antioco's residents to serve as slaves in Tunisia.

Around Sant'Antioco

A ten-minute drive north from Sant'Antioco takes you to the island's only other town, **Calasetta**, where ferries to and from San Pietro arrive and depart (see page 131). (There are buses between Sant'Antioco town and Calasetta every 30 minutes.) It was settled by Ligurian families in the late 18th century and retains a vaguely old-world feel. The town's beach, the wonderful **Spiagga Grande**, comes into its own when the southeastern *scirocco* wind blows. When the northernwestern *maestrale* arrives, locals prefer to head south towards **Maledroxia** or **Spiaggia di Coaquaddus**. Inland, you'll find numerous summer cottages and the occasional vineyard producing Carignano red wine; buy it at **Vinoteca Shardana** (see page 129).

San Pietro

San Pietro is known as Carloforte, after the island's only town. Colonized by the families of Ligurian coral fishermen from the Tunisian island of Tabarka in 1738, it retains a colonial stateliness which seems out of place in Sardinia. Its 6,500 inhabitants still speak an 18th-century Genoan dialect and blend north African recipes with their famous blue-fin tuna catch to offer one of Sardinia's most enticing dining experiences.

Carloforte

Seen from the ferry, San Pietro's only town, Carloforte, is a sea of colours: white yachts sway in the tourist port backed by green palms and pastel houses lining the quay. It's a scene straight from the Cinque Terre in Liguria: not surprising, perhaps, when you remember that Carloforte is essentially a displaced Ligurian colony.

The town's ancestors were fishermen from the town of Pegli near Genoa who were sent to the small island of Tabarka off the coast of Tunisia to harvest red coral for the noble Lomellini family in 1542. As their population grew, they became susceptible to Saracen pirate raids until, in 1736, the entire town became enslaved under the control of the Tunisian governor. Its residents pleaded with the King of Sardinia, Carlo Emanuele III, to intervene and he graciously negotiated a ransom with Tunisian officials and settled the 140 enslaved families on the deserted island of San Pietro in 1738. With northern Italian efficiency, the freed settlers built Carloforte in only two years, around a statue to honour the king. The Saracens tracked down the settlers again in 1798 and made off with 944 captives from Carloforte before the Savoyards ransomed them back to the island five years later.

Today, Carloforte remains one of Sardinia's least Sardinian towns. Its unique dialect, *Tabarkino*, is distinct from anywhere else in Sardinia. The town's main draws are its colourful alleyways and Ligurian and north African cuisine. Try the *farinata* made from chickpea flour, or the *cascà* (couscous).

Essentials

❶ Getting there & around Saremar (T892 123, saremar.it) operates up to 17 daily ferries between Portovesme and Carloforte (40 mins), and up to 14 daily ferries between Carloforte and Calasetta on Sant'Antioco (30 mins). **Delcomar** (T0781- 857123, delcomar.it) runs up to seven late-night ferries between Carloforte and Calasetta (40 mins). You certainly don't need a car in Carloforte but you can enquire about private taxi services at Carloforte's tourist office. A bus runs from piazza Carlo Emanuele in Carloforte south on the SS102 eight times a day in the summer.

Carloforte.

Around San Pietro

Like Sant'Antioco, San Pietro is largely covered in green *macchia* with few roads. Charter companies in Carloforte's harbour offer tours to the island's far-flung beaches and grottoes (such as the steep **Grotto di Mezzaluna**), accessible only by boat. The SP101 road north from Carloforte heads towards the island's tuna-processing plant and the fabulous **Cala Lunga**, whose long, placid inlet makes for a fantastic swim if you don't mind the rocky shore.

South of town, the SP103 wraps around saltpans – where flamingos nest from spring into summer – and continues to some of the island's best beaches (**Guidi** and **La Bobba**) en route to **Le Colonne**, whose two massive rock pillars jut out from the sea like columns. The road ends at the island's largest beach, **La Caletta,** where the *maestrale* wind rolls in some decent surf.

San Pietro's tuna slaughter

Unlike their Sardinian counterparts, the tabarchini have always been fisherman and have been economically dependent on the annual bluefin tuna catch since settling on San Pietro in the 18th century. To this day, the island's prosperity depends on the annual tuna harvest – a month-long affair culminating in a bloodbath known as the 'mattanza' (slaughter). Tuna fishing in the Mediterranean dates back to the Phoenicians, who prized the fish enough to engrave them on their coins. The island's multicultural history is evidenced in the mattanza's blend of archaic Ligurian trapping techniques with Arabic titles, such as 'rais' for the captain of the slaughter.

As the tuna enter the Mediterranean in early May to spawn, a series of nylon nets are placed between the northeast tip of San Pietro and neighbouring Isola Piana. The nets are laid to create six chambers covering 500 m, complete with a system of doors leading the fish through the maze-like rooms before trapping them in the final camera della morte. On the day of the mattanza, the appointed rais leads a solemn prayer before shouting to the tonnarotti (tuna fishermen) to raise the trapped tuna. Rising to the surface, the tuna are stabbed with massive hooks, dyeing the sea red as they're hauled onto large boats and brought to a nearby processing plant. The pick of the catch is snapped up by Japanese importers who ship their harvest to Rome and then fly it first class to Tokyo the following day.

Though the annual yield has decreased over the years, roughly 4,000 tuna, each weighing an average of 120 kg, were caught in 2008. Recently, the island initiated Girotonno (girotonno.org), a festival in honour of the tuna harvest, during which tourists can hire boats to witness the slaughter first hand and dine at international food stands back in town.

For displays of the mattanza's trapping techniques, visit Carloforte's **Museo Civico** (via Cisterna del Re 20/24, T0781-855880, carloforte.net/museo. Tue 0900-1300, Wed 1030-1300 and 1500-1800, Thu-Sat 1600-2000, Sun 1030-1300, €2, €1 concessions).

Heading west from Carloforte, the SS104 dissects the island towards **Capo Sandalo** and a lone lighthouse. This is the best spot to see the rare Eleonora's falcon, named after Eleonora of Arborea who loved them so much that she declared herself the owner of them all in her 1395 *Carta de Logu.*

The Iglesiente

North of Carbonia, the Sulcis' rolling countryside abruptly tilts into the sprawling mountain ranges of the Iglesiente, a contrasting territory defined by its industrial history and its undeveloped coast.
Since Phoenician times, the area's abundant iron, lead and silver deposits have lured a long list of foreigners to mine for riches, exploiting both the land and the local population. The Romans unimaginatively dubbed the area 'Metalla' and were quick to get their hands (or rather, their slaves' hands) dirty in the local mines. The mines flourished again from the mid-1800s to the mid-1900s but closed for good in the 1970s, leaving a bitter distrust among locals and a scarred landscape of abandoned villages and high unemployment in their wake. Yet, things are starting to look up. In 1997 UNESCO recognized the Iglesiente as the centre of an island-wide geological park, leading its towns to restore and reopen the mines to foreigners once again to cater to a growing tourist industry.

Masua.

Ironically, years of coastal mining have discouraged commercial or residential development, leading to de facto ecological conservation and creating a contrast where tumble-down industrial complexes and some of the Mediterranean's most unspoiled coastline meet. From Nebida north to the Costa Verde, the Iglesiente's windswept beaches and abandoned ghost towns truly make it Sardinia's wild west.

Iglesias.

Iglesias & around

Tucked at the foothills of the Monte Linas mountains, Iglesias is the heart of the Iglesiente region and the mining capital of Sardinia. Despite the region's sad tale of prosperity lost, Iglesias is far from being a gritty mining town. Its proud Pisan palaces and medieval church towers make it a charming base from which to explore the nearby mines and coastline.

During the Middle Ages, rulers from the Giudicato of Cagliari donated villas to be turned into churches (hence the town's original name, 'Villa di Chiesa'). The town later flourished under the rule of the infamous Pisan Count Ugolino della Gherardesca (see page 112) but its prosperity couldn't prevent the Aragonese from taking it over in 1324 and using it as their base to conquer the island. They renamed the town Iglesias and left a lasting Iberian influence on its architecture in the form of stately Gothic palazzi. Despite interest in the mines and sputtering prosperity under the Savoyards and again in the mid-1900s, today the southwest's capital is once again best known for its churches.

The mines were closed for political reasons. It's the same old story; a foreign company comes in here, exploits the land, takes what they need and then leaves.

Maurizio Concas, Fluminimaggiore

Central Iglesias

Iglesias' main shopping drag, the pedestrian-only corso Matteotti leads to the town's most picturesque corner, piazza La Marmora, before a left-hand turn on via Sarcidano brings you to the **Cattedrale di Santa Chiara** (closed for restoration), which honours Iglesias' patron saint. The 13th-century Romanesque-Gothic cathedral stands opposite the municipal building in Iglesias' only real square, and bares Ugolino's coat of arms by its entrance; he is said to have commissioned its construction in his will.

At the intersection of via Don Minzoni and via Pullo is the 15th-century Catalan-Gothic **Chiesa di San Francesco** (T0781-24226, daily 0800-1200 and 1700-1930). Note the statue of the rarely depicted pregnant Virgin on the church's stone façade.

The cannibal count

Iglesias will forever be indebted to its symbolic founder, Ugolino della Gherardesca, a 13th-century urban visionary. Ugolino was a Count in Pisa's pro-papal Ghibelline party and modelled the town after a self-governing Pisan *comune*, complete with its own currency and laws. He drafted the sophisticated Breve di Villa di Chiesa, a four-volume code of civil and penal laws that remains perfectly intact and is available on request at Iglesias' **Archivio Storico** (via delle Carceri, T0781-24850, Mon-Fri 0900-1300 and 1545-1815). The Count also reopened the town's mines which had lain abandoned for nearly 500 years, surrounded its centre with a wall, 26 towers and a moat, and minted Italy's first coins, transforming Villa di Chiesa into Sardinia's second most important city after Cagliari in the space of just 30 years.

Things went sour in 1288, when Ugolino was accused of treason by Archbishop Ruggieri degli Ubaldini for plotting with the Ghibelline's bitter rivals, the Milanese Guelfs. According to legend, the Count was captured along with his two sons and grandsons and imprisoned in a castle for nine months where he eventually starved to death but not before killing and eating the bodies of his family members. Various pieces of art and literature depict this horrific tale but none is more famous than Canto 33 of Dante's Inferno in which Ugolino is placed in the lowest circle of hell, gnawing on Ruggieri's skull.

Today, although Ugolino remains a popular figure in Iglesias, the world knows him best by his nickname, 'Cannibal Count'.

Inside, traverse arches raise the ceiling to a point. An impressive 11-panelled retablo by Antioco Mainas is found to the left of the entrance. Nearby, on via Manzoni, the **Chiesa della Madonna delle Grazie** (daily 0830-1230 and 1700-1900) was the site of a Byzantine church named after San Saturnino before being reworked in the 13th century.

On a hill northwest of the town centre, the **Santuario della Beata Vergine del Buon Cammino** (T0781-31427, daily 0800-0900 and 1700-1900) is a relative newcomer, built around 1730 to shelter pilgrims, and offers wonderful views of Iglesias from its elevated position.

Museo dell'Arte Mineraria

Via Roma 47, T0781-350037, museoartemineraria.it. Apr-Jun Sat-Sun 1800-2000, Jul-Sep Fri-Sun 1900-2100, €4.

Aside from the town itself, Iglesias' main draw is its mining museum. Housed in the former miners' school, the museum displays vintage photographs, tools and models of the wooden mine shafts used throughout the Iglesiente, plus roughly 8,000 rock specimens from all over the Mediterranean. Downstairs, visitors descend through the tunnels excavated by the school's students.

East of Iglesias

Ten kilometres east of Iglesias is the town of Domusnovas and the remarkable **Grotta di San Giovanni**. This 850-m natural grotto is one of only three caves in the world that you can drive through, although the paved road is accessible to scooters, not cars. Listen for birds as you walk through the twisting tunnel.

Continuing east, turn off the SS130 at Siliqua to see the crumbling walls of the 13th-century **Castello di Acquafredda**, built on top of an extinct volcano. The stronghold housed one of Ugolino della Gherardesca's surviving sons, Guelfo.

Towards Nebida

Eight kilometres west of Iglesias on the Golfo di Gonnesa is the town's beach, the vast **Funtanamare**, whose near-constant *maestrale* winds make it one of the island's best windsurfing spots. From here, the road climbs north around

Tip...

On the northwest corner of piazza Sella, a lonely tower is all that's left of Ugolino's once-imposing Castello Salvaterra. Continue past the castle on via Eleonora d'Arborea until it becomes via Fontana. Turn left at the unmarked staircase, just past via Lanusei, to walk along the medieval city walls and towers that once enclosed Villa di Chiesa.

hairpin turns with breathtaking views of green-carpeted *macchia* plunging into the sea below. Before reaching the former mining town of **Nebida**, you'll see four sharp *faraglioni* rocks jutting out of the water, dominated by the massive **Pan di Zucchero** (sugarloaf) island looming in the distance. As soon as you enter the town, turn left at the unmarked car park, from where a path wraps around the mountainside, offering unbeatable views of the sprouting islands and lumpy loaf. Just below, a path leads down to the abandoned **Laveria Lamarmora**, which was used to wash and separate the ore from Nebida's mine. A family-run restaurant is conveniently located at the path's most panoramic point, so you can order a coffee and take in the view (see page 125).

Masua

The road continues north to Masua, another former mining town whose extraordinary beach, **Portu Cauli**, faces the Pan di Zucchero and the loading dock of the old mine. One side road leads to the rather ugly mine complex, another to the beach car park, which gets mobbed in the summer. Follow the arrows from the car park for 2 km to reach the tunnels at **Porto Flavia** (T0781-491300, igeaminiere.it, guided tours in Italian daily by reservation only 0900, 1030 and 1200, €8, €4.50 under-12s), one of the Iglesiente's most popular tours. During their heyday, most of the area's mines loaded their cargo onto boats which transported

the ore to Carloforte to be sent to northern Italian or French markets, but Masua's steep incline presented a problem. After years of packing mules with the extracted minerals, engineers dug two 600-m tunnels through the cliff face and designed an ingenious mobile arm to transfer the ore onto the boats directly below. The hour-long tour culminates with a panoramic view of the nearby Pan di Zucchero and the beach.

North of Masua the road coils around mountain peaks before plunging into a valley and the turn-off for **Cala Domestica**, a beach set at the end of a long inlet pinned in by high walls. A path from the right of the beach leads through a tunnel to a sandy patch with fewer crowds, while a trail up the left cliff leads to a watchtower.

Buggerru

A few more twists up the coast and the quiet beachside resort of Buggerru appears in a steep valley. From the mid 1800s to the mid 1900s, the town's French-owned Mines des Malfidano extracted enough ore to bankroll the town, so that by 1860 Buggerru was known as 'Little Paris' and boasted an opera house, hospital and electricity. Yet, frustration over poor working conditions led Buggerru's miners to protest against their foreign employers in 1904. The *carabinieri* intervened and shot three people dead, leading to Italy's first national labour strike. A monument in the town's piazza commemorates the tragic event.

An eye-catching vista of the coast's *faraglioni* rocks at Nebida.

Around the island

These days, Buggerru's economy is linked to its windswept beach, which hosts Sardinia's surfing championship each August. However, the town is still littered with remnants of its mining history, such as the **Galleria Henry** tunnel (T0781-491300, igeaminiere.it, guided summer tours daily by reservation at 0900, 1030, 1200, 1400, 1530, 1630 and 1730, €8, €4.50 under-12s). Visitors wear a hard hat and board a train as it grates through a 940-m shaft that was dug out by hand in 1865 to transport the mine's ore to its wash house below. It's worth the admission, not for the pitch-black train ride (ask for a flashlight) but for the views during the walk back: the bare-faced rocks diving into turquoise coves rival any stretch of coastline in Sardinia.

Grotta di Su Mannau

Via Vittorio Emanuele 3, 5 km south of Fluminimaggiore, T0781-580411, sumannau.it. Guided tours daily 0930-1830 by reservation, from €8, €4.50 under-12s.

Inland from long **Portixeddu** beach and just south of the jaded town of **Fluminimaggiore**, this 8.2 km limestone grotto is the Iglesiente's largest cave. The standard tour takes you 600 m into a room used as a temple for the cult of water during the nuraghic period, past stalactites dotted with crystals, over a pond and into the 'Rodriguez Pit', where a fused stalactite and stalagmite form an 8-m column. However, the cave is best explored on a more rigorous tour lasting between four and eight hours (€40-80 per person, no experience necessary) in which visitors wade through ponds and cross 150-m tall caverns before stopping in the snow-white Sala Vergine.

Tempio di Antas

Off the SS126, south of Fluminimaggiore, T0781-580990, startuno.it.
May-Oct daily 0930-1830, Nov-Apr Fri-Sun 0930-1700, €3, €2 under-12s.

Standing alone in a field, a towering Roman temple marks the sacred grounds where the nuraghic population worshipped their original clan father, who was said to have founded the island. Punic settlers incorporated the nuraghic figure into their own religion, naming the all-inclusive god Sid Addir and building a temple to him at the site in the sixth century BC. To the Romans, the deity was known as Sardus Pater Babai, the son of Hercules and god of Sardinia. The Romans minted coins with Sardus' image and they built the current temple on top of the Punic version in the third century AD. The temple's six 8-m columns were re-erected between 1967 and 1976 and traces of black-and-white mosaics still cover part of the floor. Remains of an ancient Roman road lead to the ruins of a small nuraghic village behind the ticket office and continue to the Su Mannau cave.

Costa Verde

The 47-km shoreline stretching from Capo Pecora to Capo della Frasca is known as the Costa Verde. It's an expanse of green scrub sprinkled with golden sand dunes that has remained startlingly undeveloped. It takes some off-road effort to reach these shores but the pay-off is worth it.

Follow the SS126 north of Fluminimaggiore to the turn-off for the area's most beautiful beach, **Spiaggia Scivu**. The road winds past a gutted mining village and a few campgrounds before ending at a penal colony next to the beach. The beach has a snack bar with showers and offers views up the coast, backed by walkable dunes.

Back on the SS126, a turn-off 5 km north leads towards **Spiaggia Piscinas**. The 15-km road soon turns to dirt and passes through a ghost town where the Ingurtosu mine once flourished. The beach preserves a few tracks of Ingurtosu's railroad behind the Hotel Le Dune (see page 120), and also attracts nesting turtles in June, but the real

Beaches in southern Sardinia

❶ **Porto Giunco**, Villasimius, see page 91.

❷ **Cala Pira**, Villasimius, see page 93.

❸ **Su Giudeu**, Chia, see page 106.

❹ **Capo Tuerreda**, Teulada, see page 106.

❺ **Portu Cauli**, Masua, see page 113.

attractions are the dunes that surround the shore. Billed as 'Italy's Sahara', the mounds sprawl across 6 sq km and are the tallest in Europe, ranging from 50 to 70 m in height. The highest mounds are on the left as you arrive; park on the hard shoulder and drink plenty of water before you climb.

Half a kilometre before the Piscinas car park, take the left-hand turn (signposted 'Farmacia') for the Costa Verde's most picturesque drive. After crossing two streams, a paved road hugs the coast, passing vacation homes at Portu Maga and Funtanazza before arriving at **Torre dei Corsari**. Named after the 16th-century lookout tower to the north, Torre is a quiet village with the coast's best accommodation options. Under the tower, dunes flatten out to form the long **Spiaggia d'Oro**.

Arbus

The entire Costa Verde lies within the *comune* of Arbus, a sleepy town with some decent places to sleep and a tradition of knife-making. Arbus' handmade *s'arburesa* knives, with their ridged blades and monolithic handles carved from mouflon horns, stand out on an island that prides itself on this time-honoured craft. Inevitably, the town's main draw is its **Museo del Coltello** (via Roma 15, T349-053 7765, Mon-Fri 0900-1200 and 1600-2000, free), run by knife-maker Paolo Pusceddu. Knives are for sale (€15-€350). Upon entering the beautifully restored 17th-century home, you can't miss the heaviest knife in the world, a 295-kg dagger made by Paolo himself.

Miniera Montevecchio

Montevecchio, T070-973173, minieramontevecchio.it. Guided tours May-Sep Tue-Sun 1000, 1100, 1200, 1600, 1700, 1800 and 1900; Oct-Apr by appointment only. €6, €4 under-18s.

Up the road from Arbus, a steep mountainous pass through oak trees leads to the crumbling mansions of a vast, abandoned mining complex. This was not only one of the largest mining complexes in Italy (covering over 1,200 hectares) but was the only one in Sardinia actually owned by a Sardinian – Sassari's Giovanni Antonio Sanna. During its peak from the 1860s to the 1960s, the mine annually employed 4,500 men, women and children (many of whom commuted barefoot from Iglesias). The tour begins in the Piccalinna generator room and finishes a few steps away at the 350-m deep mine shafts.

Eleven families have held out in Montevecchio since the mine closed in 1991. In the centre of it all (next to the ticket office) a bar doubles as a tourist booth and has the rare Montevecchio beer on tap. From behind the bar, a 12.5-km trail leads back to the Piscinas dunes, while another 11-km dusty dirt road leads from Montevecchio through the abandoned Ingurtosu site to the former manager's art nouveau mansion.

Villacidro

Inland on the SS196, Villacidro is a quaint town framed by mountain ranges and is a delightful destination for a picnic or a walk. Two kilometres north of town, the **Sa Spendula** waterfall is well signposted and makes a good starting point. (The fall is at its best around Easter.)

In town, check out Villacidro's art nouveau-style wash house, which was built in 1893 to give the town's women a shady place to do their laundry, then sample the anise-flavoured Murgia brandy, which is best enjoyed from the vantage point of the municipal square, looking down at the town and up towards the forests of Monte Orno.

Sleeping

Cagliari & around

T Hotel €€€€
Via Dei Giudicati 66, Cagliari,
T070-47400, thotel.com.
Map: Cagliari, D1, p76.
Cagliari's showiest hotel is this
14-floor glass tower which
stands in the city's suburban
sprawl like a giant mirror. The
modern exterior gives way to
traditional rural Sardinian decor
in the lobby but, with spas, an
indoor pool, two restaurants and
a bar with outdoor seating
hovering over a fountain. Most
of the 207 rooms are 'classic',
with cushy amenities. Big-wigs
can upgrade to the two-level
'hi-tech suites'.

B&B Garibaldi €
Via Garibaldi 120, Villanova,
Cagliari, T331-421 0170,
bbgaribaldi.com.
Map: Cagliari, E3, p76.
Four recently renovated rooms
purposely show the building's
age with elegantly exposed
brick. The result is one of
Cagliari's most stylish new B&Bs
tucked in to Villanova's scenic
shopping district. Breakfast is
served in bed or at the art
nouveau Antico Caffè just up the
street. Owner Roberto will share
his knowledge of the city.

Hotel A&R Bundes Jack €
Via Roma 75, Marina, Cagliari,
T070-667970.
Map: Cagliari, D5, p76.

This hotel, housed in an
18th-century palace, was home
to the Fascist nobility during the
Second World War. Today, its 5-m
ceilings, hardwood bed frames
and Murano glass lamps attract
an eclectic youth hostel-type
crowd. The views facing the port
can't be topped and owner Luigi
will make you feel at home with
a taste of his *Vernaccia* wine.

Hotel Calamosca €
Viale Calamosca 50, Cagliari,
T070-371628, hotelcalamosca.it.
Map: Cagliari, H5, p76.
Guests stay at Cagliari's only
beach-front hotel more for the
fabulous setting than the bare
interior. The rooms have all the
essentials but the hotel's large
garden with private beach, and
balconies overlooking
Calamosca and Cala Fighera
make this place worth the
15-minute drive from downtown
Cagliari (private car park
provided). The hotel's impressive
restaurant may keep you away
from the city altogether.

Kastrum €
Via Cannelles 78, Castello,
Cagliari, T070-662304,
karel-bedandbreakfast.it.
Map: Cagliari, C2, p76.
This B&B is Cagliari's best lodging
option, bar none. Owner
Valentino Sanna goes out of his
way to fully accommodate his
guests' needs, offering personal
touches and unique insights

about his city that will make you
feel like a true local. The six
recently refurnished rooms are
built above Punic cisterns and
have access to a rooftop terrace
overlooking the entire city.

Self-catering
Le Suite sul Corso
Corso Vittorio Emanuele 8,
Stampace, Cagliari, T070-
680250, lesuitesulcorso.it.
Map: Cagliari, C4, p76.
Catering to the refined traveller,
these refurnished luxury suites
occupy a clay-coloured
18th-century building in the
heart of Stampace. Inside, the
modern furniture and colours are
reminiscent of an IKEA catalogue;
plasma televisions and Jacuzzis
share space with photos of
domus de janas. The balconies
offer great views of Castello,
piazza Yenne and the Corso,
making this a hotspot during the
Sant'Efisio parade in May. Rates
from €60 to €150 per night.

The Sarrabus & Gerrei

Hotel Albaruja €€€
Via Colombo, Costa Rei,
T070-991557, albaruja.it.
May-Oct only.
This is one of the area's more
tasteful hotels. The medium-
sized complex is set on a grassy
patch of land with an outdoor
swimming pool and tennis court
steps from the beach. The rooms

are rather large and resemble ranch-style villas. Minimum seven-night stay in peak season.

Simius Playa €€€
Via del Mare, Villasimius, T070-79311, simiusplaya.com. Apr-Oct only.
In the heart of Villasimius next to Simius beach, this attractive complex has an outdoor pool, tennis courts and offers numerous excursions around Capo Carbonara. All rooms have balconies overlooking the sea.

Timi Ama Sardegna €€€
Località Nottieri, Villasimius, T070-79791, accorthalassa.com. May-Oct only.
Located on a lagoon behind Villasimius' prime beach, the town's poshest hotel boasts an indoor and outdoor pool, various massage treatments and 275 rooms stocked with any amenity you can think of. Minimum seven-night stay in peak season.

Hotel Corallo €€
Via Roma 31, Muravera, T070-993 0502, albergocorallo.it.
This Muravera classic overlooks the town's main drag and predates the tourist boom. Originally built in 1957, the boxy structure received a facelift in 1996 but retains its outdated colour scheme. The rooms are pleasantly outfitted and have their own bathrooms, and the restaurant serves delicious pizza.

Sa Perda Arrumbulada €
Località Monte Porceddus, San Vito, T070-994 9157.
Make yourself at home on Denise and Antonio Marungiu's working *agriturismo* farm in the Sette Fratelli foothills. They have two basic guest rooms and serve organic meals (much of which come from the pigs you see outside) at the family table. Bring

your Italian dictionary and get ready for a crash course in all things Sardo!

Stella d'Oro €
Via Vittorio Emanuele 25, Villasimius, T070-791255.
Villasimius' oldest hotel is as centrally located as you can get and is wonderful value. Family-run since 1926, the

B&B-style outfit offers private baths in each of its 17 quiet rooms. A good restaurant serves tasty seafood. Hey, it was good enough for Ernst Jünger!

Camping
Camping Capo Ferrato
Località Monte Nai, Muravera, T070-991012, campingcapoferrato.it.
May-Oct only.
Run by the Fanni family since it opened in 1965, this is luxury camping if there is such a thing. The site sits directly on the beach and offers tennis, basketball and mini-golf along with bungalows and a decent restaurant.

Spiaggia del Riso
Villasimius, T070-791052, villaggiospiaggiadelriso.it.
Apr-Oct only.
A classy pseudo campsite-resort with private rooms and bungalows overlooking the Spiaggia del Riso beach. A bonus: there's a *domus de janas* on the site hidden by trees.

Central Campidano

Hotel Terme di Sardara €€
Località Santa Maria Aquas, Sardara, T070-938 7200, termedisardara.it.
Closed Mon-Fri Nov-May.
This is the nicer of Sardara's two hotel built above pre-existing Roman thermal baths that are renowned for their therapeutic powers. Modern facilities, a fine restaurant, and outdoor *bocce* and tennis courts make up for the rather drab façade.

Funtana Noa €
Via Vittorio Emanuele 66, Villanovaforru, T070-933 1019, hotelfuntananoa.it.
This modern take on an old country lodge is set around a courtyard surrounded by olive and almond groves. The 30 rooms all have the basic amenities. Downstairs, a spacious restaurant serves Sardinian pasta dishes, with better meat than fish.

La Lolla €
Via Cavour 49, Barumini, T070-936 8419.
These seven quiet, no-frills rooms open onto a large shaded courtyard in central Barumini. Stay in top nuraghi-touring form with a dip in the hotel pool or a set of tennis. Sardinian surf and turf is served in the restaurant; the latter is cooked on the courtyard's outdoor fireplace.

The Sulcis

Chia Laguna Resort €€€€
Località Chia, T070-92391, chialagunaresort.com
May-early Oct only.
Four complexes, three luxury hotels and a cluster of cottages, each built within walking distance of their own private beach, form this extremely tasteful resort. The complex has a beauty spa, golf course, outdoor restaurants, multiple pools, a disco and organized activities for children.

Forte Village €€€€
SS195 Km 39.6, Santa Margherita di Pula, T070-92171, fortevillageresort.com.
Easter and May-early Oct only.
Listed as one of the world's top luxury resorts, Forte Village is a world unto itself tucked behind tall pine trees amidst lush tropical gardens. No cars are allowed on site; instead, guests are whisked around on golf carts or complimentary bikes to the resort's shopping centres, pools, spas and even a football school sponsored by Chelsea. Regular guests include the players of Inter Milan and Italian delegates who come to take in the hotel's private beach and villa-like suites.

Is Molas Resort €€€€
SS195 Km 37.4, Santa Margherita di Pula, T070-924 1006, ismolas.it.
Southeastern Sardinia's premier golf resort offers non-golfers luxury villas set among flowering oleander bushes, tennis courts, an outdoor swimming pool, spa and kids' activities. Half board is obligatory. A private shuttle takes you to the nearby beach.

Hotel Baia delle Ginestre €€€
Strada Provinciale Costa del Sud, Teulada, T0342-904777, baia.to
The hotel and villas are directly on the beach and you can't beat the view over the Costa del Sud. The rooms come equipped with everything you might want. Ask reception about canoe and windsurfing courses, or just relax at one of the pools or tennis courts. Minimum seven-night stay in peak season.

Hotel Baia di Nora €€€
Località Su Guventeddu, Nora, T070-924 5551, hotelbaiadinora.com.
Nora's classiest resort is set in tropical gardens with outdoor fountains, tennis courts and an oval-shaped pool where bathers can swim up to the bar. The spacious rooms are painted in stucco tones and are steps from the hotel's private sliver of Guventeddu beach. Two restaurants serve an abundant buffet of regional specialities.

Hotel Hieracon €€
Corso Cavour 62, Carloforte, San Pietro, T0781-854028, hotelhieracon.com.
This 19th-century azure-coloured palace lines Carloforte's waterfront and once housed the Danish consulate. The lobby has a regal vibe and the rooms have mahogany armoires and bed frames. It's attached to an inner garden and a popular restaurant serving great seafood.

Hotel La Matta €€
Via Nazionale 119, Sant'Antioco, T0781-801375, hotel-lamatta.com.
The name means 'the crazy one' but this is a simple, no-surprises kind of place right on Sant'Antioco's main drag. The dark corridor is enlivened by the rooms' upbeat pastels.

Hotel Maladroxia €€
Località Maladroxia, Sant'Antioco, T0781-817012, hotelmaladroxia.com.
Located in the beach resort of Maladroxia, this hotel is 7 km from Sant'Antioco town but just steps from the beach. Most of the rooms have views of the waterfront and the restaurant downstairs serves great seafood.

Hotel Riviera €€
Corso Battellieri 26, Carloforte, San Pietro, T0781-854101, hotelriviera-carloforte.com.
This is one of Carloforte's most elegant options. The hotel overlooks the quay and is just steps from the ferry. If you don't want to pay extra for a room with a view of the waterfront, the outdoor terrace's views are free. Inside, drapes dangle over the beds and high-speed Wi-Fi keeps you connected to those in less picturesque settings.

Il Ghiro €€
Via Solferino 1, Carloforte, San Pietro, T338-205 0553, arlofortebedandbreakfast.it.
This *centralissimo* family-run B&B has two spaciously restructured rooms with private bath and air conditioning as well as great views onto piazza Repubblica's sprawling *ficus* trees. Rental bikes are available next door.

Sa Tiria €€
SS195 Km 67.5, nr Teulada, T333-351 7775.
Be sure to ask for full board at this *agriturismo* as the dinners are abundant and the main course is likely to come directly from the Ledda family's pigs outside. Save room for the homemade dessert cakes afterwards. The rooms are perfectly pleasant with wooden ceilings and comfortable beds; ask for air conditioning.

Su Gunventeddu €€
Località Su Guntenteddu, Nora, T070-920 9092, sugunventeddu.com.
This is your cheapest option among Nora's resorts: a pleasantly simple hotel-restaurant with the bare essentials. The exterior is shaded by tall pines and is within walking distance of Nora's two beaches, the lagoon and the archaeological site.

La Marea €
Via Provinciale 26, Domus de Maria, Chia, T340-929 5410, la-marea.it.
Signora Zedda's B&B is 7 km behind the beach. She's a wonderful lady who's glad to point out her favourite spots along the Costa del Sud. Rooms have TVs and air conditioning.

Sa Mitza e s'Orcu €
Località Sa Mitza e s'Orcu, 12 km from Chia towards Is Cannoneris, T070-923 6207, samitzaesorcu.it/
The Campus family has refurbished six rooms on a farm in the mountains behind Chia's beaches to make this *agriturismo*. Each room has views of the countryside down to the coast. Come prepared to drink Cannonau wine.

Camping
Campeggio Torre Chia
Località Chia, T070-923 0054, campeggiotorrechia.it.
Jun-Sep only.
Roll out of bed and sunbathe on Chia's Su Portu beach below the Torre di Chia. Surrounded by expensive real estate, the bungalows are a great deal. The site also has a tennis court and a decent pizzeria.

Camping Flumendosa
Località Campu Matta, Santa Margherita di Pula, T070-920 8364, campingflumendosa.it.
Jun-Sep only.

Occupying one of the few slivers of Santa Margherita's non-resort coastline, the campsite has its own surfing school and is only 20 m from the beach.

The Iglesiente

Hotel Le Dune €€€€
Via Bau 1, Spiaggia Piscinas, Costa Verde, T070-977130, leduneingurtosu.it.
Apr-early Nov only.
This is spectacular! Owner Sergio Caroli has turned an old warehouse from the Ingurtosu mine into a luxury hotel directly on Piscinas beach. The reception is reminiscent of a wooden ski lodge with handmade carpets and a grand fireplace. The outdoor restaurant serves a wonderful fish and meat lunch buffet (non-guests can reserve a table for €30) and is steps away from the beach and wellness spa. Rooms have their own private outdoor entrance with all the amenities you'd like.

Hotel La Caletta €€€
Torre dei Corsari, T070-977033, lacaletta.it.
Apr-Sep only.
The sand-coloured jail-like balconies facing the car park may turn you off, but the hotel's best side is towards the crescent-shaped pool built above the rocky shore. La Caletta has the most comfortable beds and best views in Torre dei

Corsari, so ask for a terrace room facing the sea. Breakfast is served in an upstairs dining hall.

Eurohotel €€
Via Fratelli Bandieri 34, Iglesias, T0781-22643, eurohoteliglesias.it.
A relatively new hotel outside Iglesias' town centre but close to the bus stop. The building's imposing white façade with swooping balconies is a bit much but the rooms are as comfortable as any hotel in town and even done up in a pseudo-regal motif, complete with faux-gilded frames and chandeliers.

Hotel Artu €€
Piazza Sella 15, Iglesias, T0781-22546, hotelartuiglesias.it.
The exterior of this central hotel is downright horrible and it's lobby harks back to the 1980s but it has clean rooms, spacious bathrooms, a private garage (rare in Iglesias) and serves a tasty buffet breakfast.

S'enna e Scivu €€
Località Campu Prama on the road to Spiaggia di Scivu, Costa Verde, T347-189 4692, sennaescivu.it.
This old colonial house is set 3 km from Scivu beach and is one of only a handful of buildings nearby. The rooms are basic and the bathrooms quite small. You can choose from either meat or fish dinners (go with meat). The pasta dishes are fantastic.

Hotel Meridiana €
Via Repubblica 172, Arbus, T070-975 8283, hotelarbus.it.
This big pink hotel located at the top of Arbus' main drag has cool rooms, private parking and even a pool. If possible, ask for a back room facing the countryside, as the rooms facing the street can get a bit noisy. The restaurant downstairs serves up pizzas.

Menhirs €
Via Repubblica 61, Arbus, T070-9758495, menhirs.it.
This Arbus B&B is part of the owner's work studio. There's no lift, two of the three rooms share a bath and only one has air conditioning, but the price is right, the family is terribly kind and the young daughters' improving English adds a charming touch that's hard to come by elsewhere.

Villa di Chiesa €
Corso Matteotti 32, Iglesias, T347-386369.
Located right along Iglesias' main shopping drag, this B&B is the town's best option for the independent traveller. There's no lift to get you to the third floor and the three bedrooms share only two bathrooms but the owners (a couple from Carbonia) add a personal charm that you won't find at any hotel. The rooms have been done up with wrought-iron beds and open onto a communal room with a television and kitchen.

Al Saraceno
Via delle Ginestre 21, Buggerru, T0781-54231, buggeru. alsaracenogroup.com.
A luxury complex of 18 apartments available by the day (from €45) or week (from €315). Most have beautiful seaside views of Buggerru's tourist harbour and beach below. Private parking provided.

Le Palme
Località Marina di Scivu, Costa Verde, T347-930 3741, campinglepalme.com.
This year-round campsite is also a small B&B with three double rooms for €70 each with breakfast. The bar rents bikes for €5 a day to get down to Scivu beach, which is a few kilometres away, and the restaurant serves regional favourites at very reasonable prices.

Sciopadroxiu
Località Ingurtosu on the road to Spiaggia Piscinas, Costa Verde, T340-572 4310, campingsciopadroxiu.com.
Jun-Sep only.
This campsite also has six apartment-style villas with living room and air conditioning (from €25 per person) and is your best option if you can't afford Piscinas' luxury hotel. The restaurant has a great setting under a veranda with very reasonable prices.

Eating & drinking

Dal Corsaro €€€€
Viale Regina Margherita 28,
Marina, T070-664318.
Mon-Sat 1300-1500 and
2000-2300.
Map: Cagliari, E5, p76.
Expect to have your best and
most expensive meal in Cagliari
here with impeccable service
surrounded by glitterati. This
refined family-owned
establishment offers over 400
types of wine and surf-and-turf
dishes so good that the Pope
chose to dine here in 2008.

Antica Hostaria €€€
Via Cavour 60, Marina,
T070-665870.
Mon-Sat 1245-1515 and
2000-2315.
Map: Cagliari, D5, p76.
Dating back to 1852, this is one of
Marina's oldest restaurants. It
houses an impressive selection
of Sardinian wines but it's the
seafood – delivered each
morning – which makes
reservations necessary. Try the
sea bass cooked with *spumante*
and a dash of saffron.

Trattoria Lillicu €€€
Via Sardegna 78, Marina,
T070-652970.
Daily 1300-1500 and 2030-2300.
Map: Cagliari, D5, p76.
Locals swear by this seafood-
only trattoria and gobble down
the daily specials (there are no

menus). If you stay long enough,
you might catch the owner,
Giampaolo, playing guitar and
singing. Try the *burrida* (seafood
stew with garlic and walnuts)
and the *stoccafisso* (dried cod).

Per Bacco €€
Via Santa Restituta 72,
Stampace, T070-651667.
Mon-Sat 2000-2400.
Map: Cagliari, C3, p76.
Tucked into Stampace's historic
narrow streets, Per Bacco is a
gem off the beaten path. Chef
Sabrina trained in Tuscany and
serves a combination of regional
specialities and Italian favourites
that change weekly. Excellent
service and quaint ambience.

Sa Domu Sarda €€
Via Sassari 51, Stampace,
T070-653400.
Tue-Fri 1230-1430 and
2030-2300, Sat 2030-2300.
Map: Cagliari, C4, p76.
The rustic handicrafts and
abundant portions of rural
Sardinian favourites make this
quaint restaurant feel like a
bucolic *agriturismo* in the middle
of Cagliari. Try the *culurgiones*
(dumplings with olive oil and
crushed walnuts) and the *fregola*
pasta with *porcini* mushrooms.

Chez Victor €
Via Ospedale 42, T070-856 3513.
Tue-Sat 1230-2400, Sun
1900-2400.
Map: Cagliari, B3, p76.

Cagliari's best non-Sardinian dive
is great value. Chef Michele Pili
adds a touch of the Barbagie to
the capital, mixing gorgonzola,
porcini mushrooms and fresh
rocket into Cagliari's best crêpes.
The 'Cristiano' is a must. Trust
Michele's imagination and let
him prepare your dessert crêpe.

Cafés & bars
Antico Caffè
Piazza Costituzione 10, Villanova,
T070-658206.
Sep-Jun Wed-Mon 0700-0230,
Jul-Aug Mon-Sat 0700-0230.
Map: Cagliari, D4, p76.
Cagliari's most sophisticated café
has an art nouveau interior and
the shaded outdoor seating is a
great spot for people-watching.

Caffè degli Spiriti
Bastione Saint Remy, Castello,
T339-882 2146.
Daily 0900-0200.
Map: Cagliari, D4, p76.
Castello's most popular bar is
packed with trendy hipsters each
summer. Lie on the cushions or
in the outdoor hammocks and
sway to music as you watch
flamingos fly overhead.

De Candia Wine & Spirits Café
Via De Candia 3, Castello.
Daily 0700-0200.
Map: Cagliari, D4, p76.
Sharing the Bastione floor space
with Caffè degli Spiriti, this
open-air bar offers outdoor beds
and a more laid-back setting.

Isola del Gelato
Piazza Yenne 35, Marina,
T070-659824.
Tue-Sun 0900-0200.
Map: Cagliari, C4, p76.
This tourist hotspot boasts a
waterfall and more than 100
flavours of ice cream.

Karel Café
Via Università 37, Castello,
T070-653821.
Tue-Sun 2100-0200.
Map: Cagliari, C4, p76.
New-age animation is broadcast
over a screen as scenesters
lounge in this underground
cavern. Parties of four or more
should reserve the VIP back
room set in a Byzantine cistern.

La Paillote
Viale Calamosca, Cala Fighera,
T070-380769.
Apr-Oct daily 0900-2300.
Map: Cagliari, H5, p76.
Found at the end of Calamosca
overlooking Cala Fighera, this
private beach bar looks like a
postcard. Terraced gardens of
oleander and cactus fall into the
sea, while clients sip cocktails on
outdoor lounge chairs.

Libarium Caffè Nostrum
Via Santa Croce 35, Castello,
T346-522 0212.
Daily 0730-0200.
Map: Cagliari, C3, p76.
Get a lift in an old English cab
from piazza Costituzione to this
chic spot with elegant outdoor
seating on the Bastione Spagnoli.

Tip...
If you sit down in many of Cagliari's restaurants or bars, chances are
you will be approached by foreign street vendors selling cheap gifts.
Although some of these entrepreneurs can be more pushy than others,
the islanders have a relatively tolerant attitude towards them and it
is considered in poor taste (a *"brutta figura"*) to shoo them away too
forcefully. Instead, just politely decline the pre-frozen rose or light-up
keychain and return to your drink.

Orso Bianco
Piazza Martiri d'Italia 1, Marina,
T347-872 5766.
Daily 1000-2400.
Map: Cagliari, D4, p76.
Cagliari's best gelateria with
no frills.

The Sarrabus & Gerrei

La Mora Bianca €€€
Via Roma 14, Villasimius,
T070-791487.
May-Sep daily 1300-1430 and
2000-2300.

An upscale pizzeria and
restaurant frequented by locals
and tourists in the know.

Il Moro €€
Via Cagliari, Villasimius,
T070-798180.
Apr-Oct daily 1230-1430 and
2030-2230.
This restaurant can seat quite a
crowd and gets busy in peak
season. Signor Melis whips up
fish and meat dishes in fixed
menus, à la carte and as
well-regarded specials. Wine
lovers won't be disappointed.

Centro Ippico del Sarrabus
Località S'Ollasteddu, via Case Sparse, Muravera, T070-999078.
Daily 1230-1430 and 1930-2230 by reservation only.
This equestrian school and *agriturismo* is set on 15 hectares with plenty of opportunities to gallop around. The meals are also fantastic: meat-lovers are in for a treat, as lamb and sausages reign supreme here.

Central Campidano

Rosy €€
Via Carlo Felice 510, Sanluri, T070-930 7957.
Wed-Mon 1230-1400 and 2000-2200.
This pizzeria and restaurant is about your only option in Sanluri. Fortunately, it serves solid rural Sardinian favourites like horse steak and *malloreddus* pasta with sausage. For something different, try a pizza topped with mussels.

Trattoria da Pieretto €
Via E Depuro 3, Orroli, T0782-847138.
Tue-Sun 1300-1530 and 2000-2200.
This unpretentious dive serves pizzas at night and is a true locals' joint but is friendly to tourists. Menus (when available) follow a set price. Pasta dishes are Pieretto's forte.

The Sulcis

Da Nicolò €€€€
Corso Cavour 32, Carloforte, San Pietro, T0781-854048.
Apr-Oct Tue-Sun 1300-1500 and 2000-2300.
People take the ferry to Carloforte just to sample chef Nicolo's *trofie* pasta, smoked swordfish and *pasticciata* with cheese sauce. Elegant seating along Carloforte's main drag is available at night.

La Ghinghetta €€€€
Via Cavour 26, Portoscuso, T0781-508143.
Easter-Oct Mon-Sat 2000-2300.
This converted fisherman's house is now a large hotel and one of Sardinia's best restaurants. Chef Ivaldo Vacca is a bit of a local celebrity, thanks to his culinary creativity: beef with red tuna, ravioli stuffed with foie gras, and olive-flavoured gelato, among other delights.

Su Furriadroxu €€€€
*Via XXIV Maggio 11, Pula,
T070-924 6148.*
May-mid Oct Wed-Mon
2000-2300, mid Oct-Apr
Sat-Sun 2000-2300.
The €45 fixed menu will leave
you loosening your belt. The
restaurant specializes in all things
Sardinian and has delicious
meats and pastas. Try the
macaroni with wild boar sauce
for your first course and the
suckling pig afterwards.

Zia Leunora €€€€
*Via Trieste 19, Pula,
T070-920 9559.*
Tue-Sun 2000-2300 (often
closed Jan-Feb).
Tucked on a side street in Pula's
residential neighbourhood, this
is the town's best seafood
restaurant. Sit in the pleasant
courtyard or under the wooden
vaulted beams inside and trust
the chef's recommendations. In
summer, it's booked up to a
week in advance, so reserve early.

Al Tonno di Corso €€€
*Via Marconi 47, Carloforte,
San Pietro, T0781-855106.*
Mar-Oct Tue-Sun 1230-1430
and 2030-2230, Nov-early Jan
Tue-Sun 1230-1430 and
2030-2200.
Less famous and less visible (a
few blocks up from the
waterfront) than 'Il Mago', this
rustic-style local restaurant
opens out to a garden and has
the town's best tuna dishes.

Da Achille €€€
*Via Nazionale 82, Sant'Antioco,
T0781-83105.*
Apr-Jul and Sep Mon-Sat
1230-1400 and 2015-2230, Aug
daily 1230-1400 and 2015-2230.
This restaurant specializes in fish
and offers spacious dining under
a vaulted wooden ceiling. Try the
grouper with saffron and ragù
sauce, and the *casizolu* cheese.

Ristorante Da Vittorio €€€
*Corso Battellieri 16, Carloforte,
San Pietro, T0781-855200.*
Apr-Sep Wed-Sun 1300-1500
and 2000-2200.
Known as 'Il Mago', this is
perhaps Carloforte's most
famous seafood restaurant with
seating along the town's quay.

Trattoria Da Angelo €€€
*Via Isonzo 3, Chia,
T070-923 6363.*
Apr-Oct Tue-Sun 1230-1500 by
reservation and 1930-2230.
Nov-Mar group bookings only.
Da Angelo is a family-run
trattoria away from the touristy
beaches in Chia. Come prepared
to eat fish and lots of it. Ask
Angelo's wife to steer you in the
right direction or play it safe and
go with the daily specials.

Pizzeria R&R €€
*Via Nazionale 42, Sant'Antioco,
T0781-800448.*
Thu-Tue 2000-2300.
Good pizza and wonderful
service await you under a
covered wooden veranda.

Regional pasta, seafood and
meat dishes are also available,
and the *penne alla diavolo* is a
pleasant starter.

Gazebo Il Medioevale €€€
*Via Musio 21, Iglesias, T0781-
30871.*
Mon-Sat 1200-1500 and
2000-2245.
The inside is done out like a cave
with exposed brick and arched
ceilings, under which plates of
abundant seafood await you. Try
the swordfish or the mussels,
which are a meal in themselves.

Al '906 Operaio €€
*Belvedere di Nebida, Nebida,
T338-916 5388.*
Mon-Sat 1230-1430 and
2030-2400.
Even if you're not hungry, sit
down and absorb unsurpassed
views of the Pan di Zucchero at
this family-run restaurant at the
end of the belvedere in Nebida.
Owner Andrea is quite
knowledgeable about the
history of the Iglesiente and,
when not hustling from table to
table, is quite happy to chat.

Villa di Chiesa €€
*Piazza Municipio, Iglesias,
T0781-23124.*
Tue-Sun 2000-2300.
Outdoor seating spills on to
Iglesias' main piazza at this
longstanding town favourite.
Chef Maria has been cooking up

Entertainment

delicious ravioli stuffed with ricotta, spinach and saffron, and snails dressed with tomato slices for the last 30 years.

Cafés & bars
Caffè Pasticceria La Marmora
Piazza la Marmora, Iglesias
Mon-Sat 0830-2230.
Built in the late 1800s, Iglesias' most stylish café has an art nouveau façade painted with murals climbing its three-storey exterior. The espresso is thick, the

pastries are sweet and the outdoor seating is delightful.

Daiquiri Bar
Corso Matteotti 68, Iglesias.
Mon-Sat 0900-0200.
This normal looking café is not particularly charming but its outdoor seating and occasional happy hours tend to attract quite a crowd of thirtysomethings on summer nights. It's the best drinking spot in Iglesias.

Cagliari & around

Clubs
Old Square
Corso Vittorio Emanuele 44a, Stampace.
Nov-Apr Tue-Sun 2100-0230.
DJs spin rap inside this two-floor Irish pub each Fri and Sat.

Tierre Mambo Tango
Via Lamarmora 45, Castello, T070-351 0598.
Tue-Sun 1300-1500 and 2100-0300.
It's hard to feel underdressed in this pseudo-communist joint. Owner and ex-Red Brigade member Giuliano DeRoma serves up live music and a strong *filu e ferru* grappa.

Festivals & events
Important events include the **Sant'Efisio** procession in May (see page 47) and **Madonna Assunta** in August (see page 48). Cagliari's **Easter** celebration is centred around *nenniris*, barley that women wear with flowers during the Good Friday procession between Chiesa di Sant'Efisio and Castello's Duomo. In July, **Mondo Ichnusa** is a three-day music festival held on Poetto beach that attracts national rock and pop acts.

Gay & lesbian

Caffè dell'Elfo
Salita Santa Chiara 6, Stampace,
T070-682399.
Mon-Fri 1300-1500 and
2000-0100, Sat 2000-0100.
Upscale, with a gay-friendly
crowd, just off of piazza Yenne.

Fico d'India
Lungomare Poetto,
T070-380908.
May-Sep daily 0800-0300.
Bus PQ or PF from via Roma.
An eccentric outdoor summer
hangout with music and dance
nights beginning at 2200.

Music

Corto Maltese
Lungomare Poetto, T070-380990.
Jun-Oct daily from 2200.
A great venue that holds nightly
ska and reggae concerts on the
beach to a mixed crowd. Drive or
take the PQ or PF bus from via
Roma to Poetto's sixth stop.

Theatre

Teatro Civico in Castello
Via De Candia, Castello, T070-677
7660, comune.cagliari.it.
This 18th-century theatre stages
dance and drama from June to
September. Check the website or
call ahead for box office hours
and ticket prices.

Teatro Lirico
Via Sant'Alenixedda,
T070-408 2230.
Box office Mon-Sat 1000-1400
and 1800-2000.

The Sarrabus & Gerrei

Clubs

El Peyote
Litoranea Panoramica Km 49,
Località Santa Maria, Villasimius,
T070-791416, elpeyote.it.
Daily 2230-0330.
Found between Villasimius and
Cagliari, this dance club bumps a
mixture of house and rap music.
Also has a Mexican restaurant.

Central Campidano

Sardegna in Miniatura
Zona 'Su Nuraxi', Barumini,
T070-936 1004.
Mon-Sat 0900-1700 and Sun
0900-1800. €12, €10 children.
A miniature park of Sardinia,
complete with ceramic
monuments from the island.
Whisk around on a boat, train or
on foot and hear audio
explanations in English.

The Sulcis

Clubs

Favola
SS126 Km 4.2, Sant'Antioco,
T347-455 3029.
Mid June-mid Sep Sat-Sun
2400-0400.
Located 4 km north of
Sant'Antioco town on the road
towards Calasetta, this is
Sant'Antioco's best club, with
three outdoor patios set in a
garden and an indoor lounge.
Usually plays dance and hip-hop.
Dress up.

Festivals & events
Sant'Antioco celebrates Sa Festa
Manna (see page 47) on the
second weekend after Easter and
hosts the Dieci Giorni Sulcitani
cultural festival from 1st to 15th
August. Important annual events
on San Pietro are the mattanza
(see page 109) and the Festa
della Madonna dello Schiavo in
November (see page 49).

Tsunami
SS195 Km 33, Pula, T070-924
6128.
May-Sep Sat-Sun 2300-0400.
Ravers and scenesters flock to
this summer club from Cagliari
every weekend. The DJs usually
spin house music for a modish
clientele. The admission charge
depends on the event, and the
bouncer can be picky.

The Iglesiente

Festivals & events
Iglesias puts on some of
Sardinia's most stirring
processions during Holy Week.
Hooded members of the Santo
Monte confraternity wear
Spanish robes and parade
through the streets each night
carrying wooden crosses,
candles and statues of the Virgin
and Christ. Highlights include the
solemn 'funeral' for Jesus on
Good Friday and the festivities
on Easter morning in piazza Sella.

Shopping

Art & antiques
Artigianato Sardegna
*Scalette Santa Chiara 2, Castello,
T070-651488.*
Mon-Sat 1000-1800.
Sells handmade jewellery, rugs
and ceramics from craftspeople
throughout Sardinia.

Books
Libreria Il Bastione
*Piazza Costituzione 4, Marina,
Cagliari, T070-650823.*
Mon-Sat 0930-2030.
Stocks a wide variety of history
and international books in Italian,
as well as travel books in English.

Ubik
*Via Roma 63-65, Marina,
Cagliari, T070-650256.*
Mon-Sat 0900-2030.
Numerous children's titles and
language books.

Department stores
La Rinascente
*Via Roma 141, Cagliari, Marina,
T070-380720.*
Daily 1000-2100.
Clothing, beachwear and home
furnishings.

Food & drink
Durke
*Via Napoli 66, Cagliari, Marina,
T070-667984.*
Mon-Sat 0930-1300 and
1630-2000.

A culinary museum of Sardinian
handmade sweets (and free
samples) that were once cooked
in the store's two giant ovens.

Il Suq
*Via Napoli 19, Cágliari, Marina,
T070-660223.*
Mon-Sat 0900-1400 and
1530-2030.
Stocks frozen seafood, Sardinian
pasta and international spices.

Souvenirs
Delizie di Sardegna
*Via Sardegna 22, Cagliari,
Marina, T349-0598988.*
Mon-Sat 0915-1330 and
1500-2030.
Sells everything Sardinian, from
T-shirts to honey, and even the
odd *launeddas*!

Sapori di Sardegna
*Via Baylle 6, Cagliari, Marina,
T070-684 8747.*
Mon-Sat 0900-1300 and
1530-2030.
Traditional masks, foods and
desserts, which come primarily
from Nuoro.

Art & antiques
Casa della Ceramica
*Piazza Costituzione 5,
Villanovaforru, T070-930 0232.*
Mon-Sat 0830-1300 and
1500-2000.
Local artist Antonio Scano
moulds clay into nuraghic-style
bronzetti, votive vases and masks.

Activities & tours

Art & antiques

Arte Sarda
*Corso Battellieri 18, Carloforte,
San Pietro, T0781-855912.*
Mon-Sat 0900-2300.
Red coral necklaces, handmade
pocket knives, silver, ceramics
and hand-woven fabrics.

Artijanas
*Via Regina Margherita 168,
Sant'Antioco, T340-812 8833.*
Mon-Sat 0930-2100.
Ceramics and traditional vases
made by two local artists.

Sa Grutta
*Via Regina Margherita 186,
Sant'Antioco, T320-723 7620.*
Mon-Sat, 930-1230 and
1730-2000.
Various handicrafts are displayed
in a grotto showroom first used
during the Punic age.

Books

Libropoli
*Piazza Italia 43, Sant'Antioco,
T0781-800086.*
Daily 0900-1300 and 1800-2100.
A small bookshop that stocks
children's, travel and fiction titles.

Food & drink

Stella Marina
*Viale Salvo d'Acquisto 58,
Carloforte, San Pietro, T0781-
855675.*
Mon-Sat 0800-1300 and
1700-2000, Sun 0800-1300.
This fishmonger is the single best

place to pick-up a can of
Carloforte's prized bluefin tuna,
which normally costs about €20
a can.

Vinoteca Shardana
*Via Regina Margherita 84,
Sant'Antioco, T0781-800484.*
Mon-Sat 0830-1300 and
1630-2030.
Sardinian wines including a great
selection of local Carignano red.

Art & antiques

Il Nuraghe
*Via Martini 27, Iglesias,
T340-001 4489.*
Mon-Sat 0900-1300 and
1700-2000.
Cork trays, jewellery, Sardinian
ceramics and T-shirts.

La Coltelleria
*Via Martini 24, Iglesias,
T0781-43499.*
Mon-Sat 0930-1300 and
1730-2130.
Elaborate handmade pocket
knives made throughout
Sardinia.

Cycling

Ichnusa Bike
T393-952 7511, ichnusabike.it.
Organizes bike rentals and tours
in Cagliari and throughout the
island. Also offers guided walks
of the capital, as well as hiking
and mountain bike tours in the
southeast (prices vary).

Diving

Air Sub
*Via Balilla 26, Cagliari,
T070-506863, airsub.com.*
Teaches scuba diving, rents
equipment and runs dive trips
from the Golfo degli Angeli east
to Villasimius. Single dives range
from €35 to €65.

Guided tours

See also Ichnusa Bike (above).

Itzokor
*Via Lamarmora 123, Castello,
Cagliari, T070-919 7909, itzokor.it.*
Offers excursions to cultural and
archaeological sites throughout
Sardinia, as well as walking tours
of Castello (prices vary).

Ufficio Turistico
*Piazza Matteotti, Cagliari,
T070-669255.*
The staff at Cagliari's main tourist
office are licensed to conduct
walking tours of the city and, if
they are not available, they can
usually provide you with an
alternative guide.

Five of the best

Drives in southern Sardinia

Each of these drives will take you through remote expanses of wilderness with nauseatingly winding turns and stunning scenery. Needless to say, do these routes on a full tank and an empty stomach.

❶ Cagliari to Villasimius, see page 91.
❷ Cagliari to Muravera on the old SS125 (not SS125 Nuovo), see page 93.
❸ Costa Sud from Chia to Teulada, see page 106.
❹ Iglesias to Buggerru, see page 113.
❺ Costa Verde from Spiaggia Piscinas to Torre dei Corsari, see page 114.

Well-being
T Hotel Spa
Via Dei Giudicati 66, T070-47400.
Daily 0930-2200.
The T Hotel's Wellness Centre is undoubtedly Cagliari's nicest spa. Choose from an array of massage options, then relax in the jacuzzis, indoor pool, hydromassage tubs or steam baths. Open to non-guests by reservation.

The Sarrabus & Gerrei

Diving
Ocean Dream
Via Speranza 8, Muravera, T070-347 6791637, divesardinia.com.
Offers dives in the Golfo degli Angeli and Villasimius north to Costa Rei and Muravera. Prices range from €90 for two dives to €390 for 10 dives. Horseback riding, boat trips, trekking, mountain biking and even private flights along the eastern coast are also available.

Morgan Diving
Villasimius, T070-805059, morgandiving.com.
Offers 17 dives exploring the wrecks, coral and underwater grottoes in the Capo Carbonara marine park (prices vary).

Sailing
Matilda
Villasimius Marina, Villasimius, T340-067 6054, matildacharter.com.
This is the best of the many boat trips from Villasimius. Captain Roberto Murgia leads daily trips around Capo Carbonara aboard a 22-m yacht between April and October. €45 for adults, €26 for children (lunch included).

Central Campidano

Guided tours
Jara
Su Nuraxi, Barumini, T070-936 4277, parcodellagiara.it.
After meeting at the nuraghic site, a bus goes to the Giara di Gesturi for walking tours of the park. Three tours leave daily at 1000, 1400, 1700 but it's always necessary to call ahead. €40 for five people (minimum).

Well-being
Hotel Terme di Sardara
Località Santa Maria Aquas, Sardara, T070-938 7200, termedisardara.it.
May-Nov only.
Fitness courses, thermal and mud massages, anti-ageing and cleansing aesthetic treatments and various oriental massages available from €16 to €53.

The Sulcis

Diving & snorkelling
Laguna di Nora
Località Nora, T070-920 9544, lagunadinora.it.
Adjacent to Nora's archeological site, this group has an aquarium for kids and offers canoe trips to turtle-breeding grounds (daily 1000 and 1700, €25, €12 under-12s) and snorkelling in the lagoon (daily 1000, prices as above), where you can see Roman relics.

Transport

Tonnare Diving Centre
Carloforte, San Pietro, T349-690 4969, tonnaradiving.it.
Between April and May you can swim with the bluefin tuna as they pass between San Pietro and Isola Piana. A single dive ranges from €30 to €63.

Fishing
Pescaturismo Barcas Amigas
Sant'Antioco, T329-424 7088, pescaturismosardegna.com.
Spend eight hours cruising Sant'Antioco's beaches, jumping in for swims or fishing with the captain for your lunch prepared on board. €50 per person; reservations required.

Sailing
Carloforte Sail Charter
Via Danero 52, Carloforte, San Pietro, T347-273 3268, carlofortesailcharter.it.
Offers day trips around San Pietro or week-long voyages along the southwestern coast in three yachts ranging from 10 to 16 m in length. Prices vary according to the number of people and the season.

Walking
Sardoa
Via Regina Margherita 188, Sant'Antioco, T320-723 7620.
Offers guided walks in town, tours to various nuraghi and trekking throughout Sant'Antioco at an astonishingly low €4 per hour per person. Call ahead for further details.

Cagliari & around

From Cagliari, there are two daily ARST buses to **Oristano** (2 hrs) and four to **Tortolì** (3 hrs). Seventeen daily trains connect Cagliari to **Oristano** (1 hr 30 mins) and eight daily trains travel from Cagliari to **Macomer** (2 hrs), for connections to **Nuoro** (1 hr 15 mins) and **Olbia** (2 hrs). Five trains and two ARST buses travel daily from Cagliari to **Sassari** (3-4 hrs), for connections to **Alghero** by train (30 mins) or bus (1 hr).

The Sarrabus & Gerrei

Up to eight ARST buses run between Cagliari and **San Vito** (3 hrs 10 mins) daily, stopping at Geremeas (50 mins), Villasimius (1 hr 20 mins), Castiadas (2 hrs 10 mins), Costa Rei (2 hrs 30 mins) and Muravera (3 hrs).

Central Campidano

Up to seven ARST buses run between Cagliari and **Villanovaforru** (1 hr 55 mins) daily, stopping at Sanluri (1 hr 10 mins) and Sardara (1 hr 20 mins). One daily ARST bus travels between Cagliari and **Gesturi** (1 hr 50 mins), stopping at Barumini (1 hr 40 mins). From Sanluri two daily ARST buses go via Sardara to **Oristano** (1 hr).

The Sulcis

Up to 14 ARST buses link Cagliari and **Teulada** (1 hr 50 mins) daily, stopping at Pula (50 mins), Santa Margherita (1 hr) and Chia (1hr 15 mins). Ferries run between Portovesme and **Carloforte** on Isola di San Pietro up to 17 times a day (30 mins) and from Carloforte to **Calasetta** on Isola di Sant'Antioco up to nine times a day (30 mins). For further details, see page 109.

The Iglesiente

Up to 15 trains daily connect Iglesias with **Cagliari** (1 hr). Up to 17 trains daily run between Iglesias and **Decimomannu** (35 mins), from where there are frequent trains to **Oristano** (15-40 mins) and half a dozen to **Sassari** (3 hrs 30 mins). There are also six ARST buses daily between Iglesias and Cagliari (90 mins), eight ARST buses between Iglesias and **Carbonia** (45 mins) and eight ARST buses between Iglesias and **Calasetta** (Sant'Antioco, 90 mins).

Bosa.

Contents

Oristano & the west

Introduction

What to see in...

... one day
Spend a day sightseeing in **Oristano** or **Bosa**; hike around **Montiferru** or **Monte Arci**, or visit the ruins at **Tharros** on the **Sinis Peninsula**.

Oristano, Sardinia's smallest province, was created from parts of Nuoro and Cagliari in the 1970s. Its territory roughly mirrors that of the island's most powerful medieval state, the Giudicato of Arborea. It lacks a major airport or port which explains why it's one of the corners of Sardinia least visited by tourists and why it has preserved its endearing authenticity. Lonely quartz sand beaches, the ruins of Tharros and the medieval castle at beautiful Bosa are among the surprises awaiting you in this refreshing part of the island. During the year, this sleepy region abandons its conservative ways for a series of daring bareback horse races that make Siena's Palio look like a child's pony ride: it's no wonder the most famous of the Palio's jockeys hail from around Oristano.

... a weekend or more
Using **Oristano** as a base, make your way to the **Sinis Peninsula** to see **Tharros** and **San Giovanni**, go birdwatching or laze on deserted beaches. From **Bosa**, head south to **Montiferru** for hiking and good food.

With more time you can visit all of the main sights – **Oristano**, the **Sinis Peninsula, Tharros, Fordongianus, Nuraghe Losa, Santa Caterina** and **Bosa** – and still have time to hang out on sparkling white beaches, go horse riding and birdwatching around the **Sinis lagoons**, hike around **Monte Arci** and **Montiferru**, and sample the region's excellent produce.

In contrast to much of Sardinia's parched landscape, the west has wetlands, including Europe's largest marsh, the Stagno di Cabras, and enough lagoons to provide Sardinia's best birdwatching and its most delicious seafood dishes. Inland, the Tirso river valley nourishes dense citrus groves and sweet Vernaccia vineyards, while the nearby Montiferru mountain range produces artichoke-flavoured olive oil and provides grazing for some of Italy's tastiest cattle. This pint-sized province packs a delectable culinary punch.

Left: The campanile of the Duomo, Oristano.

Oristano

Oristano is western Sardinia's largest town and the capital of the province. It retains a pleasant, if provincial, air and evidence of its once-illustrious past is still visible thanks to a few towering monuments and a fine civic museum.

The town was founded in 1070 when the Punic-Roman city of Tharros became increasingly vulnerable to pirate attacks. Its residents dismantled the site, hauling its granite columns and sandstone blocks inland to the new settlement of Aristanis (meaning, 'between the ponds'). Oristano had its heyday as the capital of Arborea, Sardinia's most powerful Giudicato in the 13th and 14th centuries. Led by Sardinia's greatest giudice, Mariano IV, and, later, his daughter, Eleonora d'Arborea, the struggle for Sardinian independence was born behind Oristano's turreted walls. Arborea eventually fell to Aragonese forces in 1410 and was ravaged by plague epidemics. Oristano's fortunes did not revive until the 1820s when it was connected to the SS131 highway, and, a century later, when Mussolini's land reclamation schemes led to its present urban makeover.

Essentials

❶ Getting around Oristano's centre is easily walkable. The train station is a 20-minute stroll from piazza Mariano and connects with a regular *verde* and *rosso* bus line.

❷ Bus station Stazione ARST, via Cagliari, T0783-355800, arst.sardegna.it, Mon-Sat 0600-2000.

❸ Train station Stazione Ferrovie dello Stato, piazza Ungheria, T0783-72270, trenitalia.com.

❹ ATM piazza Roma.

❺ Hospital Ospedale Civile, via Fondazione Rockefeller, T0783-3171.

❻ Pharmacy Farmacia San Carlo, piazza Eleonora d'Arborea 10, T0783-71123, Mon-Sat 0900-1300 and 1630-2000.

❼ Post office Poste Italiane, via Mariano IV, T0783-36801, Mon-Fri 0800-1850, Sat 0800-1315.

❽ Tourist information Ufficio Turistico, via Eleonora d'Arborea 19, T0783-36381, Mon-Fri 0900-1400 and 1500-2000, Sat 0900-1300 and 1500-2000. This is the main tourist office for both the town and the province. English spoken.

Modern art inside Palazzo Arcais.

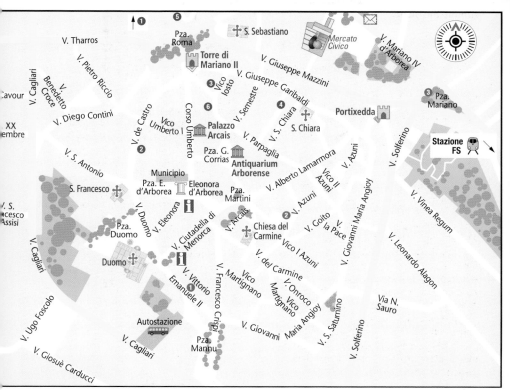

Map labels:
V. Tharros · Pza. Roma · S. Sebastiano · Mercato Civico · V. Mariano IV d'Arborea · Torre di Mariano II · V. Giuseppe Mazzini · V. Pietro Riccio · V. Cagliari · V. Benedetto Croce · V. Giuseppe Garibaldi · Cavour · V. Diego Contini · Vico Iosto · V. Semestre · S. Chiara · Portixedda · Pza. Mariano · XX embre · Vico de Castro · Corso Umberto · Vico Umberto I · Palazzo Arcais · V. S. Chiara · S. Chiara · Stazione FS · V. S. Antonio · Pza. G. Corrias · V. Parpaglia · V. Alberto Lamarmora · V. Azuni · V. Solferino · V. S. cesco Assisi · S. Francesco · Municipio · Pza. E. d'Arborea · Eleonora d'Arborea · Antiquarium Arborense · Pza. Martini · Vico II Azuni · V. Azuni · V. Vinea Regum · Pza. Duomo · V. Duomo · V. Eleonora · Pza. Arcais · Chiesa del Carmine · V. Goito · V. la Pace · V. Giovanni Maria Angioy · V. Leonardo Alagon · Duomo · V. Ciutadella di Menorca · Vico I Azuni · V. del Carmine · Vico Martignano · V. Onroco · Vico Martignano · Via N. Sauro · V. Cagliari · V. Vittorio Emanuele II · V. Francesco Crispi · Autostazione · Vico Martignano · V. Giovanni Maria Angioy · V. S. Saturnino · V. Solferino · V. Ugo Foscolo · V. Cagliari · Pza. Mannu · V. Giosuè Carducci

Detail from the church in piazza Maria Ausiliatrice.

Oristano listings

① **Sleeping**
1 Duomo Albergo *via Vittorio Emanuele 34*
2 L'Arco *Vico Ammirato 12*
3 Mariano IV Palace Hotel *piazza Mariano 50*

① **Eating & drinking**
1 Cocco & Dessì *via Tirso 31*
2 Craf *via De Castro 34*
3 Ele Café *via Parpaglia*
4 Sam House *vico Garau*
5 Trattoria Da Gino *via Tirso 13*
6 Trattoria del Teatro *via Parpaglia 11*

Around the island

Centro storico

Oristano's compact centre is designed on a wheel-like layout. Two of the town's medieval fortified gates and towers remain: the squat **Portixedda** (via Garibaldi, via Mazzini, T0783-791262, Tue-Sun 1000-1200 and 1600-1800, free), from which defenders dumped boiling oil on invaders, and Oristano's most recognizable landmark, the soaring **Torre di Mariano II** bell tower on piazza Roma, named after the *giudice* who built it.

The tower marks the beginning of Oristano's main shopping artery, **corso Umberto**, where dignified 18th-century palazzi rise high above the teens whizzing by on their bikes below. Visit **Palazzo Arcais** at No 33, which frequently hosts free art exhibitions.

The corso dead-ends at **piazza Eleonora d'Arborea**, the town's civil and legislative heart, named in honour of Sardinia's most inspirational civil and legislative champion. A 19th-century marble statue of Eleonora stands tall, clutching her famous *Carta de Logu* legal code under her cape.

Opposite the *giudicessa*, the 16th-century town hall features wrought-iron balconies and an oversized sundial on its *stile Liberty* façade.

Via Sant'Antonio takes you to the **Chiesa di San Francesco**, whose four Ionic columns and 19th-century neoclassical facelift cover the original 13th-century façade. Inside, a 15th-century carving by an unknown Valencian is one of Sardinia's most poignant religious relics: a suffering Christ nailed to a crucifix, dripping in agony. Outside, an elegant seminary built from exposed brick separates the church from Sardinia's largest cathedral, the 18th-century **Cattedrale di Santa Maria Assunta** or **Duomo**. Its bulging octagonal campanile reveals sinister gargoyles resembling Chinese New Year dragons. Engravings on the double-door entrance read like a history book of Oristano's past, showing the relocation from Tharros to Aristanis opposite Eleonora sitting on a throne. Inside the cathedral, the Cappella di San Giuseppe (second on the left) holds an impressive gilded wooden altar by Lorenzo Gerasuolo.

Piazza Eleonora d'Arborea

Antiquarium Arborense

Piazzeta Corrias, T0783-791262.
Daily 0900-1400 and 1500-2000, €3, €1.50
concessions.

Oristano's glorious past is proudly displayed
here in one of the province's most important
archaeological collections. The ground floor holds
artefacts from the Sinis Peninsula, including
Mycenaean pottery from the 15th century BC,
Carthaginian steles from Tharros' *tophet* and
rudimentary surgical tools dating from the fifth
century BC.

The heart of the museum is found on the
second floor and has exhibits, ranging from
Etruscan ceramics to Greek crafts, that testify to the
active and far-reaching commercial life of the Punic
settlement at Tharros. There's a terracotta urn from
the *tophet* with children's cremated bones inside,
and a Roman marble statue of a headless
Aphrodite. The most interesting display, however,
is the reconstructed model of the city of Tharros
during its fourth-century peak under the Romans.

The museum's **Pinacoteca** art gallery next door
has several interesting altar pieces, including the
16th-century *Santo Cristo* by Pietro Cavaro of
Cagliari's Stampace School (see page 36).

Torre Grande

Seven kilometres west of Oristano on a swampy
isthmus is the town's attractive beach, named after
its squat Aragonese watchtower. The 2-km
lungomare promenade is conveniently lined with
cafés, gelaterie and restaurants, and doubles as a
great place to stroll or jog when you're ready to
burn off the calories. In the summer the lido is
packed with windsurfers, beach volleyball players
and tanning enthusiasts, and its gentle lapping
tides make it an appealing, safe place for children.

Sa Sartiglia

Each February Oristano hosts Sardinia's most
theatrical Carnival celebration, Sa Sartiglia, in which
a masked 'king' and his followers try to lance a
suspended brass star with a tiny hole in the middle
of it, while riding a galloping horse. The event is
rooted in Moorish jousting competitions, which were
witnessed by the Aragonese during the Crusades.
The Aragonese passed both the rite and its name – a
combination of the Catalan word *sortija* (ring) and
the Latin *sors* (luck) – to Arborea's *giudicati* who
trained at the Court of Aragon.

Today, the Sartiglia is held on the Sunday and
Tuesday of Carnival under the watchful eyes of
patron saints San Giovanni and San Giuseppe. A
secret society selects the 'king', *Su Compoidori*, and
at noon each day he mounts an altar to be dressed in
a lace veil, tunic and a mask resembling a Japanese
geisha. His dressers are a trio of virgin girls called
Sas Massaieddas, monitored by the *Sa Massaia
Manna*. Once *Su Compoidori* is dressed, the virgins
sprinkle grain around the king who cannot touch
the ground as he mounts his flower-laden horse. He
is then handed a lance wrapped in periwinkles and
violets, said to symbolize fertility. He blesses the
crowd before crossing swords with his assistants, *Sa
Segundu* and *Sa Terzu Cumponis*, then gallops towards
the suspended star-shaped ring, whose diameter
is a mere 33 mm. The spectacle lasts for hours, with
droves of riders trying to pierce the ring to bring luck
for the following year. The most spectacular part, *Sa
Pariglia*, starts when *Su Compoidori* lies back on his
horse as it charges ahead. Then, riders balance upside
down on the shoulders of two other riders who stand
on the backs of their galloping steeds in a half-horse,
half-human pyramid.

Around the island

Santa Giusta

Three kilometres south of Oristano, the suburb of Santa Giusta was built on the banks of a lagoon over the remains of the Phoenician settlement of Othoca (meaning 'old town'), which was founded in 730 BC. The town, the marsh and the cathedral that stand in its centre all take their name from a local girl, Giusta, who was born between AD 117 and 138. According to legend, when Giusta proclaimed her Christianity at age 12, her pagan mother locked her in the family's cellar. After weeks of pleading in vain with Giusta to abandon her newfound faith, her mother beheaded her daughter and the girl's two followers, the family maids.

Today, the town's centrepiece is the **Basilica di Santa Giusta**, a beautifully ascetic example of Pisan Romanesque architecture built between 1135 and 1145 from local sandstone. Inside, a central nave and two side aisles are lined with columns taken from Tharros and Othoca, each subtly different. The crypt under the altar is said to be the cellar where Giusta was kept; a glass frame displays her bones.

Basilica di Santa Giusta.

The church overlooks the **Stagno di Santa Giusta**, one of Sardinia's prime fishing spots. Every year during the Festa di Santa Giusta in mid May, the marsh takes centre stage as fisherman race from end to end on traditional reed rafts called *fassonis* (see page 48) Bring your binoculars and take a side-trip to the smaller **Stagno S'Ena Arrubia**, a few kilometres south toward Arborea, to see white herons, cranes and flamingos.

Northern Campidano

The northern tip of Sardinia's Campidano plain extends just south of Oristano and is the location of some of the island's flattest terrain, straightest roads and most fertile farmland. This was an abandoned wasteland, bogged down by over 50 malaria-ridden swamps until Mussolini dreamed up a master plan to turn 18,000 ha into profitable farmland. His minions dammed the river Tirso, built canals and planted groves of eucalyptus trees to drain the land, which was then settled by experienced farmers from northern Italy. Fifty per cent of their profit went to the state in exchange for the land and the pre-built homes they were given. Unlike Il Duce's ambitious scheme to manufacture coal in Carbonia, this one actually worked and, although the pseudo-feudal system has long since disappeared, its by-products are some delicious ruby wines and Sardinia's most productive dairy region.

At the centre of the land reclamation scheme is **Arborea**, a displaced northern Italian town, which was founded as Mussolinia in 1928. The community retains its orderly grid of right-angled farm lots and evidence of its original inhabitants from Veneto, Emilia-Romagna and Lombardia can still be seen in the town's architecture and heard in the local accent. Today, Arborea is one of the top ten dairy producers in Europe, accounting for 98% of the milk Sardinians consume. Consequently, a whiff of livestock fills the air, even in stately **piazza Maria Ausiliatrice**.

Further south, the town of **Terralba** has the attractive 19th-century Cattedrale di San Pietro at its heart and is surrounded by vineyards producing red and rosé wines. Sixteen kilometres west is the unpretentious fishing community of **Marceddi**, which has a salty, purposeful air. Fisherman cast into the **Stagno di Marceddi** from jetties while seagulls flap about overhead. Forests of umbrella pines shade a prime picnic spot and you'll also find the delectable Da Lucio restaurant (see page 157).

Monte Arci

The SS131 highway divides the northern Campidano plain from soaring Monte Arci. This volcanic heap is piled 812 m high with obsidian: a hard, black volcanic glass that could be easily fashioned into arrowheads and tools, rendering it more valuable than gold until the Bronze Age. Monte Arci's endless supply of the rare substance made Sardinia's neolithic inhabitants among the most sought-after traders in the Mediterranean. Obsidian fragments from here have been found in Corsica, Tuscany and southern France. While obsidian's value has nose-dived in the past 3500 years, Monte Arci remains invaluable to thousands of wild boar who roam its slopes and it is an attractive place to explore on foot.

Turn off the SS131 at signs for Uras and Laconi, following the SS442 east to Morgongiori. Look out for brown signs to **Is Benas**, a 30-hectare pinewood forest with walking trails and wild ponies. Alternatively, continue 6 km past Morgongiori to **Ales**, the birthplace of Antonio Gramsci (see page 151), and follow another brown sign to the **Acquafridda** park, which lies in a dense oak forest with many marked paths: one leads to the peak of Trebina Longa.

Laconi

The SS442 cuts through the western Sarcidano region and into the rocky spikes around Laconi 30 km away. The ground floor of the town's neoclassical *municipio* building houses Italy's only **Museo delle Statue Menhir** (via Amsicora, T0782-866216, http://web.tiscali.it/museomenhir/,

Arborea.

Apr-Sep daily 0930-1300 and 1600-1930, Oct-Mar daily 0900-1300 and 1600-1800, closed 1st Mon of month, €3, €2 concessions), dedicated to the anthropomorphic stone statues found throughout Sardinia. Forty menhirs, a few dating back to 6000 BC, are displayed in seven rooms. The masculine statues are engraved with three-prong tridents and etched daggers; the female statues have protruding breasts.

Above the town on via Don Minzoni, the pretty 22-ha **Parco Laconi** sits in a forest of trees from four continents and is a wonderful picnic spot. Its surging waterfall feeds streams and a lake teeming with goldfish. The park belonged to the Aymerich family from the 17th century until 1990. You can see their 18th-century villa in town but the true architectural gem is the crumbling Gothic **Castello Aymerich** hidden inside the park, which preserves an original tower from 1053.

Sinis Peninsula

West of Oristano, the Sinis Peninsula is a swampy expanse of marshy lakes and ponds teeming with enough mullet, eel and shellfish to keep the surrounding fishing villages and migratory birds well fed. Between autumn and late spring, you'll see more flamingos, cranes and herons here than anywhere else in Sardinia, transforming the blue pools and green shrubs into a palette of feathery colour. This flat, watery world is ideally explored by bike or on horseback and offers enough distractions for a few days.

Cabras

At the heart of the Sinis is this unassuming fishing town whose compact centre unfolds in a warren of hobbit-sized houses and tight lanes that make cars unwelcome. It's easy to get lost in Cabras but after tasting the seafood, you won't mind. The town is built on the banks of the **Stagno di Cabras**, a 2215-hectare estuary where fresh water from Montiferru's creeks and salt water from the Oristano Gulf mix to create an ideal breeding ground for eel, bass, carp, crustaceans and five types of mullet whose unhatched eggs constitute 'Cabras' gold': *bottarga*. The town is full of *pescherie* selling Cabras' seafood: one of the best is L'Oro di Cabras (see page 159).

The small **Museo Civico di Cabras** (via Tharros, T0783-290636, daily 0900-1300 and 1500-1900, €5 with Tharros) presents an archaeological overview of the Sinis Peninsula (in Italian). The first section displays bone spear heads, obsidian shards and female divinity statues from the Cuccuru Is Arrius site 3 km west of Cabras, which was inhabited by pre-Nuraghic settlers as far back as the fourth century BC. *Tophet* steles and sarcophagi urns from nearby Tharros abound, and anchors and lead bullets from a Roman shipwreck are also on display. Don't miss the reconstructed *fassone* raft as you enter (see right).

Stagno di Cabras

Many of the Sinis' traditions relate to the Stagno di Cabras, Europe's largest lagoon, whose shimmering surface hides a complex social hierarchy shaped by strict laws and an often violent history.

In 1853 Oristano's wealthy Carta family bought the lagoon from Piedmontese nobles. For over a hundred years the Cartas operated a strict feudal system which allowed only 150 select individuals to fish the lagoon. At the top was the owner, Signor Carta, who received a 60 per cent commission from each fisherman. Below him were four *pesargus* who weighed each catch and received a salary, followed by roughly 12 *saraccius*. These 'servants' worked night and day, often nude and barehanded, striking the captured fish on the head with a piece of wood. They slept in makeshift reed huts called *barraccas* (see page 143), could only return home once a week in shifts and were paid in coins and *bottarga*. The lowest and largest class of fishermen could only fish from small *fassone* rafts made from reeds. They balanced upright on the rafts and propelled themselves through the lagoon with long poles, often wearing out five rafts in a single season (October to April).

The rest of the local population was forbidden from fishing in the lagoon but often cast nets at night. In the 1960s the killing of a watchman by two illegal fishermen resulted in a local uprising, which prompted the regional government to intervene and purchase the lagoon from the Carta family. Shortly afterwards, Don Efisio Carta, the heir of the lagoon's original purchaser, was murdered by bandits. Today, the lagoon is owned by a consortium of 300 people who remain the only ones legally allowed to fish it.

Corsa degli Scalzi

San Salvatore's *Corsa degli Scalzi* (barefoot race) is said to commemorate an event in 1506 when Saracen pirates attacked Cabras, forcing the town's faithful to flee to San Salvatore, hauling a statue of the Saviour to save it from the invaders. Like most of Sardinia's rural religious festivals held between May and September, the event is probably rooted in a remote pagan agricultural rite that was later given a Christian gloss.

Origins aside, the spectacle remains poignant. At dawn on the first Saturday in September, a town elder cries *"Currei in nomin'e Deusu!"* ("We run in the name of God!") and hundreds of barefoot Cabresi in white tunics and shorts run from the town's parish church along a rock-strewn dirt road to San Salvatore 7 km away, carrying a statue of the saint and wailing in Sardo for blessings from Christ. More emotional is the *rientra* the following dusk, when the procession is reversed: the runners, many of whom have bloodied feet, carry the statue back to the parish church while chanting *"E po' Santu Srabadoi!"* ("For San Salvatore!") before a sea of spectators.

San Salvatore

The lonely road west of Cabras skirts boggy swampland before coming to a fork marked by a crumbling nuraghe on one side and Cabras' festival village, San Salvatore on the other. Inside the town, dirt paths are lined with rows of squat Mexican *hacienda*-style houses.

The town lies abandoned all year until late August when it is roused by the arrival of families from Cabras who make the pilgrimage to their stout *domigheddas* (little houses) to celebrate the nine-day *novenario* festival in honour of San Salvatore (see box, above). The focus of this pilgrimage is the 17th-century **Chiesa di San Salvatore** (Mon-Sat 1530-1800). The church's two internal naves are divided by a staircase leading to a chamber dug out of the rock in the fourth century. The chamber encompasses a pre-existing well that was used by the local Nuraghic population to worship water. At the bottom, six dungeon-like vaults reveal scribbled ink drawings that read like a chalkboard of Sardinia's tangled religious past of pagan, Christian and Islamic influences. The original prehistoric well is preserved behind a glass case, complete with a betyl shaft (a small menhir carved with rudimentary genitalia) that was believed to spur fertility. The walls contain Greek and Punic writing and votive images of the gods Mars, Venus, and Hercules. In the far room above a Christian altar you can see 16th-century Arabic script, recounting the opening passage of the Koran.

San Giovanni di Sinis

South of San Salvatore, the Sinis Peninsula narrows to a sliver at the fishing village of San Giovanni. The stout, Middle Eastern-looking building on the left as you enter is actually Sardinia's second-oldest Christian church, the **Basilica di San Giovanni di Sinis**. Constructed from local sandstone in AD 470, the palaeo-Christian monument is built in the form of a Greek cross under a crimson dome and bears a striking resemblance to its slightly older sibling, Cagliari's San Saturnino (see page 87). The church got a complete renovation in the 10th century, only to fall into disrepair. It was used as a shelter by shepherds from the 1830s until it was restored to its original splendour in the 20th century.

Until recently, the coast of San Giovanni, from the basilica to Tharros hundreds of metres away, was lined with rows of *barraccas*. These were fishermen's huts, constructed on a wooden base that was overlaid with thick layers of sedge reeds picked from the lagoon and fastened together to resemble a straw tent. The huts were without water, electricity or plumbing, and concerns over sanitation prompted the government to demolish all of San Giovanni's *barraccas* in the 1980s… except for one. If you peer past the brush opposite Bar Palmette on the left between the basilica and Tharros, you'll see the last of an extinct breed. Its owner, a 90-something fisherman named Luigi Garau, can usually be found at the bar. Get him going and he will talk your ear off (in Italian) and may even show you around his reed residence.

Two columns preside over a Roman temple at Tharros.

Tharros

Località Tharros, T0783-370019, penisoladelsinis.it.
Daily 0900-1900, €5 with Cabras museum, €3
concessions.

A short walk from San Giovanni, where the Sinis
Peninsula's southernmost tip juts into the Gulf of
Oristano, are the remains of the Punic-Roman city
of Tharros, one of the Mediterranean's most
important trading posts for over 12 centuries. Even
those with little curiosity about Sardinia's past
should walk the 2-km trail through strawberry,
myrtle and heather from Tharros' ticket office to
the solitary lighthouse at Capo San Marco; it is one
of the island's loneliest and most evocative corners.

Like its sister city, Nora (see page 104), Tharros
was founded by Phoenician merchants on a bay
that offered safe mooring along the main trade
routes between their native Lebanon and Spain. The
Phoenicians' original settlement was built around an

abandoned Nuraghic village on Murru Mannu in
730 BC, and the name 'Tharros' probably comes
from its Sardinian predecessor, since the root *tarr*
means 'land' in Sardo. By the time the Carthaginians
showed up in 510 BC, Tharros was already trading
with the Celts, Egyptians and Etruscans.

Under Carthage, Tharros was Sardinia's
strongest naval base and wealthiest Punic city.
Things slowed down after the First Punic War (241
BC) when Rome took command, but this was
followed by a massive urban overhaul in the
second and third centuries AD: the streets were
paved with basalt blocks, aqueducts and sewer
pipes were laid, and twin thermal baths were
constructed. Raids by Saracen pirates caused the
city's population to dwindle during the late
Byzantine period until it was abandoned and
cannibalized in 1070 to build Aristanis (Oristano).

Today, 40% of the site has been excavated and
its ancient port lies underwater, so most of what is

visible was left by the Romans. As you enter, the wide street leads to a compact grid of sandstone Roman dwellings and shops on the right, with the ingenious sewer system still in place. To the left, the rectangular *Castellum Aquae* water reservoir fed the fountain in the nearby *Compitum* square, while down the hill was the city's Forum. Opposite the Forum is the older of the twin baths, with reconstructed concrete columns representing the original temple. A few steps away, the newer and better preserved thermal bath conserves its original stone columns and base. Climb the basalt road up Muru Mannu hill for wonderful views over much of the peninsula. If you look closely at the hill's summit, you'll see the original Nuraghic village lying side-by-side with a Punic *tophet* and the outline of a small Roman amphitheatre.

Rising above the site, the **Torre di San Giovanni** (May-Aug daily 0900-1300 and 1530-2000, €3) provides the best view of Tharros and is one of the few Aragonese watchtowers you can enter. (Out of season, ask the custodian at Tharros nicely and she may give you the keys to the tower.)

Above: Evidence of the Romans' sewer system remains intact. Below: San Giovanni di Sinis – walk the 2-km stretch from Tharros to the end of the cape.

Tip...

Tharros is extremely exposed to the elements and can be either blustery or burning hot, depending on the season, so bring your own shade and insect repellent. The site is at its most spectacular at dusk when spotlights illuminate the ruins.

Mari Ermi's ravishing coastline .

The coast

North of San Salvatore the road cuts through Vernaccia vineyards and fields of artichokes toward the Sinis' famous beaches, rumoured to be the cleanest in all of Italy. Follow signs to popular **Is Arutas**, 6 km north, where a dirt road follows the lonely shoreline, which is covered in rice-sized grains of pure white quartz, the result of ancient erosion from the nearby island of Mal di Ventre. The road culminates at Oristano's most spectacular beach, **Mari Ermi**. Walkers can turn left at Campeggio Is Arutas and follow a sandy trail along **Maimoni** beach, which stretches the entire length of the Sinis' protected marine park (bring mosquito repellent). Fishermen should head a few kilometres up the road to **Porto Suedda** to cast their lines with locals.

Putzu Idu & around

The seaside resort of Putzu Idu continues the Sinis' Spaghetti Western character but thanks to a handful of nearby beaches, a marsh and the potential for excursions, there's lots to do here.

The sand along Putzu Idu's long beach is finer than that at Is Arutas but you may have to contend with a fair amount of algae. Kiosks on the beachfront advertise day trips to the appealingly named **Isola Mal di Ventre** (stomach ache island) 8 km away. Constant *maestrale* render this flat island uninhabitable, but the eastern shore has sandy inlets around its granite rocks. Surfers should try the waves just north of Putzu Idu at **Capo Mannu**.

Behind Putzu Idu is the **Stagno Sale Porcus** lagoon, one of the largest reserves in the Sinis and a favourite destination for migrating cranes, cormorants, geese and pink flamingos, roughly 10,000 of which flock here in the winter and spring. There are plenty of paths along the lagoon's bank, so bring your binoculars!

What the author says

More than anywhere else in Sardinia, the province of Oristano is known for its exotic birds which feed on the region's ample sealife. It also has a proud history of horseback riding that has seeped from its daring festivals into its awakening tourism industry. While I'd advise you to watch the daredevil antics of the Sartiglia (see page 139) and Ardia (see page 152) from the sidelines, I think the best way to experience the Sinis is in the saddle.

Start by calling Sa Pedrera Hotel (see page 154) in advance to request an English-speaking guide for the trip. The hotel can also arrange transport to the nearby stable, where the Sinis' equestrian expert and your guide, Giuseppe Meli, awaits. A one-hour jaunt will explore the banks of the Mistras lagoon, a 450-hectare wetland that is home to egrets, cormorants, herring gulls and flamingos, while the two-hour excursion continues north along the Sinis' protected marine park to the glistening quartz shores of Maimone beach (no riding experience necessary). Cap off your day at Sa Pedrera's restaurant to dine on some local seafood: try the fresh bass and mullet, or the *fregola* pasta with fresh crustaceans, and don't miss the opportunity to eat 'Cabras' caviar'. You won't taste better spaghetti topped with clams and *bottarga* anywhere else.

Eliot Stein

Montiferru & around

North of the Sinis' swampy patchwork, bulging Montiferru (iron mountain) rises up to the extinct volcanic peak of Mont Urtigu (1050 m). The slopes are covered with thick forests of chestnut, holm and cork trees, which are nurtured by many springs and rivers, and the mix of rifts and rises offer some fantastic hikes around wild mouflons and cascading waterfalls. Small agricultural hamlets are surrounded by fertile lowlands that provide some of Sardinia's most prized delicacies: Vernaccia wine, olive oil and *bue rosso* cattle. There are fewer than 2000 of these auburn-tinted cows in existence and they are only found in this area.

Before roads were laid, the towns dotting Montiferru were connected by walking paths. These unmarked trails remain great for hiking: some can be followed easily without a guide; for others, guides are helpful and available (see Activities & tours, page 161).

San Vero Milis & Milis

San Vero Milis is a one-horse town at the base of Montiferru, identified by the onion-shaped campanile of its sandstone **Chiesa di Santa Sofia**. Its vineyards produce most of Sardinia's prized Vernaccia dessert wine. Originally introduced by the Punic population, the name comes from the Latin '*vitis vernacular*' (local wine) and is produced only in or near the lower Tirso river valley. Many of San Vero's residents make the wine themselves and sell it from their homes – just ask around; otherwise, head to San Vero's award-winning Cantina Josto Puddu (see page 160).

Six kilometres northeast, **Milis** is a pleasant town built from dark basalt rock and surrounded by citrus groves. These were the most fertile in the Mediterranean throughout much of the 20th century, yielding 60 million oranges a year. Look for the eighth-century **Chiesa di San Paolo**, the burgundy **Palazzo Boyl** cultural centre and the towering campanile of the 16th-century **Chiesa di San Sebastiano**.

Around the island

In early October tractors roll through the valley laden with harvested vernaccia grapes. After the grapes are processed, Milis hosts one of Sardinia's most spirited festivals, the **Rassegna del Vino Novello** (the weekend after 6th November), when visitors can stroll (or stagger) from tent to tent all night long sampling the region's new wine.

Seneghe, Bonarcado & Santu Lussurgiu

These bucolic communities cluster in a triangle on the southern slope of the Montiferru mountain and are each worth your time if you're not in a particular hurry.

There may only be 1800 people in **Seneghe** but its nickname, '*La Città del Olio*', is well deserved, since its artichoke-flavoured olive oil, *Senolio*, routinely wins the regional *Oscar dell l'Olio* competition and is judged among Italy's best.

East of Seneghe, **Bonarcado** is a tiny town of shepherds and *bue rosso* cattle ranchers. Its main attractions are its two churches, the 12th-century Romanesque **Chiesa di Santa Maria**, with its sober dark stone façade, and the more famous seventh-century **Chiesa di Nostra Signora di Bonacattu**. Only four pews fit into this pocket-sized chapel which was built over the remains of Roman baths. Inside, traces of the original second-century mosaic floor are still visible.

The road north from Bonarcado winds along Montiferru's ancient volcanic rim towards Santu Lussurgiu. After 4 km, look for a gravel car park with a faded stone sign to 'Sos Molinos' (beyond the sign for 'Chiosco Sos Molinos') and follow a steep dirt path to reach a stunning waterfall tumbling down a 20-m cliff into a pool.

Chiesa di Nostra Signora di Bonacattu, Bonarcado.

Four kilometres further along the road, **Santu Lussurgiu** nestles in a deep crater, with steep cobblestone streets snaking around the town's three churches. At the centre is the **Museo della Tecnologia Contadina** (via Meloni 1, T0783-550617, by appointment only, €3), which displays a modest collection of agricultural items collected by Maestro Salis, the town's venerated elementary school teacher. Salis taught reading and Italian here in the 1950s, when roughly half of Santu Lussurgiu's population was illiterate and only spoke Sardo. Tucked down a narrow alley, the Antica Dimora del Gruccione (see page 155) is one of Sardinia's classiest hotels and greatest surprises.

Six kilometrres north, the village of **San Leonardo** sits in a shady forest of holm and oak trees and has long been a cool summer getaway for Santu Lussurgiu's upper-crust. The tumbledown 12th-century church is where Ugolino della Gherardesca's son, Guelfo, is buried, though San Leonardo is better known for its seven natural springs that trickle down canals from the top of the park. Between Santu Lussurgiu and San Leonardo, a sign for 'Fontana Sa Preda Lada', showing a statue of the Virgin and some grazing donkeys, marks the beginning of a cobblestone path that leads to prime mouflon-spotting territory.

Tip...

From Sunday to Tuesday during Carnival, 60 of Santu Lussurgiu's most daring riders dress in medieval costume and race down the town's narrow streets on galloping horses while performing acrobatic tricks in a celebration known as *Sa Carrela 'e Nanti*.

Cuglieri

From San Leonardo, a mountain pass winds around the western slopes of Montiferru for 10 km before the crumbling remains of **Casteddu Ezzu** (old castle) come into view atop a peak. The fortress was built in 1186 by the Giudicato of Torres to defend against Arborea to the south. A steep hike up to its ruined walls rewards you with a fantastic panoramic view of the 'Iron Mountain' and nearby coastline. If scrambling uphill isn't for you, continue 3 km from the castle to Cuglieri and drive up to the 18th-century parish church, **Santa Maria della Neve**, which has views on a clear day stretching north to Capo Marargiu.

South of Cuglieri

South of Cuglieri, you'll find a trio of modest beachside resorts. The villages of **Santa Caterina di Pittinuri**, to the north, and **Torre del Pozzo**, to the south, are hemmed in by Aragonese watchtowers. Stop off at the middle town, **S'Archittu** (the little arch) where the wind has chiselled out a limestone tunnel large enough to sail through. The sight is especially dramatic at night when it's illuminated. The beaches here are decent but you can do better if you continue on the SS292 south to the 6-km strand at **Is Arenas**, said to have Europe's largest seaside pine forest.

History buffs should take the marked dirt road between Santa Caterina and S'Archittu to see the scant remains of the Carthaginian city of **Cornus**. Founded in the sixth century BC, the city took centre stage in 215 BC during the Second Punic War when Sardo-Punic forces aligned under the leadership of Ampsicora and his son Osto to rid the island of Roman occupation in the name of '*Bellum Sardum*' (see page 28). The ambitious plan didn't quite work out: Roman commander Manlio Torquato crushed the allied forces and killed Osto, causing Ampsicora to commit suicide when he heard the news of his fallen son. The few remaining relics are from a later Roman funerary site built around a temple and well.

Shortly after the SS131 highway forks northeast towards Nuoro, you can't miss Italy's largest artificial lake. It took five years and 16,000 workers to dam the river Tirso here to create the 22-sq km Lago Omodeo, which is used to irrigate the Campidano's parched wheat fields. It was a monumental feat in 1924 but not without controversy, as the plan called for the small community of Zuri to be flooded. The residents reluctantly agreed to abandon the village for the good of the island but insisted on dismantling their beloved 12th-century church, stone by stone, and reconstructing it 2 km away at the new settlement.

Sos Molinos waterfall, Montiferru.

Paulilatino & Santa Cristina

At Km 115 of the SS131, 28 km from Oristano, is the turn-off for the town of Paulilatino and its pilgrim village, Santa Cristina. Paulilatino's fine **Museo Etnografico** (via Nazionale 127, T0785-55438, Tue-Sun 0930-1300 and 1600-1900, €5 including Santa Cristina) is housed in an 18th-century building and displays traditional Sardinian items, including a beautiful exhibit dedicated to Sardinian bread. A signposted road leads 3 km away to the **Santuario Nuragico di Santa Cristina** (T0785-55438, daily 0830-2100, €5 including Museo Etnografico), a nine-day celebratory *novenaria* site that proves that Sardinians are an ancient people whose pagan roots are not far from the surface of its Christian soil. The 13th-century **Chiesa di Santa Cristina** is surrounded by small *muristenes* houses that were once inhabited by monks. These days, the otherwise dormant village awakens when Paulilatino's families celebrate the nine-day rites of Santa Cristina in May and San Serafino in October, corresponding to the times of planting and harvest on the ancient Sardinian calendar.

The sacred well at Santa Cristina.

Flashback 2,300 years by taking a 50-m path from the Christian village to the Nuraghic equivalent, with village huts inhabited by pilgrims who came to worship the cult of water. The site's centrepiece is Sardinia's best-preserved Nuraghic-age structure: a sacred well dating from roughly 1000 BC, whose dark basalt rocks are chiselled to refined perfection. Worshippers would leave votive offerings around the well's 26 by 20 m atrium before descending the trapezoidal stairwell to a 7-m high chamber enclosing the well itelf.

The well's positioning suggests that Sardinia's mysterious Nuraghic inhabitants possessed a keen knowledge of astronomy. During the equinoxes in March and September, the sun illuminates the bottom of the stairwell, and every 18½ years the full moon shines through a small opening at the top of the well to reflect in the pool below (book your flight for June, 2025).

Fordongianus

A narrow road from Paulilatino shoots south to the Roman spa town of Fordongianus on the bank of the river Tirso. Founded in the first century BC by the Emperor Trajan, *Forum Traiani* was Rome's most important inland settlement on Sardinia: a military outpost where soldiers could keep an eye on the barbaric *Sardi Pelliti* of the Barbagie and get a good scrub at the baths when off-duty.

A Roman bridge still carries cars over the Tirso and provides views of the town's trademark **Terme Romane** (T0783-60157, forumtraiani.it, Tue-Sun 0900-1300 and 1500-1900, €4 including Casa Aragonese). A series of vaults shelter a basin from which scalding (56°C) water springs, trickling down a few channels into the Tirso and sending clouds of steam billowing up from the river on a cool day.

Fordongianus' modern town is built with volcanic red trachyte stone which is also used in its annual summer sculpture competition. A few past winning pieces stand outside the 17th-century **Casa Aragonese** (via Traiano 10, T0783-60157, Tue-Sun 0900-1300 and 1500-1900, €4 including Terme Romane).

Nuraghe Losa.

Nuraghe Losa

Just off the SS131 at Km 124, T0785-52302,
nuraghelosa.net.
Daily 0900 till 1 hr before sunset, €3.50, €2.50
concessions.

From the crossroads at Abbasanta, you can see the
Bronze Age towers of the nuraghe Losa, one of the
most impressive in Sardinia. Like Barumini's Su
Nuraxi (see page 98), the edifice was originally a
three-storey nuraghe connected by internal
passages to successively built towers, all of which
were enclosed by a stone curtain wall, rendering it
a virtual megalithic castle.

Losa's nucleus is its three-tower fortress. The
central tower, which is 12 m in diameter, was built
in the 14th century BC, but its top level has since
collapsed. Inside, lights illuminate three niches that
served as closets and a passageway separates two
towers. A staircase wraps around the central tower
to the outdoor keep and the third-floor terrace.
The third tower must have been accessed by the
village's most nimble residents, since its entrance
can only be entered through a tiny door.

Outside, a turreted wall with two remaining
towers surrounded the tri-lobe structure. The
entire 3.5-hectare site is enclosed by a second wall
which preserves a small burial area by the entrance.

Casa Museo di Antonio Gramsci

Corso Umberto 57, Ghilarza, T0785-54164.
Wed-Mon 1000-1300 and 1500-1830, free.

Anyone interested in Italian politics should visit
Ghilarza where Italy's most influential liberal
political theorist, Antonio Gramsci, lived from 1898
to 1914. Gramsci was born in Ales in 1891 but grew
up in Ghilarza in the present-day museum building.
From an early age, he was deeply affected by the
plight of Sardinia's impoverished workers whom he
saw as victims of mainland exploitation, and he
favoured Sardinian independence. After studying at
the University of Turin, Gramsci joined the Italian
Socialist party and, through his speeches on
workers' rights and articles as editor of the party's
newspaper, *Il Grido del Popolo*, became one of the
party's leading figures. In 1921, Gramsci co-founded
the Italian Communist Party and worked to
encourage Italy's left-leaning parties to back the
movement. Despite his parliamentary immunity,
Gramsci was arrested by Mussolini's Fascist regime
in 1926 and received a 20-year prison sentence. He
died while imprisoned but left more than 3000
pages of writings during his sentence. Many of
these testimonies helped spur the resurgence of
Italy's Communist Party following the Second World
War and are displayed at the museum (in Italian).

Sedilo & the Ardia

If you're *anywhere* in Sardinia in early July, join the 50,000 spectators who descend on the sleepy hillside town of Sedilo for Sardinia's most reckless festival, the Ardia horse race. The event commemorates the victory of Emperor Constantine and his Christian army over Maxentius and his pagan troops in AD 312. According to legend, Constantine looked to the sky and saw a bright cross with the writing '*In Hoc Signo Vinces*' (in this sign you will conquer) before leading his daring cavalry to victory. This event led to his local canonization as Santu Antine.

Every year at dawn on 6 July and at dusk the following day, the town holds a frantic bareback horse race that circles Sedilo's pilgrim village, **Santuario di Santu Antine**. The parish priest chooses a horseman of proven courage and faith to be the race's leader, *Sa Prima Pandela*, and to carry the yellow flag baring Constantine's insignia. This jockey nominates two other flag bearers, *Sa Segunda* and *Sa Terza Pandela*, who, in turn, select three escorts to represent the Christian forces and to ensure – by clubbing their bare-headed challengers with heavy wooden sticks – that the 100 'pagan' riders chasing them don't pass the *Prima Pandela*.

The *Prima Pandela* starts the race by galloping downhill towards an arch baring Constantine's Latin dictum, while a cavalry of jockeys give chase. Dozens of riflemen then fire blanks at the horses to discourage them from tearing into the crowd and to prevent crashes into the arched wall (several jockeys have died this way). Riders pass around the curved track up to seven times while the crowd cheers.

Bosa

Bosa paints a pretty picture arriving from the east: the arching bridge crossing the river Temo in the foreground, narrow palazzi painted in warm coats of pink and pistachio like a basket of Easter eggs on the Serravilla hill, and the crowning castle perched above the valley's undulating olive groves. It's a perfect tableau from a Tuscan Renaissance painting and, if Bosa were in Tuscany, it would be crawling with tourists. Instead, this fishing port and craft town remains one of Sardinia's greatest surprises and most attractive medieval settlements.

Set on the northern bank of Sardinia's only navigable river, Bosa was founded by the Phoenicians, settled by the Romans and ruled in the Middle Ages by a line of Tuscan marquises with a prickly surname: Malaspina dello Spino Secco (bad thorn from the dry thorn). Like Alghero and Castelsardo, Bosa thrived on coral fishing. The Spanish granted it royal city status, which prompted the Bosani nobility to be the first on the island to shed their Sardinian costumes in favour of 18th-century threads.

Today, the town retains an air of urban sophistication and, although its coral and leather industries have subsided, it still produces Sardinia's best handmade lace and sweetest Malvasia wine.

Sas Conzas

This neighbourhood on the Temo's southern bank is characterized by a row of two-storey 18th-century leather tanneries, established by the Savoyard kings but abandoned in the 1960s. The tannery buildings are currently being renovated as apartments and restaurants but one houses the **Museo delle Antiche Concerie** (via delle Conce 13, T329-414 4921, Mon-Sat 1100-1300 and 1800-2300, €5), which chronicles the history of the town's leather industry.

It's a pleasant walk 2 km upriver from the museum (cross via Roma and continue on via Abate) to the rose-coloured **Basilica di San Pietro**,

Bosa.

Tip...

If you're driving, park your car in the Sas Conzas district or along via Lungo Temo de Gasperi.

one of Sardinia's oldest Lombard Romanesque churches, dating from 1062. Enjoy a good view of Bosa as you return.

Sa Piatta

Three arches carry the **ponte Vecchio** bridge across the Temo, connecting Sas Conzas to Bosa's flat Sa Piatta district. You can't miss the Baroque **Cattedrale dell'Immacolata** under a colourful dome on the Sa Piatta side of the bridge. Rebuilt in the 1800s following frequent floods of the Temo, the cathedral features an impressive mural of the Virgin watching over Bosa.

Turn left at Bosa's main street, **corso Vittorio Emanuele**, where 18th-century Savoyard palazzi with wrought-iron balconies line the boulevard. One such mansion, **Casa Deriu** (corso 59, T0785-377043, Tue-Sun 1000-1300 and 2030-2300, €4.50, €3 concessions), was occupied until 1980 and offers a re-creation of an aristocratic residence on the second floor. The third-floor art gallery and **Pinoteca** across the street are included in the ticket. The splashing fountain at nearby **piazza Costituzione** provides a soothing soundtrack for people-watching at the square's outdoor café. To the right you'll see the broken clock of the **Chiesa del Rosario** poking out onto the corso.

Sa Costa

Bosa's oldest and most famous quarter is the steep Sa Costa district, which climbs the Serravalle hill towards **Castello Malaspina** (always ring in advance: T0785-373286, Jul-Sep 1000-1300 and 1600-1800, closed during rain or strong winds, €2.50, €1.50 children), which has long been under renovation. The residents of Sa Costa remain the loyal custodians of the abandoned castle, which is reached via several medieval cobblestone alleys that ascend from various points along the corso. (You can drive up to the castle using the street that climbs the hill from piazza del Carmine.)

The Malaspina family built the fortress in 1112 and surrounded it with a stout wall and towers but the threat of Aragonese raids led Giovanni Capula, the architect of Cagliari's Elefante and San Pancrazio towers, to fortify the castle further in the 1300s with the red ochre, turreted bastion that you see today. The only building remaining inside the fortress's dilapidated walls is the **Chiesa di Nostra Signora di Regnos Altos**, with its striking 14th-century fresco cycle which brings together some VIP saints, including St Lawrence, St Christopher and St James. It appears to show Catalan influences but lacks an artist's signature.

Bosa Marina

In the summer, most of the action in Bosa shifts 2 km west to its coastal counterpart, Bosa Marina, at the mouth of the river Temo. The Marina's few hotels, bars, restaurants and a disco give the town some hop each summer but the main attraction is the wide beach dividing the harbour from one of Sardinia's largest and oldest watchtowers, the 16th-century **Torre Aragonese** (Sat 1500-1830, Sun 1030-1300 and 1500-1830). From high on the tower's terrace, the views of the coast are remarkable; two other watchtowers are visible north toward Alghero.

Sleeping

Duomo Albergo €€
Via Vittorio Emanuele 34,
T0783-778061, hotelduomo.net.
This small newly opened hotel is
as close as visitors will get to
Oristano's cathedral dome.
Rooms are decorated with
Sardinian flair and bright colours.
Most rooms have balconies and
those facing the street have nice
views of the bell tower.

Mariano IV Palace Hotel €€
Piazza Mariano 50, T0783-
360101, m4ph.isarose.net/.
A perfectly fine hotel catering to
the no nonsense business crowd.
Rooms come with satellite TV,
private baths, air conditioning
and private parking, but if you
like soft mattresses, look
elsewhere.

L'Arco €
Vico Ammirato 12, T0783-72849,
arcobedandbreakfast.it.
Located off the town's main drag
and run by a charming woman,
this B&B is a pleasant alternative
to Oristano's larger business-
style hotels. The Arco's two
rooms have modern comforts
and, between November and
June, you'll awaken to freshly
squeezed orange juice from the
family's citrus groves.

Campsites
Villaggio Camping Spinnaker
Torre Grande, T0783-22074,
campingspinnaker.com.
Apr-Oct only.
Offers traditional tent and
caravan spaces and bungalow
lodges in a pine forest directly on
Torre Grande beach. There's also
a pool, pizzeria and restaurant.

Gallo Bianco €
Piazza Maria Ausiliatrice 10,
Arborea, T0783-800241,
locandadelgallobianco.it.
Arborea's only central hotel is a
charming, old-fashioned place
with 10 rooms overlooking
Arborea's elegant square.
Mussolini stayed here in the
1930s. The hotel has since
installed colour TVs and air
conditioning, and there's a
restaurant open to non-guests.

Ferrari €€
Località Is Pontigheddus, Cabras,
T0783-290094,
agriturismoferrari.com.
Angelo Ferrari's tranquil
agriturismo has 10 en-suite
rooms with air-conditioning and
a gazebo. Rimedia Ferrari
prepares all of the restaurant's
meat dishes from the family farm
(seafood is also available).

Il Sinis €€
Località San Salvatore,
T0783-392653,
agriturismoilsinis.it.
This agriturismo is an ideal place
to book for San Salvatore's Corsa
degli Scalzi festivities (see page
143). There are six rooms
available, each with their own
bath and air conditioning. The
highlight, however, is the
home-grown cuisine eaten in a
large, vaulted dining room.

Sa Pedrera €€
Km 7.5 between Cabras and San
Giovanni di Sinis, T0783-370040,
sapedrera.it.
The Sinis' finest hotel doubles as
one of its best restaurants. Large
rooms are spread around a
compound, making it feel more
like an agriturismo than a hotel.
Play tennis, rent bikes to explore
the Sinis, or let the hotel set up
hiking or horse riding excursions
for you.

Sa Ruda €€
Località Sa Ruda, T0783-931800,
agriturismosaruda.it.
Located between San Salvatore
and Is Arutas, this agriturismo has
a U-shaped group of rooms
around scattered menhir rocks.
In fact, the residence is part
agriturismo, part archaeological
reconstruction, with rebuilt reed
huts on the property. Owner
Marcella Meli is always happy to
show you around.

Is Cortillaris €

Località Is Cortillaris, T0783-391322, iscortillaris.it.
Apr-Oct only.
A modern agriturismo set on a large knoll with low, ranch-style accommodation. Rooms are spacious and equipped with air conditioning and private baths. The restaurant serves Cabras' traditional seafood and yummy meat courses as well.

Campsites

Camping Is Arutas

Località Marina Is Arutas, T0783-391108, campingisarutas.it.
Mid May-Sep only.
Bring strong mosquito repellent to this campsite, set on a corner of one of the Sinis' most magical and least trafficked beaches. In fact, you may want to consider staying in one of the *case mobili* houses instead of a tent. There's a small play area for kids, as well as ping-pong and volleyball.

Montiferru & around

Antica Dimora del Gruccione €€

Via Michele Obinu 31, Santu Lussurgiu, T0783-552035, anticadeimora.com.
This is one of Sardinia's hidden gems! Tucked off a small street in Santu Lussurgiu, the 17th-century mansion has been in Gabriella Belloni's family for centuries and is decorated to

look somewhere between a medieval castle and rural farmhouse. There are 10 guest rooms, some with fireplaces; ask for a first-floor room overlooking the town. Dinner is an organic treat, usually involving Montiferru's prized *bue rosso* steak.

Desogos €

Vico Cugia 6, Cuglieri, T0785-369163.
Cuglieri's only hotel opened after the Second World War, when a prisoner of war returned from North Africa with no money and

started the hotel's famous restaurant. The rooms have seen better days but are perfectly fine for crashing the night.

Campsites

Europa Camping Village

Torre del Pozzo, T0785-38058, camping.it/sardegna/europa.
Set amidst Is Arenas' dense pinewood forest within walking distance of the beach. Bungalows are available for couples or families, and there's a restaurant, bar and market. The tennis courts, pool and mini-golf course are a plus.

Sardegna Grand Hotel Terme €€

SP48, Fordongianus,
T0783-605016, termesardegna.it.
Owned by the same group that
runs Sardara's spa hotel (see
page 118), the Fordongianus
version is a step up both in
comfort and modernity. It still
attracts the same elderly
clientele, however. The rooms
are large and cushy, and the
warm pools and massage
options add to the pampering.

Corte Fiorita €€

Via Lungo Temo De Gasperi 45,
T0785-377058, albergo-diffuso.it.
A hotel with the personal feel of
an intimate B&B, the Corte Fiorita
is divided between two
locations: Le Palme on the river

Temo and I Gerani in the Sa Costa
district (a golf cart drives you and
your luggage up its steep
streets). Each of the Corte's 30
rooms have been elegantly
restored. Check in is at Le Palme.

Hotel Al Gabbiano €€

Viale Mediterraneo, Bosa Marina,
T0785-374123,
hotelalgabbiano.it.
Late Jun-Sep only.
A breezy, middle-of-the-road
hotel with no surprises. Each
room has its own balcony and
those facing the sea can get a bit
noisy in high season. A 'seaside
view' means peering through a
run-down building to see the
beach.

Belvedere €

Via Belvedere 21, T349-594 7875,
bosa.it/belvedere.
Enjoy great views of the river
Temo as it zigzags toward Bosa

from this B&B high up in the Sa
Costa district. Each of the four
rooms has its own bathroom, TV
and air conditioning. Small pets
are allowed. Note: the owner
lives on site and can be a bit
intrusive.

Sa Balza €

Corso Vittorio Emanuele 45,
T0785-374391, sabalza.it.
Bosa's most conveniently located
B&B is a 17th-century charmer.
Owner Emanuele Masia has
recently restored three rooms
with modern amenities while
keeping the trademark vaulted
ceilings. Emanuele is a wealth of
local knowledge and can
suggest day trips in and around
his town; he works at the travel
agency below the B&B and
speaks fluent English.

Eating & drinking

For hotel restaurants, see Sleeping.

Oristano

Cocco & Dessì €€€€
Via Tirso 31, T0783-300720.
Tue-Sun 1230-1430 and 1930-2245.
A newly remodelled interior belies the age of this old-time restaurant that's been around since 1925. Famous for its Italian and Mediterranean dishes, including a few regional classics, such as *bue rosso* steaks and *maccarones* pasta. Sardinian cheeses are available as well.

Trattoria del Teatro €€€€
Via Parpaglia 11, T0783-71672.
Wed-Mon 2000-2300.
Located near Oristano's theatre, this trattoria has recently changed management but its new young caretakers have promised to maintain the attention to detail that has made its elegant stone interior a mainstay in town. The menu changes frequently but Cabras' *bottarga* is usually on hand. When available, try the red tuna and the pistachio gelato.

Craf €€€
Via De Castro 34, T0783-70669.
Mon-Sat 1230-1430 and 2000-2245.
Famous for its low arched ceiling, fine food and fussy service, this is one of Oristano's great restaurants. The menu has recently expanded beyond its famous ram, kid, piglet and wild boar dishes to include fish. The *pane frittau* bread doused in tomato sauce and topped with an egg white is a must.

Trattoria Da Gino €€€
Via Tirso 13, T0783-71428.
Mon-Sat 2000-2230.
Head chef Nazzaro Pusceddu serves up Oristano's best seafood dishes: *bottarga*, lobster, and sea urchin stand out. There's lots of Vernaccia wine on hand, which Gino celebrates each November during the *novello* period.

Cafés & bars
Ele Café
Via Parpaglia.
Daily 0900-0200.
A hot-spot among Oristano's fashionable crowd who come more to be seen than to drink at the café's outdoor seating.

Sam House
Vico Garau, T0783-73355.
Mon-Sat 2000-0100, Sun for football matches.
A laid-back Irish pub.

South of Oristano

Da Lucio €€
Via Lungomare 40, Marceddì, T0783-867130.
Sep-Jun Mon-Fri 1230-1445, Jul-Aug Mon-Fri 1230-1445 and 2030-2245.
You'll struggle to get fish fresher than at Lucio's, a few steps from the docks in Marceddì. There's lots of local *muggine*, *bottarga* and clams to be had, washed down with local Torralba wine.

Sinis Peninsula

Sa Funt €€€€
Via Garibaldi 25, Cabras, T0783-290685.
Mon-Sat 2000-2300.
A draped fishing net and recreated *fassone* raft welcome you as you enter this well-regarded seafood restaurant. Smoked fish, mullet, *bottarga* and clams are popular and accompanied by Vernaccia wine upon request.

Il Caminetto €€€
Via Battisti 8, Cabras, T0783-391139.
Daily 1230-1430 and 2000-2230.
The three Canu brothers preside over Cabras' most famous restaurant, hidden in its web of streets. Cabras' *bottarga* is the star, served atop spaghetti with or without clams. The restaurant also specializes in mullet, served in soups, smoked or boiled.

Montiferru & around

Meridiana €€€€
Via Littorio 1, Cuglieri, T0785-39400.
Wed-Sat 1230-1430 and 1930-2230, Sun 1230-1430.
Owner Emilio Acca is known for his seafood dishes, such as sea urchin, white mushrooms mixed with shrimp, and swordfish. The local Vernaccia wine is recommended.

Al Bue Rosso €€€
Piazzale Montiferru 3, Seneghe, T0783-54384.
Daily 1230-1430 and 2000-2200.
Housed in a converted 1910 dairy, this osteria is loved by locals who are quick to point out that it doesn't actually serve *bue rosso*. However, whatever the exact breed, we can vouch for the steaks. Seneghe's famous olive oil is splashed on many of the dishes, and the fregola pasta with mutton ragù is also tasty.

Sa Mola €€€
Via Giardini, Bonarcado, T0783-56588.
Mon 1930-2200, Tue-Sun 1300-1430 and 1930-2200.
This refined restaurant is found inside a restored 18th-century home surrounded by a garden. Try the tasty bean soup with *porcini* mushrooms or the *pane frittau*, which consists of *carasau* bread slathered in pecorino cheese and tomato sauce. The

highlight is undoubtedly the tender *bue rosso* served with potatoes. Flan is a good bet for dessert.

Bosa

Borgo Sant'Ignazio €€€€
Via Sant'Ignazio, T0785-374129.
May-Sep daily 1230-1430 and 1930-2230, Oct-Apr Wed-Mon 1230-1430 and 1930-2230.
The only way up to this restaurant in Bosa's Sa Costa neighbourhood is on foot. Try the local *alizansas* pasta with meat and vegetables, roasted eel, or the filling *impanada* patties stuffed with meat.

Cafés & bars
Birreria alla Corte del Malaspina
Corso Vittorio 39.
Mon-Sat 2000-0130.
Central Bosa's one true pub is a cosy place to drink the night away.

Entertainment

Cinema
Ariston
Via Diaz 1/A, T0783-212020.
Four screens with evening show times.

Clubs
BNN Fashion Club
Km 1.8 between Torre Grande and Cabras.
May-Sep Thu-Sun 2300-0200.
The former Banana Disco is under new management and plays trance and electronic music. There's outdoor seating in a lush garden with a modestly sized bar inside.

Cinema
Multisala Zinnigas
Località Zinnigas, Santa Giusta, T0783-359945.
Six screens with evening show times.

Clubs
Discoteca Al Paradise
Località Turas, viale Alghero 14, T0785-373776.
Jun-Sep Fri-Sun 2200-0300.
Located 1 km from Bosa Marina toward Turas, this is your best bet for house music.

El Patio Latino
Bosa Marina.
Fri-Sun in summer.
Bosa Marina's only real nightlife spot is an oddball. There's no phone number and no set hours but it's conveniently located along the main drag. The pumping electronic music lets you know when things get going.

Shopping

Books
Libreria Canu
Via De Castro 20, T0783-78723.
Mon-Sat 0900-1300 and 1630-2000.
Lots of photography books about Sardinia with a small English-language section.

Souvenirs
I Fenicotteri
Corso Umberto 50, T0783-78077.
Mon-Sat 0900-1300 and 1600-1930, Sun 0900-1300.
Sells the usual cork, pottery and masks found in all Sardinian souvenir shops; the difference being that owner Giuseppe Pippia makes most of the items in his workshop at the back.

Food & drink
L'Oro di Cabras
Via Cima 5, Cabras, T0783-290848, orodicabras.it.
Mon, Tue, Thu-Sat 0800-1300 and 1600-1830, Wed 0800-1300.
This is the most famous of the many places in town to pick up Cabras *bottarga*.

Montiferru & around

Food & drink

Azienda Olearia Peddio
Corso Umberto 87, Cuglieri,
T0785-369254.
Mon-Sat 0800-1300 and
1500-2000, Sun 0800-1300.
While Cuglieri's olive oil isn't as
prized as Seneghe's, it's still
pretty darn good. Pick up a litre
for €6.50 at this co-op.

Cantina Josto Puddu
Via San Lussorio 1, San Vero Milis,
T0783-53329, cantinapuddu.it.
Mon-Fri 0800-1300 and
1530-1830.
Josto Puddu's prized amber-
coloured Vernaccia wine ensures
he is regarded as one of the top
100 bottlers in Italy. Red wine
and *spumanti* are also on hand,
as are samples.

Oleificio Sociale di Seneghe
Corso Umberto 1, Seneghe,
T0783-54665.
Nov-Jan daily 0900-1230 and
1500-1700; call ahead at other
times.
Sells Seneghe's award-winning
Senolio oil: €5 for a half-litre
bottle. If the shop is closed,
knock on the doors at corso
Umberto 99 and 204, where the
residents sell homemade
versions.

Souvenirs

Vittorio Mura & Figli
Viale Azuni 29, Santu Lussurgiu,
T0783-550726.
Mon-Sat 0900-1230 and
1630-1900.
A family-run knife-making studio
in the heart of Santu Lussurgiu.

Bosa

Food & drink

Enoteca
Corso Vittorio.
Mar-Oct daily 0900-1300 and
1600-1930.
Owner Mario Pes sells lots of
Sardinian wines, including
Malvasia di Bosa, winner of the
region's best white in 2008.

Souvenirs

Al Vecchio Mulino
Via Solferino 12, T0785-372054.
Apr-Oct Mon-Sat 1030-1300
and 1600-2400, Nov-Mar
Mon-Sat 1030-1300.
Housed inside a 17th-century
water mill, this gift shop sells
Malvasia wine and other
souvenirs but specializes in
handmade lace.

Tip...

In the summer lace-lovers are
in for a treat. Wander along via
Carmine behind corso Vittorio
Emanuele, where women sit
outside and stitch elaborate
designs. Stop at No 161, where a
lady sells her creations from an
open window each morning.

Activities & tours

Sinis Peninsula

Diving Centre Putzu Idu
Putzu Idu, T348-694073,
divingputzuidu.
Choose from skin diving, scuba
or snorkelling courses, or trips
to 12 dive sites around the
Sinis' coast.

Naturawentura
Putzu Idu, T0783-52197,
capomannu.it.
This all-inclusive guiding
company organizes trips to Isola
Mal di Ventre, runs kite surfing,
windsurfing and surfing lessons
in the San Vero Milis marina, and
offers 4WD, mountain bike and
trekking trips throughout the
region.

Montiferru & around

Benthos
T348-062 4943,
benthos@tiscalinet.it
Raimondo Cossu's company has
been leading hikes around
Montiferru for over 20 years and
he is as knowledgeable as
anyone about the area.
Raimondo doesn't speak English,
but with advance notice he can
usually arrange a translator.
(Non-Italian speakers should
contact him by e-mail.) Choose
from single or multi-day hikes, or
various bike excursions.

La Bocca del Vulcano
Via Leonardo Alagon 26, Santu
Lussurgiu, T0783-550974,
laboccadelvulcano.it.
Treks and culinary tours around
Montiferru. Non-Italian speakers
should book by email and the
company will try to arrange a
translator for the excursion.

Towards Nuoro

Is Bangius
Fordongianus, T0783-60157.
Mon-Sat 0800-1200 and
1500-1700, Sun 0900-1200 and
1500-1700, €4 for 30 mins.
This modern-day spa is down the
street from the Roman version.
Soak in baths filled with 40°C
water while gazing at the Tirso.

Bosa

Esedra
Corso Vittorio Emanuele 64,
Bosa, T0785-374258,
esedrasardegna.it.
Architectural tours, cycling, boat
trips and other excursions
around Bosa and northern
Sardinia, including frequent trips
up Monte Urtigu, with a
4WD-vehicle doing much of the
hard work for you.

La Pagaia
River Temo, Bosa, T320-844 6120.
May-Oct daily.
Rent canoes, kayaks and paddle
boats to tour Sardinia's only
navigable river. Highly
recommended.

Transport

Oristano

Hourly trains to **Cagliari** (1½ hrs),
plus three trains daily to **Sassari**
(2½ hrs) and one train to **Porto**
Torres (3 hrs). The Azzurro bus
line connects Oristano to **Torre**
Grande while ARST buses run
throughout the **Sinis Peninsula**.

Bosa

Buses leave from the station in
piazza Zanetti hourly to **Bosa**
Marina. There are also four buses
daily to Alghero (1 hr), seven to
Macomer (50 mins), two to
Sassari (2½ hrs) and five to
Oristano (2 hrs). Bosa Marina is
the terminus for the summer
Trenino Verde tourist train to
Macomer (treninoverde.com).

Contents

Nuoro & Ogliastra

Arbatax's Rocce Rosse.

Introduction

What to see in...

...one day
Take a boat trip around the **Golfo di Orosei** from **Cala Gonone** or **Santa Maria Navarrese**. Inland, hikers should trek to either **Tiscali** or **Gola Gorroppu**.

Sardinia's rebellious character springs from its interior, a rugged patchwork of villages hemmed in by the Gennargentu and Supramonte mountain massifs on two sides and the sea on the other. A large swathe of this territory comprises the Gennargentu National Park, which extends from the Supramonte east to the Golfo di Orosei and remains one of the most remote and impenetrable pockets in the Mediterranean. Despite nearly 3000 years of invaders, this region has only been conquered in name. The Romans raided it 15 times but failed to subdue the area, dubbing it '*Barbarie*' after the barbarian-like ferocity and customs of its inhabitants. The name has stuck as 'Barbagie', the collective name for a cluster of five groups of rural communities: Nuoro, Ollolai, Mandrolisai, Belvì and Seulo. And, even today, Italian street signs are often ripped through by bullet holes, while those in Sardo are left untouched.

...a weekend or more
Check-in at **Su Gologone** to explore the caves and archaeological sites of the **Valle del Lanaittu**. Then, spend a day visiting the villages of the Supramonte, including **Orgosolo** for its *murales* and **Oliena** for its wine.
Alternatively, hop aboard the Trenino Verde, stopping at **Sadali**, hiking **Orgosolo**'s *tacchi* and finishing your jaunt by stretching out at the beaches of **Arbatax**. Then head to **Santa Maria Navarrese**, **Orosei** or **Cala Gonone** to explore the **Golfo di Orosei** and the **Grotta di Ispinigoli**.

Central Sardinia is brimming with unparalleled beauty. You won't find more imposing peaks than the Gennargentu mountains or more mesmerizing beaches than along the Golfo di Orosei. Many of the cinderblock towns folded into the hills are softened by poignant *murales* and, as you explore these provinces, you will experience the island's warmest hospitality.

Left: Oliena.

Nuoro & the north

The Barbagie's capital, Nuoro, remains a strange melting pot, in which African street vendors mingle with old women in traditional dress who cross themselves after crossing the road. In the past, Nuoro produced so many gifted writers (including Nobel laureate, Grazia Deledda) that it was once known as the 'Athens of Sardinia'. But since it was upgraded to the provincial capital in 1926, Nuoro has fallen victim to the same unsightly development that blighted much of urban Italy in the 20th century.

The area north of Nuoro and west of Siniscola is a rugged expanse of winding valleys whose cork trees shade free-range livestock under the twin peaks of Monte Albo (1127 m). Most tourists overlook this region because of its utter remoteness and rollercoaster turns but, as long as you're not in dire need of a toilet or a bed, the gorgeous backdrop is worth the hassle. Just be sure to set out on a full tank of petrol and not a full stomach.

Nuoro

At its heart, this municipal city is just a small town overgrown by government that still turns to Deledda for inspiration: look for excerpts of her writing scattered around the streets. While the cradle of *Sardità* may have received a suburban makeover, it hasn't strayed far from its roots and you'll stumble upon some of Sardinia's most staunch traditionalists and finest museums here.

Nuoro's older districts, **Santu Predu** and **Seuna**, are stacked towards the top of the mountainous crater that holds the town, with the newer development falling below. Historically, the Santu Predu neighbourhood at the top of the hill was occupied by shepherds, while the less wealthy farmers lived in the Seuna quarter.

Older *Nuoresi* remember that the two quarrelling factions would only meet on corso Garibaldi in the commercial district that connected the two areas and that the shepherds used to hurl stones at the farmers below. ('Predu' derives from the Sardo word for stone.)

Abstract statues in piazza Satta.

These days, **corso Garibaldi** is a more peaceful buffer and Nuoro's most attractive thoroughfare. The street's outdoor cafés are a prime spot to take in an afternoon espresso or an evening drink. Just off the corso is Sardinia's most serious contemporary art museum: **MAN** (via Satta 27, T0784-252110, museoman.it, Tue-Sun 1000-1300 and 1630-2030, €3, €2 concessions, free children and over-65s), which has two floors displaying over 350 paintings and sculptures from Sardinia's premier 20th-century artists, plus frequent temporary exhibits.

Nuoro's detailed, if small, **Museo Archeologico** (via Mannu 1, T0784-31688, Wed and Fri-Sun 0900-1330, Tue and Thu 0900-1330 and 1500-1730, free) is nestled near piazza San Giovanni and holds a variety of finds from the province's chief archaeological sites, ranging from an ancient skull of the monkeys that once roamed Sardinia, to *bronzetti* figurines and Roman coins.

Past the loud crimson gleam of the neoclassical **Cattedrale di Santa Maria della Neve**, via Mereu climbs the hill to shady **Parco di Sant'Onofrio** and the **Museo della Vita e delle Tradizioni Popolare** (via Mereu 56, T0784-31426, mid Jun-Sep daily 0900-2000, Oct-mid Jun daily 0900-1300 and 1500-1900, €3). Inside, galleries are dedicated to the Barbagie's bizarre Carnival celebrations (see page 171). Some of the island's earliest instruments are also on display. Yet, it's the parade of traditional Sardinian dress that steals the show. A glass case full of mannequins shows off the island's elaborately embroidered peacock-coloured costumes and filigree jewellery, which were common everyday wear until the mid 20th century. The costumes from each area are each subtly different: Desulo's sunny colours look vaguely Eastern European, while Oliena's black-fringed headwraps dangle like hair; Aggius' heavy female cloaks nearly cover the face underneath, and Macomer's male costumes look just like *Carabinieri* uniforms.

Essentials

❶ Getting around The parts of Nuoro town worth exploring are compact enough to traverse on foot. If you have a car, park in the higher part of town, as it's a steep climb from the newer development (where the ARST bus station is located) to the centre. Bus 8 runs frequently from the bus station up to Monte Ortobene.

⊖ Bus station Autolinee ARST, viale Sardegna, T0784 295030, daily 0600-2000.

◷ Train station Stazione delle FS, via Lamarmora 10, T0784-30115.

❺ ATM corso Garibaldi.

⊕ Hospital Ospedale Civile, via Mannironi , T0784-240237.

✚ Pharmacy Farmacia Gali, corso Garibaldi 65, T0784-30143.

⌒ Post office Poste Italiane, piazza Crispi 8, T0784-30554, Mon-Fri 0815-1840, Sat 0900-1300.

❶ Tourist information piazza Italia 19, T0784-30083, Mon-Sat 0900-1300 and 1600-1900.

Monte Ortobene.

Strange types wander the streets… women with Egyptian eyes in tight peasant costumes with wine jars balanced on their heads.

Grazia Deledda on Nuoro, 1901

Sardinia's Athens

It is no coincidence that the capital of a province traditionally overlooked as a harsh and impoverished badland has produced Sardinia's most affecting artists. The peasants of the Barbagie have long been at odds with the outside forces who have tried to tame them. In 1868, *Nuoresi* farmers raided the town's municipal building to protest against the Savoyards' enclosure law, which seized private lands and distributed them among wealthy barons. The event, known as the Su Connottu uprising, reignited a nascent consciousness of *Sardità* in Nuoro and inspired a miniature Renaissance.

Of the era's prominent figures, novelist **Salvatore Satta**, poet **Sebastiano Satta** (no relation) and sculptor **Francesco Ciusa** stand out, but it is **Grazia Deledda** (1871-1936), Sardinia's only Nobel laureate who stands head and shoulders above the rest.

Deledda lived the first 29 years of her life in Nuoro. She was the daughter of a recreational poet father and a strict mother who refused to let her attend secondary school. Like most people in Sardinia at the time, her family only spoke Sardo at home and she took private lessons to learn Italian. Even though the idea of a female writer was beyond taboo in 19th-century Nuoro, Deledda began publishing short stories and poetry in literary magazines at the age of 15, against her parents' wishes.

Even after emigrating to Rome in 1900, Deledda's novels remained unequivocally linked to Sardinia, its complex family ties, hardships and its hesitance to emerge from superstitious introspection into an evolving world. Despite publishing 33 novels in Italian and receiving a Nobel Prize for literature in 1926, Deledda admitted that her Italian remained poor and that she found it difficult to translate the autobiographical experiences from the Sardo-speaking Barbagie into her novels. "I will never be able to have the gift of beautiful Italian language," she said. "And it's in vain that I try with all my will."

Grazia Deledda's birthplace has been preserved as the **Museo Deleddiano** (via Deledda 44, T0784-258088, Tue-Sat 0900-1300 and 1500-1900, free), where visitors can peruse some of her letters and belongings and read her memories of the various rooms (in Italian).

Monte Ortobene

Nuoro's playground lies 6 km away at Monte Ortobene (955 m), which has beautiful views over the Supramonte and the Lanaittu valley (see page 172). At the peak, there's a shady ilex forest with picnic tables, a jungle-gym for the kids and a few pizzerias for the famished.

In 1900, the mountain was chosen by Pope Leone XIII as one of 19 throughout Italy to receive a giant bronze statue of Christ. The statue was unveiled on 29 August 1900 and thousands of Sardinians flocked to Nuoro to catch the spectacle. The tradition has stuck, and every year on 29 August, a procession of colourfully clad islanders parade through Nuoro and up to the statue in the **Processione del Redentore**. Follow signs for 'Redentore' past trickling fountains to reach the 7-m statue.

Su Tempiesu

Off the SS389, north of Nuoro, T328-756 5148, archeologiaviva.it.
Daily 0900-1900, €3.

Su Tempiesu is a well temple built with startling architectural precision for the worship of water from the 11th to the eighth centuries BC. It's the area's most fascinating Nuraghic monument and doubles as Nuoro's most scenic picnic spot.

Follow the brown signs north on the SS389 from Nuoro towards Orune before turning down a 7-km paved road to the ticket office and picnic area, which enjoys unbeatable views of the limestone massifs of Monte Albo. Two trails – take the 'Sentiero Faunistico' to pass two reconstructed Nuraghic huts – lead to the temple nestled between two canyon walls. Water from the chasm is channelled into a well under a triangular vestibule and trickles down a canal into a second basin when the spring overflows. Worshippers left votive *bronzetti* statues to the water gods on the two benches inside the atrium and studded the cornice with ornamental daggers. The entire structure is built in colourful trachyte and basalt

A sombre *murale* at Macomer.

Macomer & around

West of Nuoro, the province juts out around the granite plateau of Macomer. The town developed under the Romans as a junction along the Cagliari–Porto Torres road and remains the crossroads of Sardinia's public transport network. If you have your own transport, you probably won't want to bother with Macomer's centre but you could spend a full day driving around the archaeological sites in its environs.

Ten kilometres east of Macomer at Silanus, the **Santa Sabina** site has a strikingly well preserved single-tower nuraghe from the 14th century BC, with a climbable spiral staircase inside. A few steps away, its Christian descendant, a 10th-century Byzantine church built in black-and-white stones, is fringed by crouching *cumbessiàs* pilgrim houses, which are inhabited during a nine-day *novena* in September. Heading towards Macomer from here, the SS129 passes a graveyard of crumbling nuraghi.

Just off Highway 131 at km 144 north of Macomer, is the turnoff for **Nuraghe Santa Barbara**. A 15-minute walk from the car park will bring you to this reddish bastion whose central tower is all that remains of a four-lobed fortress. From the hillside, you can see the slanting **Nuraghe Ruiu** across the highway below.

rocks, which are found no fewer than 30 km away, and remains fully functioning 3100 years later: proof of the mysterious builders' architectural know-how and opulence.

Siniscola & the coast

Beyond Su Tempiesu, the mountain road continues past Bitti and signs for Lula and Lodè, corkscrewing as it climbs between the peaks of Monte Albo. Enjoy the views before, finally, snaking down to Siniscola, surrounded by citrus groves. To the east, the beaches along the coastal strip are popular getaways. **La Caletta** has a cluster of hotels and restaurants and some great birdwatching along its marshy canals to the south. Yet locals prefer the bathing spots south of **Santa Lucia**, off the SS125. The best of these is **Berchida**, found at the end of a long dirt road at km 242. In July and August, buy a €4 car park pass at Agriturismo Su Meriacru towards the beach.

The Supramonte

North of the granite Gennargentu mountain range (meaning 'silver gate', because of its shiny schist gleam), Cannonau vineyards erupt into the bald limestone peaks of the Supramonte. This was once a notorious bandit hideout, covered with thick forests until the Piedmontese cut the holm and oak woods to build Italy's railroads in the 1800s. Even without its leafy coat, the Supramonte and the unspoiled Lanaittu valley still keep a tight hold of their secrets, sheltering archaeological sites, karstic caves and mountain sinkholes – not to mention Sardinia's most famous bandit, the 'Scarlet Rose'. The villages in this area boast Sardinia's most famous costumes: elderly women in Oliena still walk the street in black dresses embroidered with peacock colours and, if you plan your visit right, you may also stumble upon the sheepskin tunics worn during Mamoiada's otherworldly Carnival celebrations.

Mamoiada

At first glance, this lethargic enclave looks like any rural Italian village: rows of vineyards dot the rolling countryside and old men huddle together on park benches. But look a little closer and, along the main street, you'll see a handful of *murales* depicting the woolly ghouls of Mamoiada's *Mamuthones* carnival procession (see page 171).

If you can't make it to the village during Carnival, you can still learn about the Barbagie's pagan rites at the town's **Museo delle Maschere Mediterraneo** (piazza Europa 15, T0784-569018, museodellemaschere.it, daily 0900-1300 and 1500-1900, €4, €2.60 concessions). You can also browse an impressive collection of the devilish disguises at Signor Mameli's workshop, **Maschere Mameli** (see page 192).

Orgosolo

Orgosolo has long held the distinguished title of bandit capital of Sardinia (see page 174). During the first half of the 20th century, bus hold-ups were a regular occurrence and a murder took place every

Io vi prometto di sacrificare alla vostra sete un boccione d'olente vino d'Oliena serbato da moltissimi anni in memoria della più vasta sbornia di cui sia stato io testimone e complice.

I urge you to sacrifice your thirst for a mouthful of wine from Oliena, aged for many years, in memory of the greatest drunken binge that I have ever witnessed and experienced.

Gabriele d'Annunzio

two months, leading director Vittorio de Seta to immortalize the town in his 1961 film, *I Banditi a Orgosolo*. Since then, the shepherding community has softened its image and is now more famous for Sardinia's first *murales* movement, which started in 1975 to mark the 30th anniversary of the Italian liberation from Fascism.

Orgosolo's cinderblock buildings are dressed with roughly 120 politically charged murals, rendered with precision and laced with captions in *Sardo*. Most are found along corso Repubblica and its side streets, and deal with the struggle to end corruption, violence and greed in an area which has long been a victim of all three. The murals also reflect a range of international events, from the slaying of Palestinian Mohammed Al'Durra by Israeli forces, to the condemnation of Spanish dictator Francisco Franco, to the extermination of Native Americans by white settlers.

Despite the makeover, Orgosolo has yet to shake off its past. Many of the murals' verses were penned by town poet Peppino Marotto, who was shot dead in 2007. His murder allegedly stemmed from a vendetta dating back to the 1950s.

Oliena

Oliena enjoys a picture-perfect setting under the limestone wall of Monte Corrasi (1463 m). Its backdrop drew Italian bard Gabriele d'Annunzio in 1909, who came here to drink as much Cannonau wine as possible. He was so impressed with the wine that he wrote an article about it in the *Corriere della Sera* newspaper, urging readers to follow suit. His rapture propelled Oliena's Nepente label to international fame and it remains among Sardinia's most esteemed brands.

The Jesuits left their mark in the 17th century by building the bulky **Chiesa di Saint Ignazio** on Oliena's main street and introducing the population to silk worms. These still provide the thread for the elegantly embroidered black *muncadores* shawls worn by Oliena's elderly women, who walk the streets in conservative headwraps and ankle-length dresses.

Carnival in the Barbagie

Unlike the light-hearted Christian revelry of Carnival celebrations on the mainland, the moving processions in Mamoiada and Ottana reflect the hardships of Sardinia's impoverished centre and remain gripped in mysterious pagan practices.

In Mamoiada, residents don menacing jet-black masks (*sas viseras*) made from dyed wild pear and alder wood, dark sheepskin tunics (*sas peddhes*), up to 30 kg of cowbells (*sos sonazzos*) and the rattling thighbones of sheep to transform themselves into the *Mamuthones*. These heavy beasts process through the streets, dragging their hunched frames forwards in two rows before breaking into synchronized convulsions. They are led by white-masked herders called *Issohadores* who guide them out of town while attempting to lasso any women in the crowd as an omen of fertility. (According to tradition, if an *Issohadore* accidentally ropes a man, the captured male has to buy drinks for all his companions!)

The exact meaning and origin of the *Mamuthones* procession has been lost over time and continues to baffle anthropologists. Roman invaders thought the beasts represented some kind of pagan animal worship and tried to outlaw them, but to no avail. The most accepted theory is that the *Mamuthones* represent the evil beings from the underworld that haunted Mamoiada's ancestors; the *Issohadores* capture these menacing spirits and drive them out of town in a pseudo-exorcism. In a post-Christian Barbagie, the rite has received a Catholic makeover and is now performed in January in honour of San Antonio Abate and again on Carnival Sunday.

In the town of Ottana, the Carnival procession also springs from the remote past and is probably rooted in Greek purification rites. Known as the *Sos Merdules Bezzos*, it evokes the struggle of man to keep from turning into the beasts he fights to tame. The procession's protagonist is *Su Boe*, a shaggy sheepskin-clad man draped in bells and covered in an elaborately horned mask representing an ox. The ox battles for dominance with herders, called *Sos Merdules*, each of whom wears a black mask depicting a beleaguered and fatigued expression. The herders' wives, *Sas Filanzanas*, dutifully follow their husbands, knitting wool all the way.

Mamoiada's ghoulish Carnival stars.

66

Here the Carnival is everything. It represents a struggle between man versus beast. You have to understand that up until 50 years ago we were living like people in the Middle Ages; we were dying of hunger. That's why our Carnival is so morose. 99

Franco Maritato, mask-maker, Ottana.

Valle del Lanaittu

East of Oliena, the U-shaped Lanaittu valley is one of Sardinia's truly unspoiled highlights. Although it's ringed by the steep white walls of the Supramonte, the valley is surprisingly accessible and you could easily pass days among its fascinating nooks.

Five kilometres beyond Oliena towards Dorgali, turn off the road at signs for 'Su Gologone'. A short distance past the hotel of the same name (one of Sardinia's best, see page 186), you'll see an oasis of eucalyptus trees marking the entrance to the **Sorgente Su Gologone**. It's a magical spot with weeping willows billowing above the river Cedrino. Wooden signs point the way towards a 107-m deep spring that pushes 236 litres of water per second through a narrow crevice dug between a cleft in two vertical rock walls. In the winter, the spring water floods the surrounding knoll; in summer, it slows considerably and you can see fish feeding in the deep, crystal-clear pool.

Across the road from the park is the turn-off for the Lanaittu valley, 7 km away. The asphalt turns to dirt after 2 km and a fork in the road leads left to Tiscali (see page opposite) and right to Sa Sedda 'e Sos Carros and to the **Su Bentu** ('the wind') and **Sa Oche** ('the voice') caves, so-called because of the surging wind and water that flows out of them after heavy rain. The limestone grottoes are filled with internal lakes, fed by a river deep in the Supramonte, and, although not fully surveyed, are thought to be among the deepest fissures in Europe. You will need spelunking experience to explore the caves; contact **Cooperative Ghivine** (see page 192), to find out more.

Buy tickets at the lodge next to the caves to visit the nearby Nuraghic village, **Sa Sedda 'e Sos Carros** (T347-824 9517, May-Nov daily 0930-1300 and 1500-1730, €4). Ongoing excavations are busy uncovering the 200 huts that lie underground but what is visible is impressive enough. The village must have been the height of Bronze Age urban sophistication: dozens of *bronzetti* statues have been recovered here and the whole place benefited from a plumbing system that fed water from a cistern in the site's centre via conduits into each stone hut. The site's jewel, however, is the world's earliest constructed fountain, built using five different coloured stones. Water is channelled down a canal and shoots out of seven limestone mouths into a pool. Remarkably, the whole thing still works!

The Supramonte's most famous site is undoubtedly the **Villaggio Nuragico di Tiscali** (daily 0800-sunset, €5, €2 concessions). The site is reached by climbing a loosely-laid rocky trail up the side of Monte Tiscali with breathtaking views of vertical limestone dolomites, dyed rust-red by erosion, and of the Lanaittu valley below. After nearly three hours, you descend into a fissure to find the scant remains of an ancient village hidden inside the depths of a giant sinkhole that has partially caved in. It's à moving sight, although the lack of excavation has left more questions than answers about its origins. What is known is that, while the Nuraghic population undoubtedly utilized the site, the present huts are the work of much later generations. The widely held theory is that Tiscali's utter inaccessibility is no accident, since it represented the last defensive refuge of a besieged native population forced further and further into Sardinia's depths to escape Carthaginian and Roman invaders.

There are two ways to hike to Tiscali: the first is to head a few kilometres south of Dorgali on the SS125 and turn left at the brown sign indicating 'Gola Gorroppu.' Follow the arrows towards Gola Gorroppu on the paved road for roughly 10 km, looking for signs to Tiscali. A steeper, slightly shorter and more scenic route is to follow the signs from the Valle del Lanaittu. This path is poorly marked and we strongly recommend using a guide. The lodge where you buy tickets to visit Sos Carros leads daily treks to Tiscali and is conveniently placed near the site but the guide doesn't speak English. Non-Italian speakers should call one of the companies on page 192.

A makeshift bridge at the Valle del Lanaittu and the path to Tiscali.

Bandits of the Barbagie

Chiesa di San Giacomo, Orosei.

Throughout its history, Sardinia's craggy interior has vehemently fought to resist foreign rule and retains a sense of rebellious autonomy, in which age-old traditions of kidnapping, banditry and vendettas linger on, for better or worse.

Traditionally, struggling shepherds in the Barbagie would steal sheep from rival villages but never touch herds belonging to their own town. In the 20th century, sheep rustling gradually gave way to the more lucrative practice of kidnapping wealthy landowners and keeping them hidden in the mountains for months until a ransom was met. More recently still, holidaymakers have become targets.

Bandits are often viewed as noble guardians of the Sardi's historic struggle against outsiders, ransacking the wealthy to help the less fortunate, and defying the Roman government just as their ancestors resisted the Roman Empire. However, as well as targeting foreigners, the bandits also turn on each other in a tradition of vendettas, when family members of victims murdered during robberies or heists swear to take the life of the assassin. Vendettas usually take place at Christmas, when the victim's family is together, and are performed at close range with shots to the face, so as to deny the family the dignity of an open-casket funeral.

Sardinia's most famous living bandit is Orgosolo's **Graziano Mesina**, known as the 'Scarlet Rose'. First arrested in 1956 at the age of 14, Mesina has spent 40 of his nearly 70 years behind bars and has escaped the authorities no fewer than 11 times, through such daredevil acts as fleeing from a moving train with handcuffs still on, launching himself out a third-storey hospital window and even dressing as a woman in conservative Sardinian costume and walking out of a house that was surrounded by *Carabinieri*. Each time the Scarlet Rose was on the run, he hid out in the Supramonte and received racy love letters from female admirers. In the middle of a prison stint in 1992, Mesina was used by detectives successfully to arrange the release of Farouk Kassam, a seven-year-old Egyptian boy kidnapped from the Costa Smeralda. The Rose has since become a cult hero to Sardinians everywhere and received a pardon by Italian president Carlo Ciampi in 2004. He now lives in his home town of Orgosolo and passes his days leading tourists up the mountain or hanging out at Bar Chilotto on corso Repubblica.

Golfo di Orosei

Some of Sardinia's most unforgettable beaches are found where the provinces of Nuoro and Ogliastra meet along the seaside section of the Gennargentu National Park, known as the Golfo di Orosei. Less is more on this dazzling stretch of unadulterated coastline, where the only high-rises are the limestone cliffs and you won't find a road or building for 40 km.

Cala Goloritzè, Golfo di Orosei.

Orosei

At the head of the gulf is Orosei, a beachside resort backed by mountains. Its pleasant, almost Spanish feel comes courtesy of wealthy Aragonese barons, who ruled the surrounding area (known as 'Baronie') from the 16th to the 18th centuries, erecting churches and planting citrus groves when not warding off malaria outbursts.

Orosei's centrepiece is the leafy **piazza del Popolo**. A flight of steps next to the tourist office leads to the town's most famous landmark, the **Chiesa di San Giacomo**, built by the Pisans and restored with Spanish flair in the 18th century. The church's three tiled domes and campanile look vaguely Moorish. San Giacomo shares the square with one of the other ten churches packed into the town, the impressive **Oratorio del Rosario**, which has three crosses tacked on to its sun-baked façade. Nearby, **piazza Sas Animas** boasts an oratory church of the same name and the stout **Prione Vezza** tower which, as its name suggests, was a prison left over from a 14th-century castle.

Marina di Orosei

A walking and cycling path is laid along the flat 3-km stretch east of Orosei to its beach, Marina di Orosei, a scenic spot flanked by a narrow canal with views stretching across the entire gulf. At 5 km long, there's always towel space at the beach, whose name changes from Su Barone to Isporoddai to Osalla as you go south. From May to September, boats leave from the Marina's northern end – the same port that saw DH Lawrence off to Sicily in 1921 – to cruise the Golfo di Orosei (see page 178). A more isolated bathing option is 13 km up the SS125 at **Biderrosa**. This beach is part of a protected park and only 120 cars are allowed in daily, even during peak season. Passes are sold on site and cost €10 per car plus €1 per person.

Tomba di gigante di S'Ena.

S'Ena 'e Thomes & Serra Orrios

Archaeology buffs should head inland from Orosei on the SS129 several kilometres past Galtellí to the *tomba di gigante* of S'Ena 'e Thomas. Park at the sign by the road and walk 400 m to where the 16 m by 7 m tomb rises above the overgrown vegetation. An arched central stone marks the grave's entrance; bodies were laid in the 10.9-m chamber behind.

A far more impressive Bronze Age relic is **Serra Orrios** (T338-834 1618, daily 0900-1300 and 1400-1700, €6, €2.50 concessions), a 10-minute drive southwest, just beyond the turnoff for Dorgali. This Nuraghic village was built between the 15th and seventh centuries BC and inhabited as late as 250 BC. There are roughly 70 well-preserved circular huts clustered around two rectangular temples; the larger and better preserved temple has been restored. A third structure has recently been found and is thought to be a sort of communal meeting place.

Grotta di Ispinigoli

SS125, km 32.6, T0784-963431.
Mar-Jul and Sep-Nov daily 0900-1700. Aug daily 0900-1800, Dec-Feb by appointment.
€7, €4.50 children.

Fifteen kilometres south of Orosei along the SS125, you'll see a sign at km 32 for one of the world's great caves, the Grotta di Ispinigoli. Used as a shelter by goat herders until the 1970s, the cave maintains a constant 15-degree Celsius temperature (wear long sleeves). The 45-minute tour starts at a panoramic observatory before descending 280 stairs to the base of Europe's tallest stalagmite: a single column connecting the cave's vault to its base 38 m below. Visitors then gaze down at the *L'Abisso delle Vergini* ('Abyss of the Virgins'), so-called because the Carthaginians supposedly performed a human sacrificial rite called a *molk* here, in which virgin girls were thrown down the 60-m cave to their death. Archaeologists have recovered a handful of Punic necklaces at the base of the abyss that are now displayed in Dorgali's archaeological museum.

Dorgali

Ask anyone from the Barbagie and they'll tell you the *Dorgalesi* talk like Africans. Their strikingly different dialect has led to rumours that the town was founded by Saracen pirates. Bandit blood or not, the townsfolk have evolved into a hospitable bunch with a knack for making fine handicrafts. Beneath the mountainous backdrop of Monte Bardia (882 m), **via La Marmora** and **corso Umberto** are lined with stores displaying jewellery, rugs, knives and leather accessories, not to mention Sardinia's strongest Cannonau wine from the Dorgali Cantina. The **Museo Archeologico** (via La Marmora, T338-834 1618, Tue-Sun 0930-1300 and 1530-1800, €3, €2 concessions) has Neolithic pottery, a fertility stone and Punic jewellery presumably worn by the sacrificed virgins tossed down the Grotta di Ispinigoli.

Tip…

An unforgettable way to experience the Gennargentu National Park is to hike the "Selvaggio Blu." Mapped out from early shepherds' trails, the "Wild Blue" careens south from Cala Luna to Baunei, passing through limestone massifs, karstic caves and wide-angle views of the gulf below. While the 48-km hike is considered one of the most challenging hikes in Italy, guides offer less rigorous jaunts along the path that skirt its most challenging stretches. For more information, check selvaggioblu.it (in Italian) or guidestarmountain.com.

Cala Gonone

East of town, a snaky road coils down Monte Bardia for 8 km to Dorgali's seaside satellite, Cala Gonone. This former fishing village got an economic boost in the 1930s, when flush Fascists began to build their art nouveau summer getaways here. The opening of the Bue Marino cave (see page 178) in the 1950s brought many other visitors in their wake and, today, the village has evolved into a lovely resort set under pine trees, where cascading geraniums dangle out of windows.

The family-friendly resort is centred around **Spiagga Centrale**, a pebble beach next to the harbour, where kiosks offer boat rentals and excursions to the gulf's string of immaculate beaches. For more breathing room, head to the southern end of the *Lungomare* to **Spiaggia Palmasera** or continue 300 m to sheltered **Sos Dorroles**. Walkers of any level should pack a bathing suit, drive south for 3 km along viale Bue Marino until the asphalt turns to dirt, park the car at **Cala Fuili** beach around Monte Tului (916 m) and look for green signs to the impeccable **Cala Luna** cove two hours' hike away.

One of the steepest bike excursions around (or a hairpin drive) goes from Cala Gonone in the other direction, twisting up Monte Irveri (616 m), from which you have sweeping views across the gulf, and finishing at **Spiaggia Carote** (9 km) and **Spiaggia Osalla** (11 km).

Dorgali.

Cruising the Golfo di Orosei

Sardinia's most spectacular coastline is only accessible by boat. The Golfo di Orosei stretches for 70 km, dipping to form a crescent moon along Sardinia's eastern seaboard between Punta Nera in the north and Capo Monte Santu in the south. The 40-km stretch south of Cala Gonone is completely void of civilization and characterized by vertical limestone cliffs plunging head-first into deep grottoes and by hidden beaches with water that encompasses a palette of blues, from azure to indigo. This area is one of the gems of the Mediterranean and guaranteed to be a highlight of your trip.

From May to Oct tour boats cruise the gulf daily, leaving from the ports at **Cala Gonone** (see page 177) and **Santa Maria Navarrese** (see page 183). Most run from morning until evening with lunch on board and begin at around €30 a person. The boats get crowded in peak season, so avoid the less expensive ferry services that pack up to 200 people aboard and spend a bit more to ensure comfort. Pack sandals as the pebbly beaches can be tough on the feet.

South of Cala Gonone, the first stop is the M-shaped double-arched entrance to the **Grotte del Bue Marino** (T0784-96243, Easter-Oct, book through the boat tour company), named after one of the planet's most endangered mammals, the

monk seal, which used to live in the cave's environs but has all but disappeared since the 1980s. A wooden walkway takes visitors along the cave's southern route, which, unlike the northern end, remains geologically active thanks to an underwater river. Stalactites and stalagmites abound and extend for a kilometre in the cave's saltwater lake. Look out for the Neolithic drawings showing humans dancing around a solar disc.

The coast's most famous beach, Cala Luna, is a short sail south. While you could easily pass a day lounging on its pebbly shoreline and exploring its caverns, the beach's most striking aspect is behind the shore, where flowering oleander bushes shelter a stream, forming a tranquil escape from the throngs of sun worshippers. Look for one of the last nesting spots of the elusive Eleonora falcon between **Cala Luna** and lovely **Cala Sisine**, backed by mountain walls and holm oak. Further south, **Cala Biriola** is marked by a limestone arch large enough to pass under by boat. Arguably the gulf's most gorgeous beach, **Cala Mariolu** is divided into two beaches by a white rocky outcrop that doubles as a popular high dive. Polished limestone pebbles meet limpid, sapphire water here. Don't leave without swimming into the cave and feeling the smooth limestone walls lapped by the current. **Cala Goloritzè** is the gulf's southernmost beach where a 140-m rock soars like a totem pole above a natural limestone arch stepping into the sea.

Around the island

Barbagia di Ollolai

South of Nuoro and north of the Gennargentu National Park, the sleepy mountain towns around the Barbagia di Ollolai are a place where languid locals pass hours over card games in bars and vigorous visitors come to hike to Sardinia's highest peak: Punta La Marmora.

Ottana

The striped smoke stacks of Ottana's plastic manufacturing plant are visible for kilometres in all directions but don't let them put you off visiting the town during Carnival for its *Sos Merdules Bezzos* procession (see page 171). At other times of year it's worth popping into town to watch Franco Maritato create the horned ox masks worn in the procession (see page 192). Near Maritato's studio is the multi-coloured trachyte façade of the Romanesque **Chiesa di San Nicola**, built in 1150.

Gavoi

Gavoi's tidy stone centre nestled on a sloping mountainside makes it the most attractive town in the area. At its heart is the 15th-century **Chiesa di San Gavino**, whose towering campanile soars 30 m above a Gothic rose window. The church's square looks out over the shimmering, artificial **Lago Gusana** below, which is a favourite with fishermen and boaters. Shepherding is big business in these parts and Gavoi's economic staple is spicy *fiore sardo* pecorino cheese.

Gavoi.

Fonni & the peaks

Watch out for grazing sheep in the middle of the road as you climb the SS389 to Sardinia's highest town, Fonni at 1000 m. This pastoral community is gradually awakening to tourism as hikers start to use its few hotels as a base camp from which to climb the Gennargentu's tallest peaks, **Brancu Spina** (1829 m) and **Punto La Marmora** (1834 m).

Follow the brown signs indicating the Brancu Spina trail 5 km south of town towards Desulo and, after ascending for 9 km, park the car and start hiking. It's a 3-km trek to the top, from where you can see north to the limestone bluffs of Corsica and south to Cagliari's harbour on clear days. Locals claim the 1½-hour onward trek from Brancu Spina to Punta La Marmora is a breeze but we recommend contacting guides in Fonni before you attempt it (see page 193).

For something easier, meander through Fonni's streets, where some of Sardinia's finest *murales* are painted along corso Carlo Alberto.

Five of the best

Facts about Nuoro and Ogliastra

❶ Sardinia has the world's highest percentage of people who live past 100 years' old. While centenarians are found throughout the island, the vast majority live in its interior, including five of the world's oldest 40 people.

❷ The provinces of Nuoro and Ogliastra have a ratio of nearly three sheep to every person.

❸ For hundreds of years in rural Sardinian towns, a woman known as the Agabbadòra (from the Sardo command "Accabbadda!" meaning "Enough!") was called to deathbeds in the night to strike the dying person in the skull with a hammer to put them out of their misery. The last reported incident happened in Orgosolo in 1952.

❹ Eighty per cent of Sardinians are directly related to the island's original inhabitants – a figure that increases around the Gennargentu mountains – making Sardinians among the purest ethnic groups in Europe.

❺ Residents of present-day Desulo were the last in Sardinia to convert to Christianity, continuing to worship wood and stone until the seventh century.

West of the Gennargentu

Barbagia di Mandrolisai

The compact communities of the Mandrolisai lie on the western slopes of the Gennargentu and are a soothing retreat from the high temperatures and tourist hordes that characterize the Sardinian coast each summer. **Sorgono** is known for its strong Cannonau wine but is best remembered as the place that DH Lawrence condemned as a "weary village with nothing to say for itself" in *Sea and Sardinia*, before changing his mind and romanticizing about its isolated beauty. Nearby **Tonara** prides itself as the island's *torrone* (nougat) capital. Women mix honey and eggs with hazelnuts and walnuts from the Gennargentu's forests in a giant vat for up to five hours to make Torrone di Tonara, which is sold from stands at every Sardinian festival.

Aritzo

Aritzo was a favourite haunt of the Piedmontese nobility in the 19th century who came to hunt wild boar and mouflon and to escape the summer heat in its crisp climate. It remains Sardinia's most popular mountain resort. The surrounding area, the Barbagia di Belvì, is covered in dense chestnut and walnut forests, which provide material for accomplished carpenters in Aritzo and nearby Belvì.

Apart from tourism and carpentry, Aritzo's economy has long relied on a rare commodity: snow. From the 16th to the 18th centuries, workers called *niargios* would gather snow from Funtana Cungiada (1450 m), store it in straw-lined wooden freezers and then turn it into lemon sorbet. The sorbet was delivered by mule to the island's Aragonese rulers in Cagliari. Today, Aritzo's Sa Carapigna remains Sardinia's only sorbet company. The town's **Museo Etnografico** (via Marconi 1, T0784-629801, Tue-Sun 1030-1300 and 1630-1900, €1.60) displays the *niargios'* old freezers and provides entry to **Sa Bovida**, a 16th-century Spanish prison.

Diet? Rich people diet. Physical labour is the key that unlocks your bones. If you don't work, you lose the key, and lock what's inside forever.

92-year-old Sadali woman on Sardinians' famed longevity.

Sweeping views of Gennargentu National Park.

Ogliastra

Ogliastra was carved out of the southeastern corner of Nuoro in 2005 and is Italy's least populated province. Ringed by mountain ranges on three sides and plagued with poor infrastructure that has kept it isolated, this part of the island is side-stepped by visitors. It's a shame because, between the bald massifs of the Supramonte to the north, the granite Gennargentu to the west and the sharp tacchi down south, there are plenty of caves for ramblers to explore and, on the coast, fetching little Santa Maria Navarrese is Ogliastra's gateway to the Golfo di Orosei (see page 175).

Gola Gorroppu

Ogliastra begins with a bang. Of the 355-km SS125 that ploughs south from the Gallura to Cagliari, the 20-km stretch south of Dorgali is the most magnificent. The road twists through the Gennargentu National Park with views resembling an Ansel Adams photograph of sunlight dancing on the limestone walls of the Supramonte across the Flumineddu river valley. The highway climbs steadily towards the **Genna Silana** pass (1017 m) at km 183, which doubles as the starting point for the trek down to the Gola Gorroppu gorge.

If you only have time for one hike in Sardinia, set aside half a day to explore the continent's deepest ravine, often called 'Europe's Grand Canyon'. A 1½-hour trek down the rift from the pass leads to the sheer vertical walls of the **Punta Cucuttos** (888 m) and the **Punta S'Icopargiu** (1020 m) dug out of the limestone over millennia by the river Flumineddu. Continue through patches of sand and smooth rocks for another 1½ hours until you reach a series of natural pools that mark the end of the trail.

Another way to reach Gola Gorroppu is to go a few kilometres south of Dorgali on the SS125 and turn left at the brown sign indicating the site. Follow the arrows towards Gola Gorroppu on the paved road for 10 km and leave your car where the asphalt ends. Like the above approach from the Genna Silana pass, this will take you roughly six hours (including roughly two hours to ascend from the valley) and though the hike is less steep, it is also less scenic, although the drive into the valley is drop-dead gorgeous.

Regardless of your trekking ability, guides are highly recommended as they offer keen insights about the gorge's unique plants and wildlife. The best of the bunch is **Cooperativa Gorropu** (see page 193) found at the Genna Silana pass.

Baunei & the Altopiano del Golgo

Baunei looks out on to Ogliastra's coast from a natural mountain balcony. The town was founded by goat herders and is proud of its roots, which are especially in evidence on the last Sunday in August, when the town hosts the Sagra della Capra (goat festival).

On the main street opposite the Chiesa di San Nicolo, look for signs up the hill to the **Altopiano del Golgo**, a plateau at 480 m. A steep 2-km road brings you to what seems like the top of the world. Continue beyond the turn-off for **Nuraghe Coeserra** and the top-notch restaurant, **Il Golgo** (see page 191) and, after 8 km, look for a wooden sign indicating the deep limestone cave of **Su Sterru**. You can hire guides just down the road where the road loses its asphalt and scattered donkeys and pigs come into view at **Cooperativa Goloritzè** (see page 193). This *agriturismo* offers some fantastic trekking, horseback, 4x4 and boat excursions throughout the Ogliastra's lonely landscapes but you'll need to call weeks in advance as you won't get mobile phone reception on the plateau!

Santa Maria Navarrese

Ten kilometres down the hill from Baunei, Santa Maria Navarrese is a graceful seaside retreat offering similar sea-going sprees as Cala Gonone

(see page 177) but on a much smaller scale. The Spanish name stems from the King of Navarra's kidnapped daughter, who was allegedly washed up on shore here after the boat on which she was hijacked got caught in a storm. Basque sailors built the whitewashed church that stands in the town's square in honour of the princess's divine protector in 1052. The massive olive tree nearby was supposedly planted the day the church was finished but, if you've already been to Luras (see page 215), this millennium-old tree will seem like a mere adolescent. For hundreds of years the rural church and its leafy counterpart were surrounded by a group of pilgrim houses occupied annually by Baunei's faithful. In the 1950s tourism started trickling in, the *cumbessiàs* came tumbling down and the present beach town sprang up.

No longer the protective stronghold of years past, the town's Aragonese watchtower now hosts occasional art exhibitions and caps the pebbly **Spiaggia Centrale**; for finer sand, head a kilometre south to Lotzorai. In warm months, Santa Maria's port offers plenty of excursions along the Golfo di Orosei: if you do nothing else in Ogliastra, book a trip with Fuori Rotta Baunei (see page 193).

The coast at Baunei.

Rocce Rosse at Arbatax.

Tortolì & Arbatax

Down the coast, a 3-km road lined with petrol stations, industrial zones and cheap hotels links Tortolì to its more inviting port, Arbatax. The exotic name probably stems from the Arabic word for 14 (*'arba'at 'ashar'*), since Arbatax's stout Aragonese tower was the 14th built along the coast to guard against Saracen raids. For such a small resort, Arbatax has a surprisingly well-developed tourist infrastructure: the Trenino Verde's terminus (see right) is within sight of the port, which connects the town to Civitavecchia, Genoa and Cagliari, and there's even a small airport with flights to mainland Italy. Kiosks sprinkled around the waterfront can set you up with various excursions, hotel rooms and car rentals.

The area's biggest draw are the **Rocce Rosse**, a cluster of red rocks sculpted by the wind to resemble a dribbled sand castle. It's a dramatic sight against the white sand and crystalline waters that surround it, and a tunnel drilled through its base leads to a sublime bathing spot.

Arbatax's other beaches are found behind the port, the closest being **Porto Frailis**, whose bayside setting backed by grandiose villas give it a vaguely southern California feel. The **Faro Bellavista** lighthouse perched on the beach lives up to its name with memorable views stretching along Ogliastra's coast. When Porto Frailis fills up during peak season, venture south to **San Gimignano** or the long **Orrì** beach near Tortolì.

Trenino Verde

Mandas to Arbatax, T070-343112, treninoverde.com.
19 Jun-11 Sep. €16.50 one way or €22 round-trip.

Of the four Trenino Verde routes, the most scenic is undoubtedly the 160-km track from Mandas to Arbatax, which provides an excellent opportunity to explore Ogliastra's open expanses and the often overlooked **Barbagia di Seulo**. The 10-hour round-trip is best spread out over two or more days to allow for stop-offs. Trains leave each terminus twice daily and, if you alight en route, you will have to catch the next train, seven hours later.

From Mandas, the train skirts the northern bank of **Lago Flumendosa**, before pulling in to **Sadali**. Dug deep into a gully, this 900-person hamlet is a charming place bordering one of Sardinia's largest springs. A moss-laden waterfall rushes through its centre, feeding outdoor spigots where women wash their clothes. Rangers are usually on hand as you alight from the train to escort you through the 200-m **Grotta Is Janas** (cave of the fairies) nearby,

Lawrence and the *Trenino Verde*

In 1921 DH Lawrence came to Sardinia in search of simplicity. He had grown weary of industrialization and looked to Sardinia as one of the last vestiges of human individuality, guarded by Sardinian peasants under sheepskin tunics and colourful caps. He determined it was a population without self-consciousness, where the concept of Christian grace had yet to strike a people reluctant to abandon their primitive, feral defences.

From Cagliari, Lawrence could have shot up Sardinia's western coast on the state railway but curiosity led him to pierce the mountainous backbone of the island aboard a narrow-gauge steam train, weaving 90 km from Mandas to Sorgono, while scribbling his observations in a journal that was to become *Sea and Sardinia*.

Laid in 1888, the line was later dubbed the *Trenino Verde* (little green train) by the World Wildlife Federation because its twin-car engine trundled through switchbacks, plunged into ravines and clambered up some of the island's most sparsely populated expanses on its climb to 800 m. The fact that engineers were able to suspend bridges over the route's treacherous gorges and plough through the Gennargentu mountains at a time when Cagliari's bourgeoisie still wandered the capital barefoot is remarkable.

Over 120 years later, the Trenino Verde still chugs along the same tracks but, while the passengers in Lawrence's day were predominantly shepherds and farmers, today the Trenino Verde is preserved as a summer tourist line, the longest and most popular in Italy. Diesel engines have replaced steam locomotives, cutting the jaunt from Mandas to Sorgono to a cool six-and-a-half-hour round-trip; the third-class cabins have been softened by vinyl seating, and the stench of goats that dogged Lawrence has been swept out of the crank windows. The other Trenino Verde routes are Mandas–Arbatax (see page 184), Macomer–Bosa and Alghero–Palau.

which was once a winter refuge for shepherds and their flocks. Trekkers should also alight at **Ussassai-Niala**, at the foot of the Gennargentu, and follow the path past apple trees – keeping their eyes peeled for boar, mouflon and eagles– up to a limestone ridge named **Su Casteddu 'e Joni** because of its resemblance to a castle.

Jerzu & around

West off the SS125, little Jerzu stands tall enjoying a spectacular setting under sharp limestone spires called '*tacchi*' (heels). Below the town are the Cannonau vineyards which make it famous. Coming from the south, you can't miss the white tower of Jerzu's **Cantina Antichi Poderi** (via Umberto 1, T0782-70028, Mon-Sat 0830-1300 and 1500-1830), which sells the town's prized wine.

The town seems to cling for dear life to the mountainous ridge with sweeping views of the Rio Pardu valley below. Other towns haven't been as lucky. Continue a few kilometres past Ulassai and signs for the 850-m **Su Marmuri** grotto (T0782-79707, Easter-Oct daily guided visits at 1100, 1430 and 1700) and you'll pass the rubbled remains of **Osini Vecchio** facing **Gairo Vecchio** across the canyon (*ga* and *roa* mean 'sliding earth' in ancient Greek). In 1951, heavy rains caused the gorge's base to collapse, forcing the populations of the two towns to relocate to more secure terrain nearby.

Lanusei

Lanusei is a jumble of terracotta tiles and satellite dishes nestled into the side of a mountain. The community has adopted an air of self-importance since being crowned co-capital of the province in 2005. Racks of postcards spill out of stores, a bust of Goffredo Mameli, the composer of Italy's national anthem who lived here for a few years, stands in the central piazza, and there's even a youth hostel.

A few kilometres up the hill, the **Bosco Selene** archaeological park (T0782-41051, Tue-Sun 1000-1400, €4, €2 concessions) is set in a dense oak forest at 978 m. Its crisp air, tennis courts and picnic tables make it a refreshing refuge from Lanusei. The park holds two *tombe di giganti* dating from the 15th and 14th centuries BC respectively, and archaeologists are busy uncovering **Nuraghe Genna Acilli**, which promises to be a truly unique and special Bronze Age site, unlike anything seen before. It should be open to the public by 2010.

Sleeping

Grillo €€
*Via Monsignor Melas 14, Nuoro,
T0784-38668,grillohotel.it.*
Set around a straggly new development, this is Nuoro's most central hotel. The 45 rooms are far from spacious, though they are well serviced and the downstairs restaurant seems to be quite popular for lunch and dinner. Balconies cost €10 extra.

Casa Solotti €
*Località Monte Ortobene, Nuoro,
T0784-33954, casasolotti.it.*
You'll pass this elegant B&B surrounded by spacious greenery on the way up the Ortobene mountain, a refreshing shift from Nuoro's clogged confusion. There are five rooms (most with balconies) overlooking vineyards. Walking trails and organized horse rides allow you to get out and about.

Costiolu €
*10 km north of Nuoro towards
Orune, T333-663 0740,
agriturismocostiolu.com.*
One of the oldest and most magical *agriturismi* in Sardinia. The Costa brothers' 160-ha farm has plenty of breathing room for three generations of dogs, cats, pigs, cows, sheep, hens, boars, goats, horses, and even a peacock. Rooms have postcard views across the farm's cork forest but with horse riding and

plenty of other chances to get your hands dirty, you won't want to stay in.

Testone €
*Località Testone, 13 km north
of Nuoro towards Benetutti,
T0784-230539,
agriturismotestone.com.*
Another family-run farm that offers everything from homemade honey, wine, bread and meats to Italian lessons! The rooms are modest, though they do have air conditioning and private baths, but the meals are lavish affairs served at long tables in a rustic dining hall.

Su Gologone €€€€
*Località Su Gologone, nr Oliena,
T0784-287512, sugologone.it.*
Mar-Nov, Christmas and New Year only.
Central Sardinia's finest and most famous resort. From the lobby to the temporary art exhibits to the cottage-style apartments, Su

Gologone is brimming with Sardinian handicrafts. The breakfast terrace and the outdoor pool (next to the spa and gym) both offer views of the Lanaittu valley. The rooms are equipped with a cushy lounge area and draped beds. If you can't stay the night, stop by for dinner at one of the island's most delectable restaurants, which serves suckling pig slow-roasted above ilex logs.

CiKappa €€
*Corso Martin Luther King 2/4,
Oliena, T0784-288024,
cikappa.com.*
This backpackers' lodge at the edge of town shows its age. The views across to Nuoro are appealing; the grimy showers less so, but you could do worse than eat at the hotel's restaurant. The seven rooms boast a rare commodity in the Barbagie: Wi-Fi.

Club Hotel Marina Beach €€€

Località Marina di Orosei,
T0784-999900, marinabeach.it.
Apr-Oct only.
This compound is the area's largest and most plush resort. The rooms are done up with traditional motifs and each has its own veranda, some overlooking the pool. A bridge leads to the resort's private beach 100 m away.

Costa Dorada €€

Lungomare Palmasera 45,
Cala Gonone, T0784-93332,
hotelcostadorada.it.
Mar-Oct only.
Cala Gonone's most elegant hotel has a stone patio with five suites facing the beach 10 m away. Guests have access to the hotel's private boat to shuttle them around the Golfo di Orosei's beaches. There's a 15% supplement for stays of less than three days.

Hotel Bue Marino €€

Via Vespucci 8, Cala Gonone,
T0784-920078,
hotelbuemarino.it.
Apr-Sep only.
This is one of Cala Gonone's oldest hotels but a recent makeover ensures you're in for a cushy stay overlooking the town's Spiaggia Centrale. Lounge in the rooftop hydromassage tub with views spanning the coast. Ask for a room with a sea view.

S'Adde €€

Via Concordia 38, Dorgali,
T0784-94412, hotelsadde.it.
This central, modern hotel has a mountain feel with a wood-panelled lobby and green views. A nearby park will keep children busy, and the hotel can arrange excursions throughout the area.

Su Barchile €€

Via Mannu 5, Orosei,
T0784-98879, subarchile.it.
This place is not for the claustrophobic! The 10 rooms are equipped with their own bath, air conditioning and TVs, but they're shoe-horned into pretty tight quarters. There's elegant (if very pricey) dining in the downstairs restaurant under a reed ceiling.

Codula Fuili €

Località Pranos, 3 km south of
Cala Gonone, T328-734 0863,
codulafuili.com.
Located near Cala Fuili beach, this small *agriturismo* has four rooms, each named after a different beach in the Golfo di Orosei. Cartoe and Oddoane have views of the sea and all have their own bathrooms. The owners will gladly let you help them tend their goats and can suggest trekking routes around the gulf.

Sa Corte Antica €

Via Mannu 17, Dorgali,
T0784-94317, sacorteantica.it.
This B&B is found in a traditional though recently restored *Dorgalese* house tucked in a courtyard. The Pira family have given each of their three rooms a touch of class with iron bed frames and shiny-tiled bathrooms, and their hospitality is well-known in the locality.

Il Pergolato €€

Via Roma 10, Fonni,
T0784-58455.
An attractive option located smack-bang in Fonni's centre. The few rooms are scattered around an internal courtyard draped with grape vines. The excellent restaurant serves typical meat specialities and myrtle-flavoured sorbet.

Antichi Sapori €

Via Cagliari 168, Gavoi,
T0784-52021,
agriturismodasperanza.com.
It's a family affair inside this 18th-century farmhouse in the heart of Gavoi. Signora Todde cooks delicious meals – often including suckling pig – which are served by her and presided over by papa. Above the stone dining room and hearth, two floors hold seven generous rooms with essential conveniences and private bathrooms.

Listings

West of the Gennargentu

Hotel Sa Muvara €€
Località Sa Muvara, Aritzo,
T0784- 629336,
samuvarahotel.com.
A country hotel nestled in five hectares of parkland. The rooms are generously spacious (especially the suites) with wood-panelled floors. There's a pool, gym and spa to keep you busy or staff can organize excursions in the surrounding area.

Ogliastra

Arbatasar Hotel €€€
Via Porto Frailis 11, Arbatax,
T0782-651800, arbatasar.it.
You'll find this brand new hotel with a bright yellow exterior between the port and beaches. The rooms come with modern comforts in breezy colours. If the five-minute walk to the beach is too far, there's a pool out back.

Hotel Agugliastra €€
Piazza Principessa di Navarra,
Santa Maria Navarrese,
T0782-615005,
hotelagugliastra.it.
The plain white hallways and rooms are reminiscent of a hospital ward but the beds are comfortable and the bathrooms are spacious. The hotel's terrace café is a popular spot, so on summer nights you may need to use earplugs.

Hotel Nicoletta €€
Via Lungomare, Santa Maria Navarrese, T0782-614045, hotelnicoletta.info.
Mar-Nov only.
The more upscale of Santa Maria's two central hotels, this squat rust-coloured villa is surrounded by flower beds and has 28 rooms. Some have balconies overlooking the main drag, and all have modern comforts.

La Bitta €€
Località Porto Frailis, Arbatax, T0782-667080, hotellabitta.it.
Closed Jan.
Arbatax's most graceful hotel is a few steps off the beach at Porto Frailis. Rooms come with arching ceilings, Roman-style columns and massages on your balcony.

Da Concetta €
Corso Umberto I 111, Jerzu,
T0782 70197,
hotelristorantedaconcetta.it.
This is about the only choice in town. Luckily, the elderly Concetta is beyond hospitable and has several charming rooms on offer, with air-conditioning and private baths. Guests have access to the rooftop terrace with views across the valley. When hunger calls, walk across the street to find Concetta making homemade *culurgiones* (dumplings). She can also set up trekking excursions around Jerzu's limestone *tacchi*.

La Nuova Luna €
Via Indipendenza 35, Lanusei, T0782-41051, lanuovaluna.it.
Why a youth hostel sprang up in Lanusei remains a mystery but there's no denying its charm. The large stone dining room and wood-panelled ceiling resemble a cosy lodge, and €18 for a bed in a three-to-seven-person dormitory is a steal… especially considering you'll probably have the place to yourself.

Campsites

Camping Telis
Località Porto Frailis, Arbatax, T0782-667140, campingtelis.com.
A few steps away from Hotel La Bitta, this year-round campsite boasts its own private beach with free lounge chairs for its bungalow and mobile home guests. There's also a small playground, tennis court and a dive centre on site.

Eating & drinking

Canne al Vento €€€
Via Biasi, Nuoro, T0784-201762.
Mon-Sat 1930-2300.
Named after Grazia Deledda's
famous novel, this restaurant on
the outskirts of town fittingly
serves up classic Sardinian fare,
from *prosciutto* antipasto to
pecorino and honey dessert, and
everything in between.

Ciusa €€€
*Viale Ciusa 55, Nuoro,
T0784-257052.*
Wed-Mon 1930-2330.
Nuoro's best pizzas are heated
inside Ciusa's wood-burning
ovens. For something heavier, try
the risotto with Cannonau wine
and pecorino cheese.

Da Giovanni €€
*Via IV Novembre 9, Nuoro,
T0784-30562.*
Mon-Sat 1230-1430 and
2000-2200.
It's a bit hard to find this trattoria
but the wild boar served here
since the 1950s is worth the
effort. Try it atop *gnochetti* or
fettucine noodles, or go with the
filindreu mutton broth made
famous by Lula's bandits.

Cafés & bars
Caffè America
Piazza Italia 5, Nuoro.
Daily 0700-2200.
This elegant wooden haunt is a
popular spot with locals and is
conveniently close to the tourist

office. There are lots of yummy
salads and plenty of wines
available by the glass.

Pit Stop
*Via Brofferio 19, Nuoro,
T0784-257030.*
Mon-Sat 2000-2400.
Aside from corso Garibaldi's
cafés, this is Nuoro's only other
drinking spot. Cheap prices draw
a younger crowd.

Plada Caffè
*Corso Garibaldi 141, Nuoro,
T0784-238873.*
Daily 0630-2130.
Offers good panini and
people-watching.

Masiloghi €€€
*Via Galiani 68, Oliena,
T0784-285696.*
Apr-Oct daily 1230-1430 and
1930-2245.
Choose from four fixed menus or
select à la carte specialities. The
fare, like the decor, is decidedly
Sardinian; you can't go wrong
with young boar in a fennel
sauce or *gnochetti* noodles. The
restaurant also runs a B&B.

'Sa Rosada €€
*Piazza Europa 2, Mamoiada,
T0784-56713.*
Wed-Mon 1230-1430 and
1930-2200.
A fetching little place tucked into
a veranda with an all-Sardo
menu that changes daily.

Il Pescatore €€€€
*Via Acqua Dolce 7, Cala Gonone,
T0784-93174.*
Easter-Oct daily 1215-1500 and
1900-2230.
Fish is the main melody in this
oversized upper-crust
establishment. Three women
serve *burrida dorgalese* soup and
fish any way you want it, caught
by their brother. If Vermintino
wine from Gallura doesn't find
its way into your glass, you'll
probably taste it in chef Patrizia's
sauces.

Colibrì €€€
Via Floris 7, Dorgali,
T0784-96054.
Mid Mar-mid Nov Mon-Sat
1230-1430 and 2000-2230.
This seasonal restaurant has
been a mainstay for nearly 30
years, serving typical local *pane
frattau* (Sardinian 'lasagne' made
with pecorino and *pane carasau*,
topped with an egg), goat, lamb
and wild boar.

La Taverna €€€
Piazza Marconi 6, Orosei,
T0784-998330.
Mon-Sat 1300-1530 and
1900-2100.
Sit outside surrounded by cactus
and flowers or inside where farm
tools are stuck to the wall. The
wild boar is popular, as are the
maccarose de busa pasta and the
blackberry sorbet.

Sant'Elene €€€
Località Sant'Elene, Dorgali,
T0784-94572.
Apr-Sep daily 1300-1430 and
2000-2200, Oct-Mar by request.
Two kilometres north of Dorgali
on the SS125, this hotel-
restaurant combo offers a nice
mix of surf and turf. The owners
produce their own vegetables,
olive oil, tagliatelle and wine.

Aquarius €€
Lungomare Palmasera 34,
Cala Gonone, T0784-93428.
Apr-Oct daily 1200-1500 and
1900-2300.

A family-run restaurant near the
beach serving seafood, meat and
pizzas. The *aragosta alla catalana*
comes recommended, and head
chef Sebastiano Mula will
round-up shellfish from local
fishermen if you call ahead.

Da Diego €€
Piazza Sant'Antonio 22, Orosei,
T0784-998072.
Tue-Sun 1230-1500 and
1930-2300.
Orosei's best pizzeria has a
laid-back setting. Spaghetti with
bottarga and plenty of meats are
also on hand, as is Oliena's
famous Nepente wine.

Cafés & bars
Yesterday Caffè
Via Nazionale 48, Orosei.
Mon-Sat 0830-1230 and
1630-2400.
A few bits of Beatles memorabilia
are hung inside but the outdoor
seating on the cobblestones
behind the main street is more
inviting. Come here for coffee by
day and cocktails at night.

Barbagia di Ollolai

Santa Rughe €€€
Via Carlo Felice 2, Gavoi,
T0784-53774.
May-Aug daily 1900-2200,
Sep-Apr Thu-Tue 1900-2200.
This cosy retreat serves pizzas
and more hearty fare. In spring,
try the traditional *erbudzu* soup
filled with wild herbs.

Su Ninnieri €€€
Località Bruncu Spina, Fonni,
T0784-57729.
Wed-Mon 1900-2300.
Drive towards Desulo to the
junction for Brancu Spina and
follow the signs to this country
joint. Rustic recipes abound here.

West of the Gennargentu

Su Muvara €€€€
Località Fontana Rubia, Aritzo,
T0784-629336.
May-Oct daily 1900-2200.
This restaurant is attached to a
hotel of the same name and
enjoys views of mountains and
trees from its terrace. The porcini
mushrooms and homemade
torrone dessert are good.

Moderno €€
Viale Kennedy 6, Aritzo,
T0784-629229.
Easter-Oct daily 1300-1500 and
2015-2200.
There's nothing 'moderno' about
this haunt; it was one of the
area's first hotels. Downstairs,
Signora Manca whips up
homemade pasta dishes.

Ogliastra

Da Lenin €€€
Via San Gemiliano 19, Tortolì,
T0782-624422.
Mon-Sat 1930-2245.
It's a good thing the dilapidated
façade of this joint doesn't reflect
the food. Seafood is king at Lenin

Entertainment

Mura's restaurant. Locals recommend the shrimp with ragù and the fresh lobster.

Il Golgo €€€
Località Golgo, via Bitzocoro 10, Baunei, T0782-610732.
Apr-Sep daily 1230-1430 and 1930-2245.
Perched on the Altopiano di Golgo in a typical stone hut with a wooden roof, the restaurant offers wonderful meat dishes.

Ristorante Lungomare €€€
Via Turru 10, Santa Maria Navarrese, T0782-614041,
Wed-Mon 1230-1400 and 1930-2200.
Locals rate Lungomare's seafood as the best in a town with few options. Spaghetti with clams is passable; sea bass stuffed with shrimp is better. The restaurant's rooms overlook the port below.

Lo Spiedo d'Ogliastra €€
Via Zinnias 23, Tortolì, T0782-623856.
Daily 1230-1500 and 1930-2300.
A restaurant/pizzeria run by the Scattu family. The *culurgiones* dumplings are yummy.

Cafés & bars
L'Olivastro
Via Lungomare, Santa Maria Navarrese, T0782-615513.
May-mid Oct daily 0730-0200.
A mellow drinking and mingling spot. Choose from beer, cocktails and panini.

Clubs
Il Gazebo
500 m south of Santa Maria Navarrese towards Lotzorai, Ogliastra, T0782-669581.
Jun-mid Sep.
Ravers come from all around the coast to dance the night away at this club, which is loved by hormone-driven males and hated by the sleep-deprived folk at the two campsites next door. Hours and entrance fees vary.

Lo Skrittiore
Località Iscrittiore, Cala Gonone, Golfo di Orosei, T339-330 3708.
May-Sep Fri-Sun 2300-0300.
A few kilometres up the hill toward Dorgali is this popular disco that blasts everything from reggae to revival. Check the kiosks at the port for dates.

Toma Alternative Bar
Porto Santa Maria Navarrese, Ogliastra.
May-Sep daily 2130-0300.
Live music permeates from this two-storey wooden bar with romantic views overlooking the port. The inside has a modish Middle-Eastern theme.

Festivals & events
The most important and unique celebrations in the Barbagie, take place for the **Festa di Sant'Antonio Abate** in January and for **Carnevale** in February (see page 47), with the most notable processions in Mamoiada and Ottana

Cortes Apertas

Cortes Apertas (open houses) is a wonderful way to experience the Barbagie's famous hospitality while gaining insights into the traditional customs of Nuoro's remote hamlets. The events are held each weekend from September to December in a different town and last three days each. A typical festival usually showcases the town's traditional foods and handicrafts, often with folk groups dancing *ballu sardu* in costume. Tourist offices can provide scheduling information, or consult paradisola.it/autunnoinbarbagia/.

(see page 171), Orosei, Dorgali and Gavoi. Other calendar highlights include the **S'Incontru** Easter parade in Oliena and the **Festa dell'Assunta** on the 15th August in Orgosolo. Two days later, Orgosolo hosts a Palio-style horse race that attracts jockeys from throughout Sardinia. This region also has numerous harvest and food festivals. Tonara celebrates its famous nougat on Easter Monday in the **Sagra del Torrone**, with plenty of samples, while Jerzu hosts the boozy **Sagra del Vino** in August, honouring the town's Cannonau wine. Aritzo showcases its sorbet at the **Festa di San Carapigna** and marks the chestnut and hazelnut harvest with the **Sagra delle Castagne e delle Nocciole** in October.

Shopping

The Supramonte

Maschere Mameli
Corso Vittorio Emanuele III 7, Mamoiada, T0784-56222.
Mon-Sat 0900-1230 and 1630-1900.
Ruggero Mameli is Mamoiada's leading mask maker and his workshop is a great place to buy the town's trademark souvenir.

Prodotti Tipici Sardi
Piazza Santa Maria 14, Oliena, T0784-288110.
Wed-Mon 0830-1300 and 1700-2000, Tue 0830-1300.
Local cheeses and meats, and Oliena's famous Nepente wine.

Golfo di Orosei

Arte Sarda
Via Nazionale, Orosei, T346-700 0694.
May-Sep daily 0900-1300 and 1630-2000, Oct-Apr closed Sun.
The best stocked of three neighbouring souvenir shops, with a good selection of hand-woven baskets.

EnoDelizie
Via Lamarmora 149, Dorgali, T0784-96633.
Mon-Sat 0900-1300 and 1630-2000.
A great place to pick up Dorgali's famously strong Cannonau wine, as well as leading brands from throughout Sardinia.

Barbagia di Ollolai

Maschere Tradizionali Ottanesi
Piazza Sant'Antonio, Ottana, T328-652 0069.
Daily 0800-1300 and 1400-2000.
Franco Maritato is the man behind Ottana's bizarre Carnival masks (see page 171). His horned and snouted designs run from €35 to €130.

Sos Zillonarzos
Via Roma 227, Gavoi, T349-198 2731.
Mon-Sat 0730-1200 and 1630-2030.
A family-run operation, selling homemade breads and desserts, meat and lots of Gavoi's *fiore sardo* pecorino cheese.

Activities & tours

Golfo di Orosei

See also **Fuori Rotta Baunei**, page 193.

Cooperative Ghivine
Via Lamarmora 69, Dorgali, T349-442 5552, ghivine.com.
Dorgali's leading outdoor specialist leads daily summer excursions up to the Supramonte, around the Golfo di Orosei, through Ogliastra's *tacchi* and into a variety of archaeological sites.

L'Argonauta
Via dei Lecci 10, Cala Gonone, T0784-93046, argonauta.it.
Apr-Oct only.
Choose from 30 dives through the underwater cliffs or sunken Second World War ships scattered around the Golfo di Orosei. The guides are a friendly, English-speaking bunch who also run a few area treks and can suggest lodging options.

Orosei Diving Center
Località Marina di Orosei, T349-598 3533, oroseidivingcenter.it.
Explore several sunken ships and red coral reefs around Orosei with this young, energetic, English-speaking dive team. Courses are available for both adults and children.

Transport

Barbagia di Ollolai

Barbagia No Limits

Via Cagliari 85, Gavoi, T0784-529016, barbagianolimits.it.
This adventure operator offers canyoning, canoeing, trekking and week-long camping trips into the Barbagie's hinterland.

Gennargentu Escursioni

Via Porrino 15/B, Fonni, T0784-589038, gennargentuescursioni.it.
Arrange for an English-speaking guide to lead you on various trekking excursions throughout the Gennargentu and Supramonte mountain ranges lasting from one to three days.

Ogliastra

Cooperative Goloritzè

Località Golgo, Baunei, T0782-610599, coopgoloritze.com.
This is one of Sardinia's most established excursion companies, offering one- to three-day jaunts on horseback, 4x4 or boat from Tiscali to the Golfo di Orosei with English-speaking guides. Their lodge serves appetizing dishes and is a wonderful place to make camp for a few days.

Cooperative Gorropu

Via Sa Preda Lada 2, Urzulei, T333-850 7157, gorropu.com.
If you want to explore Gola Gorroppu, put your faith in

Sandra, an upbeat German expat who knows the canyon like the back of her hand. She and her husband, an Urzulei local, also lead other trips around central Sardinia.

Fuori Rotta Baunei

Marina di Santa Maria Navarrese, T339-838 7788, fuorirottabaunei.it.
This class act can't be recommended highly enough. Cruise the Golfo di Orosei aboard a converted fishing vessel that holds a maximum of 15 people, remodelled by Captain Antonello himself. Antonello speaks functional English and leads informative and interesting tours of the gulf's beaches, gladly accommodating any preferences to go to one beach over another. Sign up for the three-course lunch on board: the fresh seafood salad and shrimp pasta are outstanding!

Nuoro

Two ARST buses run daily from Nuoro to **Olbia** (2 hrs 30 mins/3 hrs) and to **Cagliari** (2 hrs 30 mins/5 hrs). There are fairly frequent daily buses between Nuoro and **Mamoiada** (20 mins), **Ottana** (30 mins), **Gavoi** (1 hr 10 mins) and **Fonni** (40 mins-1 hr 30 mins), plus four buses to **Orosei** (50 mins), one to **Tortolì** (2 hrs 40 mins) and one to **Aritzo** (1 hr 55 mins). There are also regular trains between Nuoro and **Macomer** (1 hr), where you can connect to Cagliari and Sassari.

Ogliastra

From Tortolì one daily ARST bus travels to **Nuoro** (2 hrs 40 mins) and five to **Cagliari** (2 hrs 45 mins). See page 184 for information on the Trenino Verde to Arbatax.

Contents

The Gallura

Capo Testa.

Introduction

What to see in...

...one day
Base yourself in **Santa Teresa** and spend the day exploring the granite formations at **Capo Testa** or puttering around **La Maddalena** archipelago by boat.

Sardinia's northeastern corner, the Gallura, is a blend of wealth and wilderness. For 600 years it was the most impoverished and isolated pocket of Sardinia, until, in the 1960s, the development of the Costa Smeralda catapulted Sardinia onto the world stage. However, the arrival of the international jet-set created an island within an island, one that belies Sardinia's true character. While the Emerald Coast remains Sardinia's most famous tourist attraction, Gallura's charms lie elsewhere.

... a weekend or more
Find an ATM and venture to Sardinia's theme park, the **Costa Smeralda,** to laze on the beaches and do some celebrity-spotting. Alternatively, check-in at one of the *agriturismi* near **Arzachena** and visit the area's archaeological ruins.

Shop for hand-woven rugs in **Aggius**, modern art in **San Pantaleo** and cork in **Calangianus** and **Tempio**. Bike through the **Valle della Luna**, hike up **Monte Limbara**, and marvel at Europe's oldest tree outside **Luras**.

The region's proximity to Corsica means its culture is as much rooted in France as it is in Italy. In the 1700s, so many shepherds crossed the Strait of Bonifacio from the neighbouring island that Corsicans comprised three-quarters of Gallura's population. Many of Gallura's villages resemble Corsican towns, and the *Gallurese* dialect is almost identical to that spoken across the strait.

But it is Gallura's granite formations that distinguish it from the rest of the island. From the rias around Olbia and La Maddalena archipelago, to the boulders of the Valle della Luna and Capo Testa, nature has moulded Gallura's granite into sensual arches, striking columns and dramatic spires that rival the gorgeous beaches nearby.

Left: A lighthouse in the Gallura.

Around the island

The northeast's capital, Olbia, is a transit town first and foremost. Set at the end of a carved inlet, its natural harbour has always been the obvious point of arrival and departure to and from the Italian mainland, as the Phoenicians, Carthaginians and Romans all found. The influx of tourists flocking to the Costa Smeralda and surrounding resorts ensures that Olbia's port is the busiest in the country. Cars, trains and aeroplanes also converge on this overdeveloped town, creating a chaotic traffic pattern that has hidden much of its ancient charm.

Greek merchants called the settlement 'Olbios Polis' (happy town), leading many people to think that the Greeks established their only Sardinian colony here, but it is more likely to have been founded by the Phoenicians between the sixth and fourth centuries BC. Their successors, the Carthaginians, surrounded the town with towers and a wall (still partly visible on modern-day via Torino) in 350 BC before the Romans made it their most important naval base in Sardinia. After its brief incarnation as Phausania under the Byzantines, and Civita as the capital of the impoverished Giudicato of Gallura, Mussolini restored Olbia's Greek name in 1939. Since the tourist boom of the 1960s, Olbia's population has tripled, leaving its quaint historic district surrounded by causeways and construction but also ensuring it has plenty of accommodation and some great restaurants.

In town

Olbia's main drag is the pedestrian-friendly **corso Umberto**, a wide avenue running from the waterfront to the train station, lined with designer stores and cafés with outdoor seating. Beyond the Biblioteca Comunale near the harbour, a series of narrow alleyways shoot off from the corso into the town's compact historic district, offering a pleasant, if brief, stroll past shops and 19th-century homes. A right turn at via Cagliari takes you to piazza Santa Croce and the **Chiesa di San Paolo**, whose granite façade and belltower are enlivened by the tiles on its Spanish-accented cupola, built after the Second World War. **Piazza Margherita** is a good place to stop for a drink. Look for reminders of Roman aqueducts near the square.

The corso turns a bit seedy ascending from the piazza but turn right just past the train station onto via San Simplicio for Olbia's main draw, the 12th-century Pisan-Romanesque **Chiesa San Simplicio** (T0789-23542, daily 0900-1300 and 1600-1900).

Around Olbia

Olbia's city beach is **Lido del Sole**, but a better option lies 5 km up the road at **Pittulongu**, a crescent-shaped strand with a sailing school and views of Isola Tavolara. (To get there catch bus 4

Chiesa di San Paolo.

from the city centre or, by car, follow the brown signs north toward Golfo Aranci.) One kilometre before Pittulongu is Olbia's most famous Nuraghic monument, the **Pozzo Sacro di Sa Testa** (T340-811 9340, www.iolao.it, 15 May-15 Oct daily 0900-1930, reservations necessary out of season, €2.50). Discovered by shepherds looking for water in the 1930s, the well-preserved site contains a large courtyard with 17 steps descending to a sacred well that dates back to 1150 BC .

Golfo Aranci

Continuing north around the Golfo di Olbia, you'll come to Golfo Aranci, the last affordable beachfront resort before the Costa Smeralda. This former fishing enclave has been expanding since 1882 when a track was laid linking its port with the national railway 18 km away in Olbia. Today, the town is really a sprawling collection of hotels and resort condos that descend past via Libertà's souvenir shops towards the train station and port, which has regular ferry services to the Italian mainland. There's an attractive seaside *lungomare,* with a playground for kids but, on the whole, Golfo Aranci's appeal lies in its proximity to 24 dazzling beaches that compensate for its lack of urban dazzle. The best is **Spiaggia Bianca**, a kilometre away towards Olbia, which entices a lively young crowd to its seaside kiosks.

Essentials

❶ Getting around Olbia is small enough that you won't need a car. Buses 2 and 10 run from the airport to corso Umberto every 30 minutes from 0730 to 2000. ARST buses serve destinations along the coast and inland (see page 229).

❷ Bus station Stazione ARST, corso Umberto 1, T0789-553000, arst.sardegna.it.

❸ Train station Stazione Ferroviaria, via Giacomo Pala, T0789-21197.

❹ ATM Banca di Sassari, corso Umberto 7, T0789-22371, Mon-Sat 0830-1300 and 1445-1600.

❺ Hospital Ospedale Civile, via Aldo Moro, T0789-552200, is 5 km north of town.

❻ Pharmacy Farmacia Lupacciolu, Corso Umberto 134, T0789-202461, Mon-Sat 0900-1300 and 1630-1930.

❼ Post office Poste Italiane, via Acquedotto, T0789-207400, Mon-Fri 0800-1300, Sat 0800-1315.

❶ Tourist information There is a tourist booth on piazza Matteotti, Mon-Sat 0900-1400 and 1700-2000.

Adventurous travellers should take the dirt road behind the train tracks as far as you can go, then park and walk 500 m to the twin coves of **Cala Moresca**, whose hidden beaches face the nearby **Isola Figarolo**. A 4-km dirt path behind the second beach leads to the wildlife preserve of **Capo Figari**, where a band of mouflons have thrived since their recent reintroduction. The path finishes with a view from below an abandoned lighthouse.

Golfo Aranci.

South of Olbia

Beyond the concrete jungle of Olbia's suburbs lies Gallura's pretty southern seashore. From Porto San Paolo south towards the province of Nuoro, clusters of oleander and bougainvillea drape over holiday villas facing massive Isola Tavolara and its squat twin, Isola Molara. Unlike the swanky northern resorts, southern Gallura has been slow to awaken to tourism. The action does, however, accelerate in mid June, with late-night summer raves at San Teodoro, but slows again at the end of August, when these sleepy beach communities return to hibernation.

Isola Tavolara.

Porto San Paolo

The quaint beach town of Porto San Paolo has developed as a gateway to Isola Tavolara, which looms just offshore, and is a fantastic base for scuba diving and snorkelling. The surrounding coastline from Capo Ceraso to Cala Finocchio is a protected marine reserve that includes over 20 islands and rocky outcrops, plus two shipwrecks.

Two companies offer daily ferry shuttles between Porto San Paolo's dock and Tavolara during Easter and between June and September (every 30 mins daily 0900-1300, return ferries 1215-1830, journey time 25 mins, €12.50 round trip). Longer trips, with bathing stops at the crystal-clear waters of nearby **Isola Molara** and at Tavolara's eastern limestone walls, cost €25.

Tip...

Divers shouldn't miss the Secca del Papa, a 40-m bank off Tavolara's extreme eastern end with an underwater rock resembling the Pope, where deep crevasses and rainbow-coloured fish make for one of the best dives in Sardinia; contact Porto San Paolo Dive Centre, see page 228.

Isola Tavolara

The steep limestone stack of **Isola Tavolara** makes quite an impression as you approach it. Rising to 565 m at its peak, the craggy dolomite is visible well beyond the Gulf of Olbia, highlighted by a dramatic cloud that hovers above its crest, creating the island's own microclimate and, fittingly, resembling a crown placed atop the world's smallest kingdom (see box, opposite).

Boats from Porto San Paolo land at **Spalmatore di Terra**, a sandy tongue sprinkled with summer houses and two restaurants (including Da Tonino). The boomerang-shaped **Spiaggia Spalmatore** and its transparent water is Tavolara's main draw (for great snorkelling, head behind the pink house on the left) but be sure also to visit the nearby cemetery, where the tombs of the island's former kings are marked with a crown.

San Teodoro

San Teodoro's natural setting tucked between a large mirror-like lagoon and several celestial beaches lends itself to tourism. Yet, it is only in the past decade that the quiet town has become one of the hottest summer destinations for Italy's vibrant under-30 crowd. The town's piazzas are lined with enough pizzerias, bars and discos to

The world's smallest kingdom

Giuseppe Bertoleoni was the first settler to arrive on the uninhabited island of Tavolara in 1807, intending to live there with one of his two wives after fleeing his native Genoa where he had been charged with bigamy. Bertoleoni soon realized that he was sharing his island home with a rare species of goat, whose teeth were dyed a golden colour by the grasses they ate. Word of these goats spread to Carlo Alberto, king of Savoy and Sardinia, who eagerly travelled to Tavolara to hunt the animals in 1836. Giuseppe's son, Paolo, guided the hunting excursions with apparent success, since Carlo declared Paolo the official 'King of Tavolara' on the spot and sent a confirming scroll a few days later.

The mini-monarchy was recognized by both the Italian king, Vittorio Emanuele III, who signed a treaty with the nation, and England's Queen Victoria, who placed a photo showing Tavolara's 'royal family' in Buckingham Palace, where it is still displayed with the caption, 'World's Smallest Kingdom'.

The installation of a NATO base on the island in 1962 effectively ended Tavolara's sovereignty and made roughly a quarter of the kingdom off-limits to the island's residents. Among them is Tonino, a 70-something part-time fisherman and the current King of Tavolara. When he's not fishing or transporting tourists around, Tonino rules over the island's 15-strong population, a few nimble goats, cormorants and a species of prickly knapweed flower found nowhere else on Earth.

keep tanned young cocktail-seekers fed, watered and dancing well into the early hours. A quieter alternative is to stroll the town's outdoor handicrafts market, which is held each night from 2000 between June and September.

You can't go wrong at any of the town's beaches, but you won't find anything more stunning than the 3-km isthmus of **La Cinta**, which threads through the **Stagno di San Teodoro** (home to herons, gulls, flamingos, and other birds), and the shallow crystalline sea and powdery white shores just up the road at **Cala Brandinchi**.

Costa Smeralda & around

From Porto Rotondo to Baia Sardinia, northeastern Gallura's glamorous beachside resorts represent some of the most expensive real estate in the whole Mediterranean. The Costa Smeralda was created by the Aga Khan in the 1960s as a clandestine playground for aristocrats and multi-millionaires (see page 202). However, in recent years, the Emerald Coast has outgrown its 'exclusive' aura. As some sensibly priced hotels, restaurants and discos have sprouted up around this once-elite Babylon, models and CEOs now have to share beaches

and dance floors with camera-toting tourists. Never mind the exaggerated prices and faux Arabian villas, the beauty of the Costa Smeralda's jagged coastline and emerald beaches trump its most beautiful clientele and you don't need a full wallet to enjoy them. A series of deep inlets divided by dramatically wind-carved granite is enough to make even the most jaded billionaire lower his shades in astonishment.

Liscia Ruja.

From prince's playground to tourist theme park

Sixty years ago the Emerald Coast and its surroundings were little more than a swathe of *macchia*-covered knolls, lacking plumbing or roads. The area's only inhabitants, a few struggling shepherds, considered the arid badlands too dry even for their herds, and the deep fjords around which football gods and their wives now putter in their three-storey cruisers were once breeding grounds for malaria. The coast's fortunes began to change in 1951, when the Rockefeller Foundation recruited 32,000 Americans to spray 10,000 tons of DDT around Sardinia's coastal swamps, thus ridding this 55 km coastline of malarial mosquitoes and preparing the ground for a prince with a full wallet to dream up a jet-setters' paradise.

By the late 1950s, a few wealthy financiers had decided that Sardinia's hidden inlets and translucent waters made a great place to park their yachts. In 1962, Prince Karim Aga Khan IV, the 22-year-old spiritual leader of Ismaili Muslims worldwide and an international playboy, came to see what all the fuss was about. He fell in love with Sardinia's rugged beauty and convinced his high-rolling cronies to invest in an ambitious project to transform the barren landscape of the northeast coast into a world-class hideaway.

The Aga Khan bought more than 3000 acres of coastline from local impoverished shepherds at the equivalent of €150-220 a hectare and set to work. His Emerald Coast Consortium imposed strict building regulations, prohibiting the introduction of non-native plants and stipulating that all water pipes and electrical lines be hidden underground. The prince hired Robert Trent Jones to design the world-class Pevero Golf Club, and top European architects Jacques Couelle and Michele Busiri Vici to incorporate the best elements of North African, Spanish, Italian and Greek architecture to grace the resort's pastel-coloured centre, Porto Cervo. The result is a striking pseudo-idealized Mediterranean village, whose petrified artificiality leaves nary a bougainvillea out of place.

The Costa Smeralda has not traditionally catered to Sardinians and has done little to boost their stagnant economy. The nightly cost of many hotel suites in high season tops the average Sardinian's monthly salary; many of the area's high-rolling vacationers never leave the confines of Costa Smeralda's private, foreign-owned resorts, and residents of its Moorish-kasbah-meets-Mykonos architecture turn up their noses at the Gallura's indigenous *stazzu* ranch-style homes. However, although this ersatz wonderland may be divorced from Sardinian culture, the Costa Smeralda does attract day trippers eager to spot or even mingle with a movie star. And, since the Olbia-Costa Smeralda airport was enlarged in 2004, new budget airline routes have made Italy's flashiest playground more accessible to average tourists. Sardinians, too, are finally benefiting from the influx: several locally owned B&Bs and *agriturismi* have opened in the area, signalling a new chapter in a prince's gilded fairy tale.

Porto Cervo

The heart of the Costa Smeralda is Porto Cervo, home in high season to mega yachts, plush villas and people who actually wear what you see on catwalks. For all the celebrity hype found in gossip tabloids each summer, Porto Cervo is a clever marriage of glamour and laid-back cool. It has enough flashy lights to keep you interested, at least for a day, although, if you come out of season, you'll find the scene is far more bare than bling.

Unless you arrive on your own boat, Porto Cervo first reveals itself along its **Passeggiata**, a pedestrian street lined with a string of cream-coloured designer boutiques where you can drop €1500 on a handbag. Make a detour away from the

shops to visit the **Chiesa di Stella Maris**. This striking ode to North African architecture was completed in 1969 by Busiri Vici, and provides great views of the harbour. Its interior holds El Greco's painting of *Mater Dolorosa*.

A path leads from the church to the fan-shaped **Piazzetta**, overlooking the port below. This is the town's main hub and is thronged with yachties at dusk, who return from a tough day of beach-hopping to sip €5 coffees, €15 beers or €22-80 cocktails. Two stairways descend from the *piazzetta* to more boutique stores in the **Portico Sottopiazza**, from where a wooden bridge connects the town to the port. For a dose of culture outside the realms of Gucci or Fendi, climb the road away from the port towards the **Promenade du Port**, where two impressive art galleries have opened in the past year: **Louise Alexander Gallery** (via del Porto 1, T0789-92090, louise-alexander.com, mid Jun-mid Sep daily 1100-1300 and 1800-2400, free) has presented work by the likes of Andy Warhol, Jean-Michel Basquiat and Roy Lichtenstein, while the **Monte di Mola Museo** (via del Porto Vecchio 1, T0789-92225, gocilgroup.com, mid Jun-mid Sep daily 1800-2400, free) has the Moët & Chandon wine bar inside.

Beaches south of Porto Cervo

The best bathing spots are south of Porto Cervo and are clustered close enough to let you visit them all in one day.

About 1.5 km from Porto Cervo towards Arzachena, the floury sand and light green bay at **Pevero** make it a favourite haunt for VIPs. Turn right from the main road towards Abbiadori and follow signs for Cala di Volpe and Capriccioli. **Liscia Ruja** is the first beach signposted and the largest and busiest in the area. The 2-km dirt road leading to its car park will seriously test your car's suspension but the narrow sandy strand framed by offshore islands is extraordinary. (Don't park along the dirt road or you may be fined.)

Leaving the beach and turning right toward Capriccioli, you'll spot the 5-star Hotel Cala di Volpe and the Pevero Golf Club. A sign soon afterwards indicates a left turn to Hotel Romazzino but before arriving at the hotel, turn right on to via degli Asfodeli to reach the coast's most renowned beach, **Il Principe**. You'll have to park and descend a lovely brush-lined path to reach this unspoiled gem. Back on the main road, a left turn leads to the twin beaches of **Capriccioli**, which are backed by juniper trees and offer one of the best views of the Costa Smeralda.

Five of the best

Ways to spot a celebrity on the Costa Smeralda

❶ Hang around Porto Cervo's **marina** at dusk, when many VIPs return from a day aboard their yachts (see below).

❷ Work on your tan at **Il Principe** or **Pevero** beaches (see page 203).

❸ Stroll around the grounds of **Hotel Pitrizza** (see page 218).

❹ Book a table at the **Yacht Club** restaurant (see page 223).

❺ Brave the bouncers at the Costa Smeralda's three biggest nightclubs: **Billionaire**, **Sopravento** and **Sottovento** (see page 227).

Porto Cervo Marina.

Tip...

Don't leave Porto Cervo without taking a detour to its 720-birth marina, the largest in Sardinia. Set at the end of the resort's natural bay, this is really a sight to behold in high season, with 55-m yachts from all over the world bobbing at the quay, many with their own security guards outside.

Porto Rotondo.

Five of the best

Ways to enjoy the Costa Smeralda on a budget

❶ Check out the temporary art exhibitions at Porto Cervo's galleries (see page 203).

❷ Hang out on the beaches, all of which are public and free (see page 203).

❸ Dine at Porto Cervo's **Ristorante Pomodoro**, where the pizzas cost as little as €10 (see page 223).

❹ Sip a €3 glass of local Vermintino Piras wine at the **Pina Colada Bar** and chase it with €10 champagne during the 1900-2100 happy hour (see page 223).

❺ Head to Baia Sardinia's best club, **Phi Beach**, between 1900 and 2400 for free live music, dancing and an electrifying sunset above the granite outcrops (see page 227).

Porto Rotondo

Just down the road, Porto Rotondo isn't officially part of the Costa Smeralda but it doesn't deviate much from the area's theme… except that it boasts its own heli-pad.

In 1959 two Venetian Counts, Luigi and Nicolò Donà delle Rose, sailed their yacht from Tuscany to Sardinia on an underwater hunting expedition. Bewitched by the same shimmering potential for development that enticed Prince Karim Aga Khan, the brothers returned to Sardinia in 1963 with two suitcases full of *lire*, displaced some sheep and their owners, and got to work on what was supposed to be a few villas for their aristocratic friends. As demand grew, the brothers invited artisans to expand the resort, until their glitzy getaway was complete with six piazzas, arching bridges, Roman columns, the inevitable luxury port and private residences owned by the likes of Silvio Berlusconi, Shirley Bassey and Umberto Agnelli.

Like Venice, the village is closed to cars and has a central square named **piazza San Marco**. Just behind it, the rather ugly granite **Chiesa di San Lorenzo** houses 24 biblical scenes masterfully carved from wood by Mario Cerioli: don't miss the *Last Supper* on the church's right wall. Cerioli also designed the town's Greek-inspired granite theatre nearby, which hosts outdoor films and concerts most nights in August.

Baia Sardinia

The 5-km stretch of road north of Porto Cervo passes through soaring granite walls before reaching **Baia Sardinia,** often billed as the coast's family-friendly getaway. Prices may be slightly lower here but, aside from the Acquadream water park for kids (see page 226), there's little evidence to support this claim.

The community is centred around a predictably gorgeous beach looking out towards the La Maddalena archipelago. The area's main restaurants, hotels and shops are all found on the **Piazza**, which is designed to resemble a Mediterranean ranch-style compound. For wonderful views of the Costa Smeralda and unbeatable sunsets, head up to the **Battistoni** hill just east of the piazza.

Arzachena.

Arzachena & around

The entire Costa Smeralda lies within the territory of Arzachena, a former agricultural community settled in the 1700s by Corsican shepherds with a knack for making Vermintino wine. The town itself is a far cry from its plush coastal Mecca but a wave of tourism and prosperity has been blowing inland since the 1960s, leaving Arzachena's attractive centre suffocated by the sprawling development of retail stores and bumper-to-bumper traffic. Today, Arzachena's main appeal lies in its proud past. Five fascinating Neolithic monuments, including the two most impressive tombe di giganti in Sardinia, are clustered just outside the town, shedding light on the area's distinct 5,500-year history and culture. Nearby, the communities of Cannigione and San Pantaleo are an authentic antidote to the resorts that dot the coast: Sardo is still heard in the streets and things cost roughly what they're worth. North of Cannigione, a stretch of wind-sculpted granite rocks marks the way to Palau, gateway to the islands of La Maddalena.

Arzachena

On summer nights, when other Italian towns are getting ready for the *passeggiata*, Arzachena becomes a congested thoroughfare of commuters returning from the Costa Smeralda to more humble accommodation. Its charms are not easy to spot when you're crawling through the chaotic modern suburbs in first-gear traffic, but make your way up to Arzachena's *centro storico* and you're in for a pleasant treat.

In the middle of it all is **piazza Risorgimento**, a quaint square with a fountain and the elegant 18th-century **Santa Maria delle Neve** granite church. From here, go down via Ruzittu and turn left at via Limbara to reach the **Roccia il Fungo**, a granite rock that looks strikingly similar to a mushroom; it was used as a shelter by Neolithic tribesmen. A series of narrow lanes fan out from Arzachena's prettiest street, **via Garibaldi**, before dead-ending at 75 steps leading up to the **Chiesa di Santa Lucia**, whose panoramic views of the town and valley below make up for its lacklustre façade and bare interior.

chamber. The frontal stones of the burial chamber were added around 1400-1100 BC and form a semi-circular exedra court, which was a place of profound cult worship. Legend has it that the area's Bronze Age inhabitants would eat hallucinogenic herbs in the exedra, entering a trance-like state that lasted for five days in order to communicate with the departed; a practice known as *incubazione*.

Coddu Ecchju

T335-127 6849, legambientegallura.it.
Apr-Oct daily 0900-2000; reservations required out of season. €3, €5 including Nuraghe Albucciu or Tempietto di Malchittu (see page 207), €7.50 for all three sites.

Li Muri & Li Lolghi

West of Arzachena, T338-378 7751, anemos-arzachena.it.
1 Apr-30 Oct daily 0900-2000, reservations required out of season. €3 for each site/€5 for both.

Head west of Arzachena towards Luogosanto for 3 km and follow the signs for the megalithic necropolis of **Li Muri**. Dating from 3500 BC, the site preserves a series of stone slabs fixed vertically into the ground like knives, outlining four circular tombs and one rectangular tomb. The tombs were originally covered with a horizontal slab and marked with a menhir, thought to serve as a tombstone or to represent the symbol of a deity. Though only small fragments of human bone have been excavated, the flint blades, oval-shaped beads and other offerings recovered suggest that those buried inside these single-chamber graves were the heads of a late Neolithic tribe.

Back on the main road, a right-hand turn leads to the massive *tomba di giganti*, **Li Lolghi**. As you approach on foot, you'll see 14 upright slabs placed in ascending order of height towards a central stele, 3.75 m in diameter, with a remarkable carved border. The small hole at its base served as a symbolic door to the afterlife. Behind, a rectangular burial chamber held roughly 100 bodies. In other parts of Sardinia, tombs were accessed from behind the vault but in Arzachena's tombs, the bodies were inserted by lifting the top slabs off the rectangular

Returning on the road towards Arzachena from the previous sights, signs indicate the area's most spectacular megalithic monument, the Coddu Ecchju *tomba di giganti*, dating from 1600-1200 BC. Located in front of a lovely rolling vineyard, Coddu Ecchju's two-stone stele rises to 4.04 m, making it a shade taller than Li Lolghi's single slab, and its burial chamber behind the exedra is better preserved. Like Li Lolghi, Coddu Ecchju's exedra was the setting for obscure rituals in which locals would place their leftovers in terracotta jars and smash them on the ground to wish their recently deceased relatives luck in the afterlife: a precursor to many modern wedding traditions worldwide.

Above: Coddu Ecchju. Top left: Li Lolghi.

Nuraghe Albucciu & Tempietto di Malchittu

T335-127 6849, www.legambientegallura.it.
Apr-Oct daily 0900-2000; reservations required
out of season. €3 for each site, €5 for both, €7.50
including Coddu Ecchju.

Three kilometres east of Arzachena towards Olbia,
take a tunnel under the road to reach the
two-storey Nuraghe Albucciu. The nuraghe was
inhabited from 1400 to 900 BC and lacks the
distinctive cone-shaped design of Sardinia's usual
Bronze Age towers. Instead, it's built on a horizontal
plane around a granite mound. It is thought that
the nuraghe's maze of tight alleyways and walled
barriers was designed to confuse its invaders; you
can still walk through its cool chambers and
stairwells to its rooftop deck.

Take the footpath next to the nuraghe's car
park and follow a dirt track for 2 km to reach the
Tempietto di Malchittu, dating from the 16th
century BC. The site consists of the remains of a
stone wall, a large hut once covered in timber and
a building with a small temple. Anthropologists
remain baffled as to what exactly went on here but
it's an eerily beautiful place with fantastic views
over jagged granite ranges.

San Pantaleo

This delightful pint-sized town is best measured
from end to end in human steps; rows of squat
houses enhance its scale. Its dramatic setting at the
base of towering granite spires provides a natural
inspiration for the various sculptors, painters and
craftsmen who have descended on the village
since the 1970s, turning it into an artists' haven.

The long piazza della Chiesa is the centre of
the village, where you'll find two art galleries and
the lovely Caffé Nina (see page 224) facing the
granite Chiesa di San Pantaleo. The main draw
here is to stroll the streets, draped in oleander and
wisteria flowers, and to dip into the art galleries
sprinkled around town; among the more
interesting are at piazza della Chiesa 1, via Caprera
18 and via Azuni 2.

What the author says

When Corsican shepherds started
settling in Sardinia in the early 1700s,
they lived in isolated self-sustaining
farmhouses called *stazzi*. The owners of
neighbouring *stazzi* clubbed together
to form groups known as *cussoghjas*,
in order to help each other gather
crops or to donate their own livestock
when an animal was lost. The arrival
of the Costa Smeralda tourist boom
effectively ended the *stazzu* culture
but, in recent times, the owners of
these scattered cottages have restored
their farmhouse's traditional granite
façades and juniper roofs and converted
them into *agriturismi*. There are more
concentrated around Arzachena than
anywhere else in Sardinia.

As with most *agriturismi*, these farm
stays are usually modest affairs. Cell
phone reception is often non-existent,
televisions are rare and hot water can
be unreliable. But what *stazzi* lack in
refinement, they make up for in country
charm and rural hospitality. The owners
of most *agriturismi* genuinely want
to get to know their guests and are
passionate about sharing their own
culture, enabling visitors to experience
a local way of life that would otherwise
only be glimpsed through a car window.

I particularly recommend Ca' La
Somara (see page 219). Alberto and
Laura are an English-speaking couple
from mainland Italy who have converted
an old stable into a tranquil paradise,
complete with hammocks, a pool and
yoga by request. It's a laid-back place
where cats usually lie around inside
and a donkey keeps the property's
landscaping in check.

Eliot Stein

Cannigione

Found at the western end of the deep Golfo di Arzachena, Cannigione developed slowly as a quiet farming community that supplied La Maddalena archipelago with food in the 1800s. Its main road, via Nazionale, wasn't paved until the 1970s and wraps around a series of pleasant public beaches: among the nicest are **La Conia** (look for a restaurant on the left with the same name) and **L'Ulticeddu**, past the village of Tanca Manna. The town is a less crowded base than Palau from which to visit La Maddalena; make reservations at the very helpful bi-lingual tourist office at via Nazionale 47.

Palau

The scenic road north of Cannigione passes through a dramatic landscape of wind-moulded granite formations en route to Palau. Located a stone's skip away from the islands of La Maddalena, Palau has long served as a gateway to the archipelago, with a ferry and chartered excursions (see page 228). Yet, it is also a classic beach town, with an attractive setting cradled around warped granite boulders, and recent luxury residential development has rendered it a prosperous resort in its own right.

Palau's most famous landmark is a 122-m granite block shaped like a bear, known as the **Capo d'Orso** (5 km east of Palau, T329-604 1373, Easter-Oct daily 0900-sunset, €2, €1 concessions). Ptolemy used the promontory to help him navigate in the second century AD. From the land, you can't make out the form of a bear but a hike up to the beast's underbelly provides views across to the archipelago, especially in the morning.

Just west of town, the 19th-century **Fortezza Monte Altara** (T329-604 1373, Jun-Aug daily 0900-1200 and 1700-2000, Apr-May 0900-1200 and 1500-1800, Sep-Oct 0900-1200 and 1500-1700, €3.50) stands guard over Palau and the offshore islands from a blustery rock stack. More attractive are the eye-catching views and imaginatively built villas scattered down the hill in **Porto Rafael**, a resort village that pre-dates the Costa Smeralda.

From the small car park, head to the miniature whitewashed church and descend the stone path to a gorgeous piazza opening on to a seaside cove; it is perhaps the prettiest square in all of Sardinia.

Porto Pollo & Isola dei Gabbiani

Seven kilometres west of Palau, constant *maestrale* winds blow in throngs of watersports' lovers to the narrow isthmus separating Porto Pollo from Porto Liscia. This small point jutting out into the Strait of Bonifacio hosts the European Windsurfing Championships each summer and is scattered with outfitters offering kite surfing lessons, kayak hire, dive excursions and sailing classes for everyone from experts to complete novices. The rounded cape at the head of the isthmus is known as **Isola dei Gabbiani** (Seagull's Island) and is the location of Sardinia's most popular campsite (see page 220), which attracts far more tourists than sea birds.

Parco Nazionale dell'Arcipelago di La Maddalena

The 63 islands of the Arcipelago di La Maddalena stretch north toward Corsica and are the peaks of a land mass that once joined Sardinia with its French neighbour. When waters flooded the Strait of Bonifacio millions of years ago, winds were channelled through the strait and any granite mounds tall enough to poke their heads above water were whipped into warped contours. The result is a marine playground that outshines anything the glittery Costa Smeralda has to offer. The archipelago was made a national park and marine reserve in 1996. Of its seven major islands, only La Maddalena and Caprera are inhabited year-round but daily boat tours allow you to putter to beaches on the other islands.

The archipelago's shimmering shores and strategic location have long attracted foreign attention. The islands were the first Sardinian territory to be disputed between Pisa and Genoa and were left virtually abandoned until Corsican shepherds arrived in the mid-1600s. In 1793, a 24-year-old colonel named Napoleon Bonaparte failed to conquer La Maddalena island, thanks to the actions of its most famous native son, Domenico Millelire, who hauled his cannon from peak to peak, firing at Napoleon's troops until they retreated. Millelire was awarded the first gold medal for heroism by the future Italian navy. More recently, the archipelago's residents have fought to rid themselves of a NATO base that occupied much of the park's territory (see box, page 210).

La Maddalena

Ferries from Palau arrive at La Maddalena town, a languid place of 11,000 inhabitants, where palms hang over prosperous 18th-century homes in eggshell-colours. A column dedicated to Garibaldi stands tall in **piazza Febbraio XXIII**. Two blocks up, **piazza Garibaldi** is the location of a lively indoor morning market and of the town's **Municipio**, which houses one of Napoleon's unexploded bombs. **Via Garibaldi** is the main shopping drag and affords prime people-watching from its many cafés. **Piazza Santa Maria Maddalena** is home to the island's parish church of the same name and displays two candlesticks and a crucifix donated by Nelson in 1805 in gratitude to the island's residents.

The town's waterfront offers plenty of options to cruise the archipelago by private boat (see page 228) but consider captaining yourself along La Maddalena's **Panoramica** road instead. This 20-km route rings the island, passing a virtual sculpture garden of bizarre granite shapes and stunning beaches, so pack a snorkel! Two kilometres east of town 'Panoramica' signs lead to the **Museo Archeologico Navale** (T0789-790660, May-Sep Tue-Sun 1030-1230 and 1530-1900, Oct-Apr Tue-Sun 1030-1230, €2.50), which displays over 200 wine amphorae from a Roman cargo ship that sank in the Strait of Bonifacio in 120 BC. Soon after, you arrive at the placid (and packed) **Cala Spalmatore** at the end of a deep bay. Hooking around to the west, the larger twin beaches of **Monti d'Arena** and **Bassa Trinità** are popular with locals.

Essentials

❶ Getting around Ferries, operated by **Delcomar** (T0781-857123), **Enermar** (T0789-708484) and **Saremar** (T0789-727162), run from Palau to La Maddalena roughly three times every hour and take 20 minutes. A return trip costs €10-12 for foot passengers or €25-30 for a vehicle including passengers. On La Maddalena, buses leave from the intersection of piazza XXIII Febbraio and via Giovanni Amendola nine times a day and take the Panoramica route, stopping at each of the island's beaches; others continue to Caprera (13 times a day). Boat trips to the other islands depart from Cannigione, Palau, La Maddalena and Santa Teresa di Gallura.

Views of La Maddalena from Capo d'Orso.

Saying no to NATO

Sardinia's position at the crossroads of two continents has long been coveted for military means. While tourists are lured by postcard images of sweeping valleys and lonely shores, NATO has recognized that the island's lack of development makes it a perfect location for testing weapons. Today, Sardinia has 23 military bases, which occupy more land per square kilometre of the country than anywhere else in the world, and they are found in the most unlikely of places, including La Maddalena national park.

While the military's presence contributes over $40 million annually to Sardinia's economy through jobs and construction contracts, many Sardinians feel that these bases are the latest chapter in the island's history of outside control. It's a stormy subject on a sunny island and one that recently came to a head.

The US has had a NATO nuclear submarine base on the island of Santo Stefano since 1972. In 2003, an atomic submarine from the base hit a reef in the Strait of Bonifacio and, although no radioactive waste was leaked, this near catastrophic event, which was kept secret for days, outraged local residents and triggered Sardinia's then-regional president, Renato Soru, to strive to remove all US military bases from Sardinia.

Sardinia is effectively powerless to intervene in the national treaties that regulate the military bases but Soru's campaign to transform these garrisons into resorts accessible to Sardinians didn't go unnoticed and, in February 2008, the United States ceased its military operations in the archipelago. While an Italian military base is still active on La Maddalena, work has begun to convert the old military hospital and arsenal into hotels.

Caprera

A clanky wooden bridge connects the islands of La Maddalena and Caprera, revealing tall rows of pine trees and signs kindly asking you not to feed the wild boar. A left-hand turn at the end of the road brings you to the **Compendio Garibaldino** (T0789-727162, compendiogaribaldino.it, Tue-Sun 0900-1330 and 1600-1830, €5, €2.50 concessions), home of Italian revolutionary Giuseppe Garibaldi, until his death in 1882.

Nicknamed the 'Hero of the Two Worlds', Garibaldi dedicated his life to fighting for independence movements throughout South America and Europe. Following the fall of the Roman Republic in 1849, he fled to Caprera where he spent a month hunting from a hut. He returned to the island in 1855 to build Casa Bianca, his home away from the battlefield, before leading his 'Redshirt' army in battles across Sicily and the Italian mainland – a campaign that paved the way for Italian unification.

Today the compound is a national monument. Inside Garibaldi's rather cramped house, visitors can see his trademark red shirts and his deathbed, preserved inside a glass vault. Outside are Garibaldi's grave and an olive press.

Caprera's relative flatness and shade are in stark contrast to La Maddalena, making it a wonderful place for cycling or walking. Among numerous footpaths, the best goes up to the lookout tower at **Monte Teialone**. The island's beaches are among the most renowned in the archipelago. A right-hand turn at the fork leading to Garibaldi's house passes the **Borgo Stagnali** and continues down a dirt road to the popular **Due Mari** and **Punta Rosa** beaches but we suggest turning left at the intersection and taking a dip in the sublime **Cala Andreani**.

Other islands

The five other main islands in the archipelago (Santo Stefano, Spargi, Budelli, Razzoli, and Santa Maria) are each worth a day trip of their own. Boats leave from Cannigione, Palau, La Maddalena and Santa Teresa di Gallura, or you can hire your own craft and splash around at your own pace.

The abandoned NATO base at **Santo Stefano** remains a military zone and much of the island is off-limits, though a private resort is set on the dazzling turquoise **Spiaggia di Pesce** (visible from the ferry between Palau and La Maddalena).

Most excursions stop at **Spargi** and, if you have your own boat, you'll want to spend as much time here as possible, since the deep inlet at the south of the island, **Cala Corsara**, is among the most photogenic spots in the archipelago.

The deserted islands of **Budelli** and **Razzoli** are marked by prickly *macchia*, fierce *maestrale* winds and rough bathing spots, with the lone exception of Budelli's **Spiaggia Rosa**. Named after its pinkish sand, the beach is among the most famous in the Mediterranean but, alas, has become a victim of its own beauty and has been off-limits to the public since 1999 because tourists started stealing the sand.

The needle-thin **Passo degli Asinelli** threads between Razzoli and **Santa Maria**, whose **Cala Santa Maria** is a must-visit.

Northwest coast

Around the popular resort of Santa Teresa, nature has whipped Sardinia's northernmost point into a contorted jungle-gym of grey stepping stones, creating some of the best walking trails on the island in the process. This coast looks across the Strait of Bonifacio to southern Corsica, just 12 km away, so it's no surprise that much of Gallura's population and dialect are rooted in a shared history with its near French neighbour.

Santa Teresa di Gallura

Each summer, the modest 4000-strong population of Santa Teresa swells to 50,000 as vacationers descend on its attractive pistachio-coloured centre overlooking the sea. The town was founded in 1808 by Vittorio Emanuele I, who designed it as a 'small Torino', but, aside from Santa Teresa's right-angled intersections, it bears no resemblance to its Piemontese model. Much of Santa Teresa's present character sprang up in the 1960s during Gallura's tourist boom and its economy still revolves around the summer surge, with most hotels and restaurants only open from Easter to mid October.

The town's hub is the enormous **piazza Vittorio Emanuele I**, whose tourist shops and gelateria pulse with energy on warm nights. The streets surrounding the piazza offer some great shopping, and are an especially fine place to buy local red-coral jewellery. Nearby, the massive **Torre Longosardo** was built by the Aragonese in the 16th century as a lookout but now only guards **Rena Bianca** beach directly below, whose setting, hemmed in by coarse granite, makes it one of Gallura's finest. If you do nothing else in Santa Teresa, take the stone path from the right of the beach, which winds through a rocky wonderland covered in wildflowers each spring to a lonely headland with views toward Corsica's white limestone bluffs. One kilometre east of the centre

What the author says

From Santa Teresa, follow the brown signs along via Capo Testa on foot or drive 1.5 km west along the same route and park at the small car park in front of a wooden 'Ente Foreste' sign. From the car park, a path descends through wildflowers and offers views of the coast (bring a camera) before reaching the sandbar isthmus that separates Capo Testa from Santa Teresa.

Climbing up the hill, look for the brown 'Colonne Romane' sign that leads to shallow Spiaggia Levante. From the shore, a stumpy column to the far left marks the Roman quarry where granite was extracted to build the columns on Rome's Pantheon. Snoop around these rocky building blocks and you'll find a few more Roman remains, particularly on the highest promontory.

Continue up the cape, because Capo Testa saves its best for last: a lighthouse built above a granite 'playground' that plunges into the crystal-clear sea. The area is ideal for scrambling and from the top of the granite piles, Corsica looks close enough to touch. If you show up at dusk, consider buying a bottle of wine from the make-shift snack bar in the car park, finding a free rock and watching the best sunset in Gallura.

Eliot Stein

is Santa Teresa's lovely tourist port, with its arching wooden bridge, from where ferries to Bonifacio and summer excursions to French islands in the Strait depart (see page 228).

Capo Testa

Of all the wind-whipped rocks strewn about Gallura, the crowning glory is arguably Capo Testa, 3 km west of Santa Teresa, where the *maestrale* winds have chiselled the entire cape into something resembling a cross between a Henry Moore sculpture and a Dr Seuss picture. One of the more pleasant walks you can take in Sardinia is the 3.5-km trail from Santa Teresa to Capo Testa (see box), especially in the springtime when the *macchia* turns into a sea of wildflowers (in summer, bring water and your own shade). If you can't get enough granite, head between Santa Teresa and Capo Testa to the beach at **Baia Santa Reparata**.

West of Capo Testa

The coast west of Capo Testa is largely undeveloped. A strand of tall pines marks the *comune* of Aglientu, whose attractive **Rena Majore** beach is less crowded than those closer to Santa Teresa. From the beach car park, you can walk a scenic dirt trail for 7 km along the coast to the sleepy resort community of **Vignola Mare**, named after its Vermintino vineyards. Alternatively, the road between Rena Majore and Vignola Mare passes three more beaches found at the end of dirt roads (the bumpier the road, the better the beach) before turning inland towards a series of private holiday villas called the **Costa Paradiso**.

The ocean reveals itself again as you approach **Isola Rossa**, where crags shelter a tourist harbour and beach below a 16th-century Aragonese tower. This fishing town was founded by Neapolitan immigrants in the early 20th century and gets its name from the cluster of rocks visible offshore. To escape the crowds, head west to the 10-km patch of deserted sand dunes at **Badesi Mare**, where the surfcasting is said to be among Italy's best.

Spiaggia Levante.

Capo Testa.

Unlike Gallura's coastal resorts, change has been slow to penetrate the mountainous spurs that characterize its interior. The towns dotting these pinnacles are little affected by tourism and proudly retain Gallura's unique character, as handicrafts, not holidays, continue to drive the economy. Where granite permits, the countryside is awash in burgundy from the stripped oak trees of Italy's cork capital, and myrtle, cistus and juniper herbs lend their colours to Aggius' hand-woven rugs.

Tempio Pausania

The heart of Gallura and co-capital of the Tempio-Olbia province, Tempio Pausania was little more than a place to change horses on the road to Olbia in Roman times. It first gained significance after Gallura's coastal population fled inland to escape Barbaric raids following the collapse of

Rome. When malaria decimated Olbia in the 1600s, Tempio became Gallura's capital for the next 200 years, only to see most of the regional authority gravitate back to Olbia in succeeding decades. Tempio's low-key profile has spared it from the sprawling growth that has affected its seaside counterparts and, like many inland towns in Gallura, it preserves a venerable granite *centro storico* similar to many Corsican villages.

Tempio's main promenade begins along **corso Matteotti**, where rows of cafés and designer stores entice pedestrian shoppers. A right turn at **piazza Italia** leads to **via Roma**; pop in to the shop at No 36 to see the world's only dresses made from cork (see page 228). The town's centrepiece is **piazza San Pietro**, where three churches are jumbled together in a cluster of granite and form the focal point of Tempio's poignant Holy Week celebrations. The most famous is the 15th-century **Cattedrale di San Pietro**, which has two wooden Baroque altars inside.

Aggius.

Past the stately **piazza Gallura** and *municipio* building on via Nino Visconti is the **Casa Nino di Gallura**, home to the last ruler of the Giudicato of Gallura (1275-1298), Nino Visconti. (Visconti was placed in Purgatory along with other careless leaders in Dante's *Divine Comedy*.)

Just north of town, you might spot locals filling up water jugs at the trickling **Fonti di Rinaggiu**, which is renowned for its therapeutic qualities. Far more impressive, however, is the **Fonte Nuovo**, set at the end of a park built by prisoners with views towards the dramatic peaks of the Valle della Luna.

Aggius & the Valle della Luna

Six kilometres northwest of Tempio, the delightful village of Aggius enjoys a spectacular setting at the base of serrated granite massifs where bandits used to hide. These days it's famous for being one of the last towns in Gallura where women still hand-weave wool rugs on a loom, a tradition that's fervently displayed throughout the town's warren of grey stone streets. To witness the weaving process and buy a rug, visit **ISOLA** (via Criasgi,

T079-620299, Mon-Sat 0900-1230 and 1500-1930) and **L'Albero Padre** (via De Cupis 11, T079-620196, Mon-Sat 0900-2100), where a family of women and girls weave the town's traditional designs.

Aggius is also home to Sardinia's largest **Museo Etnografico** (via Monti di Lizu 6, T079-621029, museomeoc.com, mid May-mid Oct daily 1000-1300 and 1500-2030, mid Oct-mid May Tue-Sun 1000-1300 and 1530-1900, €4). Set inside a former *stazzu* (traditional *Gallurese* farmhouse), the fascinating museum displays regional clothing and agricultural tools, as well as an exhibit showing how various local herbs and berries are soaked in a cauldron for a month to create the vibrant colours used in the town's rugs.

North of Aggius' centre, past the picturesque pond and walking trails at **Santa Degna**, is the **Valle della Luna**, where nature has strewn colossal boulders to create an otherworldly lunar landscape; to explore, follow the **Panoramica** route by bike or on foot.

Calangianus & around

You'd never guess it from Calangianus' austere exterior but this humble town is Italy's cork capital; its wooded surroundings produce 90 per cent of the stoppers used in the country's wine bottles.

Cork is thought to have been harvested in Sardinia since Neolithic times and today it is produced in every region except Oristano. When the island's summer humidity kicks in, the bark of a cork oak tree loosens, allowing trained craftsmen to extract it with a hatchet. (By law, this process can only take place between 15th May and 15th August.) After nine or ten years, the stripped cork will have grown back and is ripe for harvesting again. Much of the cork is sold in its raw state and is used as serving trays for *antipasti* meats; cork for bottle-stoppers and souvenirs is boiled to render it more elastic. **Arte Sughero** in Calangianus has a good selection (see page 228).

Between Calangianus and nearby Luras, you'll see mountains of cork bark lying piled high as it awaits shipment. **Luras** itself is an attractive town with a fine ethnographic museum, **Museo Galluras** (via Nazionale 35, T079-647281, galluras.it, daily by request – phone in advance, €5, €2.50 children) and four dolmen graves scattered around its outskirts: the easiest to find is **Alzoledda**, while the most impressive is **Ladas** (follow the brown signs from Luras' centre).

For something extraordinary, follow signs from Luras to **Olivastri Millenari** (14 km northeast, T368-337 6321, Easter-Oct daily 0900-1900, €2) to see the oldest tree in Europe. Take a dirt road uphill towards **Lago di Liscia** until you reach a hut and three olive trees in a field. The youngest, a mere 550-year-old stripling is really just coming into its own; another is 2,000 years' old, while the third is (wait for it…) between 3,800 and 4,000-years-old and has a trunk measuring 11 m in circumference!

The view towards Monte Limbara.

Berchidda

South of Monte Limbara on the main road towards Olbia, Berchidda is best known for its Vermintino wine, which can be sampled at the **Museo del Vino** (via Grazia Deledda 151, T079-704587, museodelvino.net, Apr-Oct Tue-Fri 0900-1300 and 1500-1800, Nov-Mar Tue-Fri 1000-1400 and 1600-1900, Sat-Sun 1000-1400 and 1600-1900, €3). It's also the birthplace of Sardinia's most famous musician, trumpeter Paolo Fresu, who hosts the international Time in Jazz festival in the area every August (see page 49).

Monte Limbara & Lago Coghinas

One of the most rewarding outdoor excursions in this area is a day trip to the province's tallest mountain, Monte Limbara, and its largest lake, Lago Coghinas, a jaunt which can be tailored to suit the sporty and the indolent alike.

Travelling south of Tempio towards Oschiri, Monte Limbara's base reveals itself under tall pines. There are many ways to ascend to the mountain's summit, **Punta Balistreri** (1359 m), which is occupied by RAI satellite antennae. The most demanding option is to turn left at the Coradureddu sign, 7 km from Tempio, then trek along a dirt path up to **Vallicciola**, roughly 6 km away, before taking a paved road to the mountain's peak. The climb, from top to bottom takes roughly four hours, though the first part is a bit of a scramble. Less strenuous is to wind up to the mountain's peak by car: just past Coradureddu, look for a brown sign indicating **Vallicciola**. A third alternative is to park at Vallicciola and continue on foot to the top (1½ hours).

However you arrive, Punta Balistreri is a magical place, with sweeping views of the whole of Gallura. A few benches create a shady spot for a picnic, and there's even a small church, the **Madonna della Neve**. Don't descend without taking the stone path to the **Punto Panoramico**, where a statue of the Madonna holds the infant Jesus up to see the vista out to La Maddalena archipelago and Corsica.

Once you've regained your vehicle, continue towards Oschiri. After a stomach-churning drive through the **Passo della Limbara**, the shimmering **Lago di Coghinas** appears. You'll soon arrive at a bridge where the wonderful agriturismo **La Villa del Lago Coghinas** is located (see page 221). Drop your bags and take a dip in the outdoor pool, play a game of football, ping-pong or mini-golf, or, better yet, let Signora Caterina and her charming family organize a kayak or canoe trip on the lake for you. After a full dinner, loosen your belt and star-gaze from the terrace of your room: a modern *tholos*-style nuraghe built steps from the lake.

Sleeping

Olbia & around

Gabbiano Azzurro €€€€
Via dei Gabbiani, Golfo Aranci, T0789-46930, hotelgabbianoazzurro.com. May-Oct only.
Overlooking the striking Spiaggia Terza, this modern resort has fantastic views from its cheery pink rooms and from the poolside terrace. The hotel runs sailing and scuba lessons and organizes horse-riding excursions.

Hotel Cavour €€
Via Cavour 22, Olbia, T0789-204033, cavourhotel.it.
If you can get past the wafting perfume as you enter, this friendly, centrally located hotel will keep you perfectly happy for a few days. The recently renovated rooms are all well insulated, refreshingly quiet and done up in soft colours.

Janas €
Via Lamarmora 61, Olbia, T339-109 2836, janasaffittacamere.com.
This charming B&B is tucked into Olbia's *centro storico* in an early 1900s home. Three rooms, two sharing a bathroom and each with air-con, look out onto a pleasant garden with lemon and orange trees.

South of Olbia

Hotel L'Esagono €€€
Via Cala d'Ambra 141, San Teodoro, T0784-865783, hotelesagono.com. May-Sep only.
Set around a lush tropical garden steps away from Cala d'Ambra beach, L'Esagono's rooms are spacious and full of character. The nearby summer disco is a perfect fit for those young at heart, but a drawback for those who like to sleep early.

Hotel Bonsai €€
Via Golfo Aranci, San Teodoro, T0784-865061, hotelbonsai.com.
There are no bonsai trees on hand here but the hotel does have a nice garden, a heated pool, Turkish baths and comfortable, if minimal, tile-floor rooms with good air conditioning. It's a short walk from San Teodoro's nightlife.

Campsites
La Cinta
Via del Tirreno, San Teodoro, T0784-865777, campingsanteodoro.com. May-mid Oct only.
Found steps away from La Cinta beach, this shady campsite has a modest market, five stone bungalows and is well suited to those who don't demand much in the way of comfort on a shoestring budget.

Costa Smeralda & around

Some of the plushest resort hotels on this coast (Cala di Volpe, La Bisaccia, Pitrizza, Romazzino and Sporting) are regularly listed among the world's best, with rooms that can top €2,000 per night in high season. For details see starwoodhotels.com, hotellabisaccia.it and sportingportorotondo.it.

Residence Rena Bianca €€€
Località Baia Sardinia, T0789-950060, renabianca.com. Apr-Oct only.
These pastel-coloured villas sprinkle the hillside 100 m from the beach, forming a miniature resort community with its own central square. The management organizes numerous coastal excursions including diving trips.

San Marco €€€
Piazzetta San Marco, Porto Rotondo, T0789-34110, hotelcolonnasanmarco.it. Jun-Sep.
Situated in the middle of the resort, this hotel has beautifully manicured gardens with a waterfall, luxurious rooms (some with seaside views), a pool with whirlpool spa, and a fabulous restaurant.

Hotel Baja €€

Via Nazionale, Cannigione,
T0789-892041, hotelbaja.it.
Cannigione's newest and most
luxurious hotel has the feeling of
a Costa Smeralda resort without
the heavy-handed price tag.
There's a separate palm and
rooftop garden, an outdoor pool
and a beauty spa.

Ca' La Somara €

Località Sarra Balestra,
T0789-98969, calasomara.it.
Nestled in a pasture between
Arzachena and San Pantaleo is a
converted stable with 12 rooms.
Inside, the large hearth,
tapestries and cacti give it a
vague feel of the American
southwest. The English-speaking
owners serve hearty mainland
Italian dishes. Burn off each meal
with a dip in the pool, or ask
about walking excursions.

La Quercia €

8 km west of Arzachena towards
Luogosanto, T079-652302,
turismolaquercia.it.
Even if you don't spend the
night, call ahead and book a
meal at this out-of-the-way rustic
spot. It's run by a young couple
who cook up *Gallurese* favourites
fused with recipes from their
native Iglesiente. The results are
so delicious and abundant, you'll
want to book one of the modest
rooms and pass out.

Rena €

Località Rena, 3 km north of
Arzachena, T0789-82532,
agriturismorena.it.
This *agriturismo* is located in a
converted *stazzu*, owned by the
English-speaking Ruzittu family.
Juniper beams preside over a
fireplace and wooden rooms
have views out to fields with cork
and olive trees. Purchase farm
honey and ham, and don't miss
the bountiful dinner!

S'Olias €

Località Ancioggiu, Cannigione,
T0789-88303, solias.it.
This revamped granite
stazzu-style house is set in a
large pasture dotted with olive
trees and feels a lot more like
an *agriturismo* than a hotel.
The 10 rooms each have air
conditioning, comfy beds and
terraces leading out to the green
surroundings. Dinners are served
in a stone dining room.

Tenuta Pilastru €
Località Pilastru, 5 km west of Arzachena, T0789-82936, tenutapilastru.it.
Thirty-two *stazzu*-style cottages are sprinkled throughout a granite wonderland bordered by livestock pastures at this impressive *agriturismo*. Each room has satellite TV and air conditioning. The wines are home-produced and the *zuppa gallurese* is sensational.

Campsites

Campeggio Isola dei Gabbiani
Località Isola dei Gabbiani, T0789-704019, isoladeigabbiani.it.
Mid Mar-Oct only.
Occupying the entire 18-ha island, this site is a village unto itself with bars, a disco, restaurant and its own windsurfing school. Your best bet is to stay in one of the wind-resistant bungalows.

Capo d'Orso
Località Golfo delle Saline, Palau, T0789-702007, capodorso.it.
Jun-Sep only.
This camping village has bungalows and cottages, as well as spaces for camper vans and tents. The site is found directly on the placid Golfo delle Saline beach and boasts its own dive centre, football and tennis courts.

Golfo di Arzachena
Main road between Arzachena and Cannigione, T0789-88101, campingarzachena.com.
Mar-Oct only.
You won't find a cheaper deal this close to the Costa Smeralda. The campsite's large pool, air-conditioned apartments, games room and pizzeria make for a pleasant stay surrounded by world-class luxury.

Parco Nazionale dell'Arcipelago di La Maddalena

Cala Lunga €€€
Località Porto Massimo, La Maddalena, T0789-794001, hotelcalalunga.com.
Jun-Sep only.
Found 15 minutes from town among La Maddalena's poshest resorts. The 74 rooms are modern with a seaside view. Relax in the pool, rent scuba gear and scooters, or tour the coast from the resort's own port.

Miralonga €€
Via Don Vico, La Maddalena, T0789-722563, miralonga.it.
This modern-looking cream hotel is set just off the Strada Panoramica. The functional rooms have balconies facing an attractive bay. A decent restaurant serves good seafood next to the hotel's square swimming pool. The diving centre by the shore is a plus.

Sa Bertula €€
Via Indipendenza, La Maddalena, T0789-727425, sabertula.com.
Colourfully painted *murales* enliven the atmosphere of this country-style B&B. The three rooms each have en suite facilities and air conditioning.

Hotel Corallaro €€€
Rena Bianca, Santa Teresa di Gallura, T0789-755431, hotelcorallaro.it.
May-Sep only.
You won't get any closer to the beach than in this complex overlooking Corsica. Private boat excursions, an indoor and outdoor pool, satellite televisions and a Turkish bath make this Santa Teresa's most chi-chi option. Most rooms have balconies and those facing the sea have top-notch views.

Hotel Moderno €€
Via Umberto 39, Santa Teresa di Gallura, T0789-754233, modernoweb.it.
Apr-Sep.
This *centralissimo* hotel is run by a charming woman from Genoa. The top rooms have their own balcony offering wonderful rooftop views across town. The decor throughout has an attractive traditional motif with classic Sardinian animal designs in lively colours.

L'Agnata €€
Località l'Agnata, between Tempio Pausania and Oschiri, T079-671384, agnata.it.
In the middle of a 6.5 km road leading nowhere is Sardinia's most famous and luxurious *agriturismo*, created by the Italian

singer, Fabrizio de André, in 1973. Grapes dangle above as you approach the getaway's ivy-covered centrepiece: an elliptical pool ringed by granite rocks. Around it are the cosy rooms, each with balconies and oak chests. There's no working farm here but there are enough cats to convey a rural feeling, and the exquisite cuisine is a sophisticated arrangement of *Gallurese* delicacies.

Petit Hotel €€
Piazza De Gasperi 9/11, Tempio Pausania, T079-631134, petit-hotel.it.
This hotel's austere exterior belies its warm furnishings. Inside, French doors and wooden trimmings abound and the rooms are quite spacious, with dramatic views from the back toward Aggius' granite mountains.

Il Muto di Gallura €
Località Fraiga, 1 km from Aggius, T079-620559, mutodigallura.com.

Named after a famous bandit, this *agriturismo* remains a working *stazzu* where donkeys, sheep and cows are bred to make the farm self-sufficient. There's an outdoor pool and horseriding is available, or you can try your luck hunting quail or wild boar. Rooms have modern conveniences and dinners come with home-produced wine.

La Villa del Lago Coghinas €
Località Mandras, Oschiri, T338-7145131, riturismovilladellagocoghinas.it.
This charming *agriturismo* on the shores of Lake Coghinas is an outdoor lover's paradise. Bring your own gear and fish in the lake, bike through the mountains or trek around the hillsides. The farmhouse has an outdoor pool, ping-pong, mini-golf, football, and can organize excursions around the lake by boat. At dinner, Signora Caterina prepares *malloreddus*, kid or suckling pig.

Eating & drinking

Olbia & around

Gallura €€€€
*Corso Umberto 145, Olbia,
T0789-24648.*
Tue-Sun 2000-2230.
One of Sardinia's, if not Italy's,
best restaurants. Owner and
head chef Rita Denza has been
cooking *Gallurese* specialities
since the 1940s and adds a
unique creativity to traditional
classics. Her pasta dishes with
sage and saffron are
extraordinary, and she
recommends that her diners
choose their *secondi* based on
the seasons: mussels or goat with
olives in summer, Gallura's
famous *mazzafrissa* (semolina
pasta with cream) in autumn,
and lamb during the winter.

Miramare €€€€
*Piazza del Porto 2, Golfo Aranci,
T0789-46085.*
Sat-Thu 1930-2300.
Located smack bang on the port,
this was the first restaurant in
town and still serves the area's
best seafood nearly 100 years
later. Sit under the veranda to
taste the always-good mussels
filled with mortadella, or the
subtle octopus, and ask for the
house Vermintino wine.

Da Bartolo €€€
*Via Aldo Moro 133, Olbia,
T0789-51348.*
**May-Oct daily 1930-2230,
Nov-Apr Mon-Sat 1930-2230.**
Located inside the Stella 2000
hotel, Da Bartolo is well
respected for its fresh fish

courses. Call ahead for the spicy
lobster *a la catalana*, or show up
and try the more subtle
spaghetti with sea urchin.

La Lanterna €€
Via Olbia 13, Olbia, T0789-23082.
**May-Oct daily 1930-2230,
Nov-Apr Thu-Tue 1930-2230.**
Set in one of Olbia's quaint
narrow alleys, La Lanterna serves
up enormous steaks, tasty pizzas
and beautifully presented
seafood . The *baccalà* is
especially good, as are the
lemon-scented ravioli stuffed
with ricotta.

Cafés & bars
Café Mary
*Piazza Regina Margherita 10,
Olbia, T0789-608005.*
Daily 0700-0200.
A popular people-watching spot
at the corner of Olbia's
passeggiata thoroughfare.

South of Olbia

Da Tonino €€€
*Località Isola Tavolara,
T0789-58570.*
Easter-Oct daily 1100-2200.
Tavolara's king, Tonino, runs this
pricey but yummy seafood
restaurant on Spalmatore beach;
his sister runs the island's other
restaurant. Go for the novelty,
but stay for the seaside views,
fresh clams and well-cooked fish.

Il Covo €€€
Località Puntaldia, 8 km north of San Teodoro, T0784-863043.
Apr-Sep daily 1900-2400.
Head here for a break from San Teodoro's string of pizzerias and sample the area's best seafood. The lobster and clams are both tasty.

Cafés & bars
Café Florian
Via Sardegna 5, San Teodoro.
Tue-Sun 0800-0200.
Serves salads, bruschetta, cocktails and gelato in an art nouveau setting.

Costa Smeralda & around

Lu Stazzu €€€€
Località Monte Ladu, Porto Rotondo, T0789-34837.
Easter-Oct daily 1930-2300.
Porto Rotondo's best restaurant is located about 1 km outside the centre in a converted *stazzu*. Sit back as waiters serve you with trays of traditional Sardinian cuisine. Fixed menu €40.

Ristorante Yacht Club €€€€
Via della Marina, Porto Cervo, T0789-902200.
May-Sep only.
People take themselves pretty seriously here. Dine outdoors facing some of the largest yachts you've ever seen while peering over at their owners next to you. The seafood cuisine is delicious and outrageously expensive.

Ristorante Pomodoro €€€
Piazza Cervo, Porto Cervo, T0789-931626.
Mon-Fri 1900-2300.
Pizzas from €10, tasty shellfish, good local cheeses and romantic outdoor seating add up to the best-value dining on the Costa Smeralda.

Cafés & bars
Pina Colada Bar
Portico Sottopiazza, Porto Cervo.
Jun-early Sep daily 1100-2400.
Porto Cervo's discount bar-café keeps plenty of wine on ice and has €5 panini.

Arzachena & around

Agriturismo La Colti €€€
Between Arzachena and Cannigione, T0789-88440.
Apr-early Nov daily, dinner only, reservations essential.

This converted granite *stazzu* sits on an enormous 120-ha lot among rolling hills. Inside, the beautifully displayed agricultural tools are reminiscent of an ethnographic museum. Dine on typical *Gallurese suppa cuata* (Gallura's version of lasagne, made with pecorino, broth and bread), *mazzafrissa* (semolina pasta with cream) and the award-winning pigs and cows that are bred outside. Fixed menu €30.

Da Franco €€€
Via Capo d'Orso 1, Palau, T0789-709558.
Tue-Sun 1230-1430 and 1900-2330.
Palau's best restaurant was opened in 1961 by Salvatore Malu; his grandson, Alessandro, now carries on the family tradition. This elegant establishment has Murano lamps

and stiff tablecloths to accompany the fresh fish bought daily from the market. The prawns in a ginger cream are excellent, as is the *zuppa arcipelago*: a soup of fish and shellfish.

La Vecchia Arzachena €€€
Via Garibaldi 15b, Arzachena, T0789-83105.
Mon-Sat 1230-1500 and 1900-2300, Sun 1900-2300.
This attractive restaurant's two rooms are awash with opulent ceiling murals under which waiters flit back and forth efficiently. Choose from seafood or meat dishes, among which the tagliatelle in a tomato sauce is delicious. Regulars recommend the fish of the day.

Ristorante del Porto €€€
Via Nazionale 94, Cannigione, T0789-88011.
Easter-Oct daily 1300-1530 and 2000-2200.
Inside the hotel of the same name, this restaurant has been in the same hands for over 50 years and is a Cannigione staple. A fine wine list complements well-prepared seafood dishes, such as local lobster and sea urchins, prepared by Bartolomeo and Bastiana.

Cafés & bars
Caffè Nina
Piazzetta San Pantaleo, San Pantaleo, T338-368 7288.
May-Oct daily 0900-0230.
This cutesy café in the middle of the town's art scene has pleasant outdoor seating facing the granite church.

Parco Nazionale dell'Arcipelago di La Maddalena

Perla Blu €€€
Piazza Barone des Geneys, La Maddalena, T0789-735373.
Wed-Mon 1230-1500 and 1930-2230.
The restaurant's terrace seating overlooks La Maddalena's port and is conveniently located next to the tourist office. Locals slurp up mussels and pick their fish bones dry. Try the ravioli stuffed with fish and pesto.

Garibaldi €€
800 m after bridge, Caprera, T0789-727449.
Lunch and dinner by reservation. This *agriturismo* is surrounded by potted flowers and run by a couple from Nuoro who make

their own pecorino and ricotta cheeses from the farm's sheep. Come hungry and prepare to eat a four-course meal topped off with a shot of homemade *mirto*. (€23 lunch, €30 dinner).

Northwest coast

Riva €€€€
Via del Porto 29, Santa Teresa di Gallura, T347-294 8196.
Easter-Oct Thu-Tue 1930-2330. Owner Vittorio Riva is among Santa Teresa's most highly-regarded seafood connoisseurs. Inside the warm, yellow restaurant, try the spaghetti with crab meat, the spicy lobster, or the mussels with saffron.

Il Grottino €€€
Via del Mare 14, Santa Teresa di Gallura, T0789-754232.
Easter-Sep daily 1200-1530 and 1900-2330, Oct-Easter Fri-Wed 1200-1530 and 1900-2330. This small restaurant tucked down towards Rena Bianca has been growing in popularity for the past few years. Choose from fresh fish, meat or delicious pizza from a wood-burning oven. The mussel soup and grilled lamb are both good choices.

Cafés & bars
Caffè Conti
Piazza Vittorio Emanuele I, Santa Teresa di Gallura, T0789-754271.
Thu-Tue 0800-0230. Cosy wooden interior with cool outdoor seating that's great for

people-watching. Happy hour (1900-2100) has yummy freebies.

Mediterraneo Caffè
Via Amsicora 7, Santa Teresa di Gallura, T0789-759014.
Daily 0730-0230. Two art deco-styled floors house the largest bar in town. In the summer, the open-air veranda is a welcome respite from the heat.

Interior Gallura

Il Purgatorio €€€
Via Garibaldi 9, Tempio Pausania, T079-634042.
Wed-Mon 1900-2230. A relative newcomer to Tempio, this restaurant is run by the town's well-respected *pasticceria* owner, Francesca Suelzu. Inside,

wooden floors and granite walls add a touch of class to the delicious servings of mushrooms, *bottarga* and boar prosciutto served with pecorino cheese (by advance request).

Bisson €€
Via San Luca 18, Tempio Pausania, T079-632876.
Mon-Sat 2000-2300. Chef Pina Bisson tends to change her menu by the week, but usually carries sausage-based antipasti, ravioli with ricotta and a hint of lemon, and calamari. The restaurant also has a good selection of local wines from the Cantina Sociale di Tempio.

Entertainment

Olbia & around

Cinema
Cinema Olbia
Via delle Terme 2, Olbia,
T0789-82773.
Two screens with evening shows, right off the town's main drag.

Clubs
Capricorno Club
Via Catello Piro 2, T0789-24700.
Tue-Thu 2100-0100, Fri-Sun 2100-0400.
Central Olbia's only happening nightspot is this disco/bar, which plays anything from house to pop. Good cocktail selection.

Festivals & events
During July and August, Olbia hosts **L'Estate Olbiense**, with concerts and films in piazza Margherita.

South of Olbia

Clubs
Bal Harbour
Via Stintino, San Teodoro,
T0784-851052.
May-Sep Fri-Sun 2000-0400.
This fashionable beachside restaurant and bar heats up at night when a swarm of well-dressed hipsters descends on its outdoor pool.

Jamila
Via del Tirreno, San Teodoro,
T339-251 2549.
May-Sep Fri-Sun 2200-0400.
San Teodoro's most central disco is one of its most popular. Plop down on comfy red beds or dance the night away in this Arab-looking fantasy world.

Festivals & events
Isola Tavolara hosts a week-long film festival (cinematavolara.it) in mid to late July, at which Italian-language films are projected onto a giant outdoor screen by the beach.

Costa Smeralda & around

Children
Aquadream
Località Baia Sardinia,
T0789-99511.
Mid June-mid Sep daily 1030-1900, €18, €12 children.
Never mind the pamphlet showing a woman in a thong being hosed down, this water park is actually geared towards children and has plenty of slides, pools and games to keep kiddies busy for a day.

Shopping

Clubs

Billionaire
Località Alto Pevero,
T0789-94192.
Jun-Sep daily 0000-0500.
As decadent as the name
suggests, this is Costa Smeralda's
plushest club. €30 gets you in
with a drink… if the bouncers
think you have what it takes.
Splurge on a Methuselah of
Cristal champagne for €35,000.

Phi Beach
Località Baia Sardinia,
T320-488 5180.
Jun-Sep daily noon-0300.
An outdoor lounge with free
music and dancing… although a
Coke costs €10.

Sopravento
Località Abbiadori, T0789-94717.
Jun-Sep daily 2300-0500.
More of a rave-style club than
Billionaire, with a mixed crowd.

Sottovento
Località Abbiadori, T0789-92443.
Jun-Sep daily 2300-0500.
Across the street from
Sopravento, this older, more
famous disco has a more
intimate and typically Italian vibe.

Festivals & events

The **Offshore Grand Prix** is an
annual sailing competition
based in Porto Cervo in April.
Each June, racing cars descend
on Porto Cervo's sandy paths for
a leg of the **Italian Rally
Championship**.

Parco Nazionale dell'Arcipelago di La Maddalena

Festivals & events
On 22 July La Maddalena's
residents parade through the
streets to celebrate their patron
saint, followed by music and
plenty of food for all.

Interior Gallura

Festivals & events
The character 'Giorgio', who
represents a different political
leader each year, is honoured as
the king of Tempio Pausania
during **Carnival** (31 Jan-5 Feb).
He is burned on Shrove Tuesday
to make way for the new king the
following year. On **Good Friday**,
the town's confraternity
members don hoods and parade
the streets carrying massive
crucifixes. At the end of July,
Tempio hosts international folk
groups for the annual **Festa
Internazionale del Folklore**.

Shopping

Costa Smeralda
There's plenty of high-end
shopping to do in and around
the Costa Smeralda. Your best
bet is along **Porto Cervo**'s
pedestrian *Passeggiata*.

Arzachena & around

Clothing & accessories
In Gyru
Via Caprera 18, San Pantaleo,
T338-432 2944.
**May-Oct daily 0930-1300 and
1700-2330.**
Sells handmade women's
dresses, sarongs and jewellery.

Northwest coast

Clothing & accessories
La Corallina
*Via XX Settembre 4, Santa Teresa
di Gallura, T0789-754364.*
**May-mid Oct daily 0930-1300
and 1600-2000.**
This place has the best selection
of jewellery made from the local
coral that is gathered offshore.

Food & drink
La Bottega
*Via XX Settembre 5, Santa Teresa
di Gallura, T0789-754216.*
**May-mid Oct daily 0830-1300
and 1430-2300.**
Displays products from
throughout the island: tuna from
Carloforte, *bottarga* from Cabras,
plus typical wine, cheese and
spices.

For hand-woven rugs, visit **Aggius** (see page 214).

Clothing & accessories
Atelier Anna Grindi
Via Roma 34-36, Tempio Pausania, T079-631864.
Mon-Sat 0900-1200 and 1630-2000.
This imaginative designer makes dresses entirely from cork! Outfits range from €800 to €1600 and are fully washable. Also cork belts, travel bags and jewellery.

Food & drink
Pasticceria Luigi Carta
Piazza Italia 1, Tempio Pausania, T079-632974.
Mon 0900-1230, Tue-Sun 0900-1230 and 1630-2030.
A mouth-watering assortment of handmade cakes, cookies and gelato await you in this culinary tribute to Sardinian sweets.

Souvenirs
Arte Sughero di Sandra Cossu
Via Tempio 19, Calangianus, T079-660505.
Mon-Sat 0900-1300 and 1600-2000.
A collection of trays, jars, moulded *nuraghi* and other creative designs made from cork.

Activities & tours

Boat trips
Chartered excursions from Palau around La Maddalena archipelago cost €35 with lunch included but they're packed with over 100 people aboard. For more breathing room, consider paying a bit more and hopping on the **Rumbera** (Porto di Palau, T348-006 2569, rumberacharter.com), a 13-m yacht that caters for a maximum of 14 people (€70-85 per person). Lunch and wine are served on board and frequent stops allow you to swim around the island's beaches.

Santa Teresa also offers numerous cruises around the archipelago and to Corsica; for details, visit the two tour companies at the corner of piazza Vittorio Emanuele I and via XX Settembre.

Diving
Porto San Paolo Diving Center
Via Nenni 14, Porto San Paolo, T0789-40414, portospaolodiving.it.
This is the best of the town's numerous scuba outfits. Most dive trips visit the waters between Tavolara and Molara. Classes are available and gear can be rented. Non-certified divers can rent snorkel gear for just €15.

Horse riding
Sardigna Equitours
Località Schifoni, San Teodoro, T329-414 8015, sardignaequitors.it.
Located between San Teodoro and Budoni, this stable organizes two and three-hour excursions into the mountains west of San Teodoro for views of the offshore islands and coast.

Transport

Sporting Club Sardinia
Località Porto Pollo, T0789-704016, portopollo.it.
Mid Mar-mid Sep only.
This all-inclusive outfitter is your best bet of the three on the isthmus, offering diving, sailing, kitesurfing and windsurfing classes, plus laid-back boat excursions. The group also rents out bikes and mopeds and holds yoga classes. The California-style beach bar comes alive at night for music and dancing.

Well-being
Hotel Baja
Via Nazionale, Cannigione, T0789-892041, hotelbaja.it.
Choose from full-body, hand and foot massages (€20-130), to mud baths (€12-60) and beauty facials (€40-70).

From **Olbia** ARST runs frequent daily buses along the coast, including to **San Teodoro** (40 mins) and Arzachena (35 mins). From **Arzachena**, buses continue to **Porto Cervo** (30 mins) and **Baia Sardinia** (40 mins). There are several daily buses from Olbia to **Santa Teresa** (1 hr 50 mins) and **Tempio-Pausania** (1 hr 20 mins) and a morning (0615) bus from Olbia to **Sassari** (1 hr 35 mins).

Trains connect Olbia with Cagliari (4 hrs) and Sassari (1 hr 50 mins). From June to September, the **Trenino Verde** tourist line runs twice daily between Tempio and Sassari (2 hrs 30 mins).

There are ferries from Olbia to **Civitavecchia** (8 hrs), Livorno (10 hrs) and Genoa (11 hrs), and from Golfo Aranci to **Fiumicino** (4 hrs 30 mins), Civitavecchia (7 hrs) and Livorno (6 hrs). Four to ten ferries leave Santa Teresa daily for Bonifacio, Corsica (55 mins).

Contents

Alghero's harbour.

Sassari & the northwest

Introduction

What to see in...

...one day
Spend the morning strolling **Alghero**'s medieval kernel and shopping for coral. Go for a swim at one of the hidden beaches along the **Alghero–Bosa** coastal road in the afternoon and dance the night away at **Il Ruscello** or **El Tró**.

Northwest Sardinia offers so much rich evidence of its medieval past that much of it feels more Italian than Sardinian. More than anywhere else in Sardinia, the province of Sassari benefited from the bitter tug-of-war for power between rivals Genoa and Pisa. In addition to its provincial capital, Sassari, the Genoese gave the northwest two of the island's most attractive medieval towns: Castelsardo and Alghero, although the latter is renowned for having retained the distinctive Catalan spice and language it would learn from its later Aragonese rulers. For their part, the Pisans left a series of dazzling Romanesque churches in the Logudoro and Anglona regions, a reminder of the influence of Sardinia's independent *giudicati*.

...a weekend or more
After a day in Alghero, visit the **Grotta di Nettuno** or **Nuraghe Santu Antine**. Alternatively, you could spend a day at **La Pelosa** beach or drive or cycle the panoramic coastal route to Bosa.
  After exploring the west of the province around **Alghero**, head to **Sassari** to wander its Genoese alleyways and learn about Sardinian history in the **Museo Sanna**. Continue east to tour the **Logudoro**'s **Romanesque churches** and to climb the hill to **Castelsardo**'s castle.

There's ample evidence around Ozieri to suggest that the northwest corner was the earliest Sardinians' favourite part of the island. Their Bronze Age descendants built their finest work at Santu Antine and enough basalt towers around Torralba to warrant the name 'Valley of the nuraghi'. Elsewhere, you may find yourself scratching your head at the truncated pyramid of Monte d'Accodi, admiring the coastline of La Pelosa, and gripping your seat as you drive along nature's rollercoaster between Alghero and Bosa.

Isolotto con Torre.

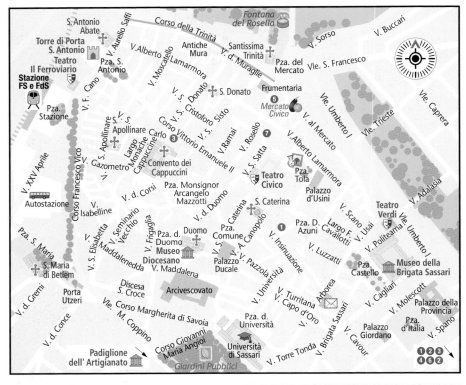

Sassari listings

① Sleeping

1 Casa Chiara *Vicolo Bertolinis 7*
2 Frank Hotel *via Diaz 20*
3 Vittorio Emanuele *corso Vittorio Emanuele 100/102*

① Eating & drinking

1 Caffé Roma *via Roma*
2 Il Cenacolo *via Ozieri 2*
3 L'Antica Hostaria *via Cavour 55*
4 Mocambo Café *via Roma 97*
5 Pizzeria Cocco *via Rosello 25*
6 Trattoria Da Antonio *via Arborea 2B*
7 Trattoria L'Assassino *Vicolo Ospizio Cappuccini 1A*

Home to 130,000 people, Sassari is the provincial capital and Sardinia's largest city after Cagliari, a fact that has created a certain rivalry between the two drastically different towns. While Cagliari basks in a soft beachside breeze, Sassari retains an inland air of legislative formality that has lingered from its proud past as a centre of political action.

Like Oristano, Sassari rose to prominence when pirate raids and disease forced residents of *Turris Libisonis* (modern-day Porto Torres) to retreat inland. By 1294, Sassari (then known as *Thathari*) was a power base from which Genoa could control commerce and expand its influence. However, unlike elsewhere in Sardinia, Sassari enjoyed legislative independence as a free commune, governed by a *Consiglio di Anziani* (group of elders). The *Sassaresi* soon outgrew their Genoese overlords and turned to Aragon in 1323 to help them rid the city of the Ligurians. The proud *Sassaresi* were not about to relinquish their autonomy, however, and rose up against the Aragonese in several rebellions before being finally subdued in 1420. Jesuits founded Sardinia's first university in Sassari in 1558 but a 17th-century malaria outbreak decimated half the population, creating widespread discontent that lingered long after. Only in the 19th century, when Sassari was connected to the SS131 highway, did it awaken again from its economic and cultural lull. During the First World War, the courageous Brigata Sassari regiment (see page 237) did much to rekindle Sassari's political fire, and the city produced two Italian presidents (Antonio Segni and Francesco Cossiga) as well as Communist leader Enrico Berlinguer in the 20th century.

Today, urban sprawl has surrounded Sassari's alluring, if crumbling, medieval quarter, but below its surface, the city remains the heart of Sardinia's political consciousness.

Essentials

❶ Getting around Sassari is built on a long, walkable slope with the modern development to the east and the medieval quarter to the west. A single road that changes names from via Roma to largo Cavalotti to corso Vittorio Emanuele passes a series of piazzas, joining the new to the old. Up to nine ARST buses daily run between Alghero-Fertilia airport and Sassari's bus station (30 mins). Local ATP buses to Platamona beach depart from the Giardini Pubblici.

⊖ Bus station Stazione Bus, via XXV Aprile, T079-263 9203, T079-241301.

◐ Train station Stazione Ferroviaria, piazza Stazione, T079-260362, T079-245740, trenitalia.com.

❸ ATM There are three banks in piazza Italia where you can change or withdraw money.

⊕ Hospital For emergency assistance, contact Sassari's **Guardia Medica** ("ambulance/emergency response") at T079-206 2222 to be taken to various medical emergency sites.

✛ Pharmacy Via Roma 14, Mon-Fri 0915-1300 and 1630-2000, Sat 0915-1300.

⟁ Post office Poste Italiane, via Brigata Sassari 19, T079-234380, Mon-Fri 0800-1850, Sat 0800-1315.

❶ Tourist information Teatro Civico, corso Vittorio Emanuele 35, T331-437 7156, Mon-Fri 0900-1400 and 1500-1800.

Left: Detail from Basilica San Gavino. Above: Castelsardo.

Museo Nazionale GA Sanna

Via Roma 64, T079-272203.
Tue-Sun 0900-2000. €2, €1 concessions, free
children and over-65s.

Inside this neoclassical garden villa is Sardinia's
most important historical museum after Cagliari's
Museo Archeologico. The museum's two floors
present a chronological history of Sardinia, from its
Neolithic origins to the Roman conquest. The first
room holds statues of the chubby mother
Goddess, obsidian arrowheads and a *domus de
janas* grave with carved bull's head from Sardinia's
Ozieri culture (3500-2700 BC). In the adjacent room,
a display is dedicated to the Monte d'Accodi
sanctuary (see page 242), with illustrations showing
its rise from a Neolithic village to a raised temple.
Menhirs feature prominently in the back room,
many with carved daggers and trident-shaped
human figures etched in their stone surfaces. Note
the punctured skull in glass case No 18,
demonstrating Neolithic and Copper Age surgery
techniques used to 'release' the patient's illness.

Upstairs there are plastic recreations of
nuraghi, sacred wells and *tombe di gigante* graves
characteristic of Sardinia's Bronze Age. Most
interesting are the mysterious *bronzetti* figurines,
which raise one palm in peace while carrying a
dagger in the other hand. Back downstairs, the
museum concludes with Punic and Roman
artefacts, such as tophet steles (see page 107),
necklaces and mosaic tiles.

Via Roma to Piazza Italia

Most of Sassari's social life takes place along via
Roma, an attractive palm-lined avenue of cafés and
bars. Across the street from the Sanna museum are
the city's prison and courthouse. (On via Cavour
you can often see prisoners looking out of their cell
windows). Via Roma concludes at Sassari's
enormous centrepiece, the 18th-century piazza
Italia, presided over by a statue of Vittorio
Emanuele II. The regal **Palazzo della Provincia**
houses the local government and makes Cagliari's

Tip...

Don't miss the art gallery to the left as you enter
the museum. It displays a selection of paintings,
including work by many Sardinian artists, such as
Nuoro's Antonio Ballero. Especially interesting is
Gerolamo Giovenone's piece showing a woman
serving two human eyes on a platter.

Palazzo Regio look provincially pedestrian by
comparison. Inside, the bi-level **Sala Consiliari**
(Mon-Thu 0815-1330 and 1600-1800) has impressive
frescoes of historical events in Sassari and pillars of
the blinded Moor slaves depicted on Sardinia's flag.

Piazza Castello

To the northwest, piazza Castello symbolizes the
city's history of foreign exploitation. Most
noticeable are the two towering eyesores built by
Fascist architects from the mainland in the 1940s
(known tongue-in-cheek as Sassari's 'skyscrapers').
More significant, however, was the castle, built here
by the Aragonese in 1330 and used as a Court of
Inquisition. Its brutal torture regime included the
decapitation of non-Catholics, the rape of young
girls and the hanging of blonde men and women,
who were once believed to represent the devil,
upside down until blood gushed from their
mouths. Animosity lingered long after the Spanish
packed their bags and, in 1877, the *Sassaresi*
demolished the structure. In late 2008, the square
was being excavated in order to lay a glass walkway
above the castle's ruins below.

A more positive chapter of Sardinian history
can be found inside a working military barracks on
the piazza. The modest **Museo Storico della
Brigata Sassari** (piazza Castello 9, T079-208 5308,
Mon-Thu 0800-1630, Fri-Sat 0800-1200, free) is
dedicated to the decorated Brigata Sassari
regiment that fought valiantly in the First World
War (see page box, opposite) and displays sandbag
trenches, helmets, rifles, photographs from the
front and letters from international officers
commending the Brigata's courage.

Corso Vittorio Emanuele

From piazza Castello, corso Vittorio Emanuele shoots west into Sassari's oldest and most appealing neighbourhood: its medieval district. The *corso* was part of the ancient Roman road connecting Cagliari and Porto Torres and later became the prime address for Sassari's medieval elite. Today, it is one of Sassari's main shopping thoroughfares, with modern boutiques interspersed between medieval Aragonese buildings. For many years, Sassari's once proud *centro storico* was in a state of neglect and its Gothic *palazzi* were falling into disrepair. However, serious restoration is now underway and it's not uncommon to see entire streets uprooted and awaiting repair, forcing pedestrians to use wooden beams to cross the street.

The 15th-century **Casa Farris** at No 23 certainly shows its age, retaining (if barely) two Catalan-Gothic double windows. Much better preserved is the Casa di Re Enzo at No 42, in the same style and from the same period. It houses a clothing store

Brigata Sassari

"Pro defender sa patria italiana, distrutta s'este sa Sardigna intera."
"In order to defend the Italian heritage, we've killed all of Sardinia."
Anonymous, Brigata Sassari

The Brigata Sassari was comprised of Sardinian soldiers who defended the northern Italian border from 1915 to 1918. During this time 1595 of their men were killed and 8745 were injured, a greater percentage than any other regiment in Italy. Prior to the war, most of the soldiers were shepherds or farmers had yet to encounter Sardi from other parts of the island. On the battlefield, they learned about each others' villages, lifestyle and customs, creating camaraderie and an island-wide pride and consciousness. Following the war, many soldiers returned to Sardinia with a new political outlook, disenchanted with the foreign-based rule that had plagued the island. Led by former commander Emilio Lussu, the soldiers helped form the *Partito Sardo d'Azione* party whose goal was Sardinian autonomy.

Piazza Italia.

but you can step inside its portico to admire the sculptured capitals and ceiling frescoes. The bottom of the corso is marked by the di Sant'Antonio column, engraved with historical scenes from Sassari by Sassarese Eugenio Tavolara in 1954.

Teatro Civico

Corso Vittorio Emanuele 35, T331-4377156. **Museum Mon-Fri 1600-2100, with guided visits in English (call ahead). Free.**

Restored in 2006 and reopened in 2008, Sassari's civic theatre holds the city's tourist office (see page 235) as well as a first-rate museum of *Sassarese* culture. The neoclassical theatre was built between 1826 and 1829 above the 13th-century Palazzo di Città where Sassari's *Consiglio di Anziani* held court in the 13th and 14th centuries.

Inside, the museum wraps around the theatre's ballroom on three levels, allowing visitors a backstage pass to its stage and seating and providing computer touch-screen graphics that detail the city's sights with videos (in Italian). Upstairs, you can look down on the corso from a wrought iron balcony, just as Sassari's mayor does on the day of the *Candaleri* (see page 239). If you can't make it for the real thing or for Sassari's Holy Week, the museum has videos of both events as well as small-scale statues depicting the festivities' various participants. The tour concludes with a display of peasant costumes worn in 19th-century Sassari, revealing a decidedly Spanish influence.

Duomo di San Nicola

Piazza Duomo, T079-232067. **Daily 0900-1200 and 1600-1900, free.**

In the middle of Sassari's narrow beehive of medieval streets, the magnificent Baroque façade of the San Nicola cathedral stands head and shoulders above its surroundings. The towering 18th-century front shows the Giudicato of Torres' coat of arms and the three martyred saints, Gavino,

Proto and Gianuario (see page 240). A statue of San Nicola presides over the saints, while God the Father blesses the cathedral from its highest point. The façade was tacked on to the 15th-century Catalan-Gothic church, which in turn was built over a 13th-century Romanesque original. Today, only parts of the campanile and the façade's base survive from the 13th century.

The Gothic interior is not nearly as flashy as the exterior but it does contain some impressive pieces. The second chapel on the right has a 17th-century canvas of the Virgin dedicated to saints Cosma and Damiano, while, beside the altar, another 17th-century canvas shows San Elgio with scenes of Sassari. The cathedral's small **Museo del Tesoro** in the sacristy holds the fine 14th-century *Madonna del Bosco* painting, as well as a silver statue of San Gavino.

Duomo di San Nicola.

Li Candaleri

The most important date on Sassari's calendar is its thanksgiving celebration on 14th August, known as *Li Candaleri*. The festival honours the Virgin for allegedly saving the city from three plague epidemics between 1528 and 1652, each of which is said to have ended on 14th August.

To thank their protector, eight candle-bearers from each of Sassari's nine medieval guilds (known as *Gremi*) haul a 5-m tall wooden 'candle' from piazza Castello to the Chiesa di Santa Maria di Betlem (see below). The candles weigh between 200 and 300 kg each and are festooned in flowers and ribbons. Children hold the ribbons and dance to the rhythm of drum beats and the tune of the *pifferario* flute. The parade stops in front of the Teatro Civico on corso Vittorio Emanuele (see box, opposite), where Sassari's mayor greets the *Gremi* with the *Sassarese* expression "*A zent'anni!*" ("May you live a hundred years!"). The response is either applause, if he's governing well, or whistles, if not, and marks the start of the most important part of the procession, *Sa Faradda* ('the descent') down to the church. Traditionally, the farmers' *Gremio* was the most important guild, as the city depended on it for food, so they enter the church first. Once inside, each guild places its candles around the image of the Virgin and a city-wide celebration of music and feasting ensues.

Chiesa di Santa Maria di Betlem

Piazza di Santa Maria, T079-235740.
Daily 0800-1200 and 1600-1930, free.

Built by Benedictine monks in 1106 and enlarged by Franciscans in the 13th century, this church actually predates the city around it. A series of heavy restorations from the 16th to 19th centuries has greatly altered the church's appearance, so that the lower part of the façade is all that remains of the original 12th-century structure. A 15th-century rose window highlights the Gothic façade's capitals and columns, though the Catalan architects also showed hints of Islamic influences in the large dome and slender campanile.

Inside, the church has fallen victim to some clumsy Baroque facelifts but it preserves its 15th-century plan of cross-vaulted Gothic chapels lining the church's single nave. Each chapel is dedicated to one of Sassari's craft guilds, which parade during the *Li Candaleri* procession; the most impressive is the bricklayers' *Cappella dei Muratori* to the left of the entrance.

Sassari's fortifications

By the mid 14th century, Sassari was surrounded by a moat, defensive walls and 36 towers, which gave their name to the region's independent authority, the Giudicato of Torres. The fortifications had largely fallen down by the 19th century when city planners toppled them, but a few remnants still survive. **Piazza Sant'Antonio** holds the last remaining tower with full battlements, while **corso Trinità** preserves the largest stretch of Sassari's walls, complete with *Thathari's* coat of arms. At the eastern end of corso Trinità is **Porta Rosello**, the only surviving medieval gate of the four that allowed entrance through the walls.

Fontana di Rosello

Opposite Porta Rosello.
Park May-Sep Tue-Sat 0900-1300 and 1730-2030, Sun 1730-2030, Oct-Apr Tue-Sat 0900-1300 and 1600-1900, Sun 0900-1300, free.

In a park opposite the Porta Rosello is this white marble fountain, built by the Genoese in 1295 over a natural spring. Makeovers in 1606 and 1828 gave the structure its present shape, with four statues at the fountain's corners representing the seasons and open-mouthed lions shooting water into a basin. The fountain is capped by two arches and a statue of San Gavino riding a horse – all of which bares an uncanny resemblance to a shopping bag. Fittingly in a politically charged city, those unhappy with Sassari's government in the past have unearthed the surrounding cobblestones and pelted the fountain with them, which perhaps explains the structure's frequent restorations.

Porto Torres & around

On the coast north of Sassari, Porto Torres is littered with petrochemical refineries that spoil first impressions of the island when approached from the sea. However, the area boasts two of Sardinia's archaeological gems, spread ten minutes and nearly 4000 years apart: the island's finest Romanesque church and a mysterious truncated pyramid predating those in Egypt.

Porto Torres was founded by Julius Caesar in 46 BC as *Turris Libisonis*, after his victory in a battle in Libya, and remained a key port well into the Middle Ages when it was the capital of the Giudicato of Torres. The pirate raids and malaria that ravaged coastal Sardinia under Aragonese and Spanish rule hit hard here, and the port waned until the Savoyards relaid the ancient Roman road from Cagliari to Porto Torres, pumping new life and industry into the town.

Basilica Romanica di San Gavino.

Basilica Romanica di San Gavino

Porto Torres, T347-400 1288.
Mon-Sat 0900-1300 and 1500-1800, Sun 1100-1300 and 1500-1900.
Free, €1.50 to visit the crypt.

Signs at the top of corso Vittorio Emanuele point towards the oldest and largest Romanesque church in Sardinia, the Basilica di San Gavino. It's a real diamond in the suburban rough, an imposing limestone structure finished in 1080 by the Pisans which, oddly enough, has two rounded apses at its ends instead of a façade. The basilica owes its name to a Roman soldier, Gavino, who was charged with watching over two priests, Proto and Gianuario, who had been sent by the Pope to Christianize the Sardinians but were jailed by the Romans. After witnessing their faith, Gavino released the two prisoners and converted to Christianity. The three were soon captured, decapitated in 304, and have remained the subject of religious rapture in Sardinia ever since.

Inside the limestone exterior, the basilica's central nave is flanked by 11 marble columns on each side taken from the Roman settlement nearby. Small windows let faint light slip through, illuminating a few frescoes and statues in a hauntingly dim glow. A staircase leads to a 17th-century crypt containing five statues in Carrara marble and the urns of the three martyrs resting in Roman sarcophagi.

Antiquarium

Via Ponte Romano 99, T0795-14433, ibiscoop.com.
Tue-Sun 0900-2000, €2, €1 concessions.

Dwarfed by an octagonal Aragonese watchtower directly behind it, the Roman column at the intersection of corso Vittorio Emanuele and the Lungomare marks the official end of the Romans' Karalibus–Turrem highway (the modern-day SS131). To the left by the railway station is the Antiquarium archaeological museum and an excavated area, showing what remains of the Roman port of Turris

Libisonis. In spring, 2009 the archaeological site was still closed for repairs with no plans to re-open anytime soon but, peering through the museum window, you can make out rows of *insulae* flats, columns, streets and a massive thermal spa that had hot, cold and tepid baths. The thermal monument is known as the **Palazzo di Re Barbaro** (Barbarian King's Palace) because, before archaeologists got their hands on it, Porto Torres' citizens had thought the structure was the fortress of the king who martyred the town's three saints.

The museum displays artefacts from the site and has an excellent second-floor model of the Roman settlement. Highlights include an altar dedicated to the Egyptian god Bubastis from AD 35 and some well-preserved mosaic tiles.

Cutting-edge crafts

In the past 30 years, the handmade knives long used by Sardinian shepherds have become coveted for their craftsmanship. Traditionally, different villages produced their own trademark style of blade, with Arbus' *arburese* and Guspini's *guspinese* both being popular. Today, the most famous Sardinian knife is the renowned *pattadese* from the village of **Pattada**, 15 km east of Ozieri.

Characterized by a metallic ring between the handle and its myrtle leaf-shaped blade, the classic *pattadese* design is the *resolza* (razor). Historically, shepherds used a single *resolza* jack-knife to sheer wool, kill their sheep and cut their meat. Although most shepherds can no longer afford these increasingly popular blades, its style hasn't changed since the 1840s. A ram's or mouflon's horn that has been aged for at least four years is used to make the knife's handle, which is heated to become more malleable, straightened in a vice and separated. A stainless steel blade is placed inside the two-piece handle, which is joined together at the sides with screws to allow it to fold.

There are over 15 knife-makers in Pattada and, while you can't go wrong with any of them, the most famous is unquestionably the Fogarizzu family. Plan on paying a pretty penny for these labour-intensive crafts: high-quality knives take about 10 hours to make and usually cost between €150 and €200.

Note that Italian law forbids the carrying of knives with blades longer than the width of four fingers in public places. Check with your airline's luggage specifications regarding knives before you pack.

East of Porto Torres

The *Sassaresi* have adopted nearby **Platamona** as their city beach. By Sardinian standards it's nothing special but it's a perfectly pleasant and lively place, capped by a crumbling Aragonese tower. A wooden walkway runs along the bird-friendly **Stagno di Platamona** marsh. The road east cuts through more pines and sand dunes until you reach **Marina di Sorso**, reputed to be a great surf-casting spot. Inland, **Sorso** is known for its Cannonau wine.

The Aragonese watchtower at Platamona.

Around the island

Monte D'Accodi

Km 222, SS131 (only accessible from the south-bound carriageway) between Porto Torres and Sassari, T334-807 4449.
Late Jun-Sep Mon-Sat 1000-2000, Oct and late Feb-late Jun Mon-Sat 0900-1900, Nov-late Feb Mon-Sat 0900-1400, free.

This often overlooked structure is one of the most intriguing ancient sites in Sardinia. In the middle of a pasture sits a truncated pyramid temple built with limestone rocks rising to 11 m that perfectly resembles a Mesopotamian ziggurat (a terraced altar from ancient Babylon). Dating from 2800 BC (nearly 200 years before the oldest Egyptian pyramid) and attributed to the Ozieri Culture, it's the world's only example of such a Copper Age structure outside Babylonia (modern-day Iraq). How and why Sardinia's indigenous population built such a structure remains unknown. During the Second World War, the Nazis used the holy shrine's elevated terrace as a cannon launching pad to shoot down aeroplanes!

The temple, which was destroyed by a fire and rebuilt in 2600 BC, consists of a long ramp rising to meet the three-tiered sanctuary whose 30 m by 38 m rectangular apex aligns perfectly with the cardinal points and was once crowned by a shrine. Inside the temple, a statue of the pre-Nuraghic chubby mother goddess was found inside a single room painted in red ochre.

To the left and right of the ramp, respectively, are a large menhir and two sacrificial altars dating from between 4500 and 4300 BC. You can still see the holes punched through the tops of the altars to secure animals for sacrificial slaughter. By the larger altar, there are two perfectly smooth, circular *omphalos* (navels of the world) stones commonly used in ancient Greece – on which shells were placed as votive offerings.

The ancient sanctuary at Monte D'Accodi.

The area southeast of Sassari is a relatively flat expanse of farmland whose vast grain fields have given it the name Logudoro ('golden place'). The few communities sprinkled throughout this area preserve the purest form of Sardo around, the mellifluous Logudorese. Bronze Age nuraghi builders left their highest concentration of towers around Torralba, and also their most spectacular monument at Santu Antine. In the Middle Ages, the Logudoro thrived under the Giudicato of Torres and reminders of its splendour are visible in a string of Romanesque churches rivalling anything on the Italian mainland.

Ozieri

Built in a natural amphitheatre between two hills, Ozieri was the home of Sardinia's most celebrated prehistoric civilization, the so-called Ozieri Culture (3500-2700 BC. Many artefacts from these Neolithic people have been retrieved from the **Grotte di San Michele** (vicolo San Michele, T329-266 9436, Tue-Sat 0900-1300 and 1500-1800, Sun-Mon 0930-1230, €3.50, €2.50 children or €5/4 including museum), near the top of town, and are on display, alongside relics from the subsequent Nuraghic to Byzantine periods, at the **Museo Archeologico** (piazza San Francesco, T079-785 1052, Tue-Sat 0900-1300 and 1600-1900, Sun 0930-1230, €4, €3 children or €5, €4 children including cave).

Above: Ozieri. Below: Chiesa di Sant'Antonio di Bisarcio, Ozieri.

Modern Ozieri is set on a slope leading from the bus depot at piazza Garibaldi to its main square, **piazza Carlo Alberto**, where tall 18th-century houses retain their *suttea* (verandas), lined with Doric columns. From the piazza, via Vittorio Emanuele III ascends to the 12th-century marble **Fontana Grixoni**, named after the *Ozierese* who funded it. In nearby piazza Duomo is the neoclassical **Cattedrale dell'Immacolata**, whose campanile stands tall, topped by a multi-coloured dome. Inside, there's a famous 16th-century retable by the 'Maestro di Ozieri'.

The Logudoro's Romanesque churches

During the Middle Ages, Sardinia's autonomous *giudicati* hired Pisan merchants and religious orders to work alongside local artists in the construction of churches. The result is a series of Romanesque masterpieces that now lies abandoned in fields, adding to their mystique.

Many of the churches are conveniently clustered along the SS597 making for a great day trip from Sassari if you have your own wheels. The tour lasts several hours, and it's hard to digest history on an empty stomach, so pick up supplies at Sassari's Antica Salumeria Mangatia (see page 265) before you head out; you'll need them later.

The tour starts, high up, 15 km southeast of Sassari on the SS597, at the **Chiesa della Santissima Trinità di Saccargia** (T347-000 7882, Apr-Oct daily 0900-1900, by reservation only at other times, €2). Horizontal bands of white limestone and black basalt cover the building like zebra stripes. The church was consecrated in 1116 by the *giudice* of Torres to thank the Virgin of Saccargia for helping his wife conceive, and is allegedly named after a 'dappled cow' (*sa acca argia* in Sardo) that would kneel in prayer at the site; look for four carved cows on the front capital. Inside, the church is built on a T-shaped cross with a single nave and transept. Thirteenth-century frescoes adorn the central apse with scenes from the Old and New Testaments. Three kilometres east, there's no sign for the abandoned **San Michele di Salvènero**, but you'll see it on your right after the 4-km marker. Take the gravel road from the SS597 to get a closer look.

Ten kilometres further, follow signs to Ardara and **Santa Maria del Regno** (T079-400193, daily 0800-1200 and 1600-1900, free). The 12th-century church and its squat bell tower face south, presumably so that the sun can illuminate its deep red trachyte façade. Inside, paintings adorn each of the columns lining the central nave. The church is said to hold the remains of many *Logudorese* rulers, including its last *giudicessa*, Adelasia.

At Km 22 on the SS597, look for the left-hand turning to **Chiesa di Sant'Antonio di Bisarcio** (daily 0900-1300 and 1500-1900, €1.50), perched on a bluff. Rebuilt between 1170 and 1190 after a fire destroyed the 11th-century original, it incorporates French influences, such as its atrium porch, into the Pisan-Romanesque design. Though a lightning bolt severed the church's campanile, the interior's three narrow naves are well preserved.

You may hit sheep traffic on the 20-km stretch east to **Nostra Signora di Castro** (daily 0900-1700) on the shores of the Lago del Coghinas. The church is surrounded by *cumbessiàs* (dwellings for pilgrims), which are still used between 13th and 19th April each year, when Oschiri's faithful carry a statue of the Virgin to the site from their church. Hungry? Find a table near the church's car park, unwrap your picnic and enjoy the lakeside vista.

Top: Chiesa di Sant'Antonio di Bisarcio.
Left: San Michele di Salvènero.
Above: Santa Maria del Regno.

Nuraghe Santu Antine & Valle dei Nuraghi

Off the SS131 at km 172, south of Torralba,
T079-847298, nuraghesantuantine.it.
Daily 0900-sunset, €3 including Torralba
museum, €2 children.

The town of Torralba is surrounded by 32 nuraghi
and numerous *tombe di giganti*, making it the
centre of the densest concentration of Nuraghic
sites in Sardinia and earning it the title, 'Valle dei
Nuraghi'. But if you only see one of Sardinia's more
than 7000 Bronze Age towers, it should be
Nuraghe Santu Antine, the crowning opus of this
mysterious culture.

The site is surrounded by 10 circular Nuraghic-
age huts and six rectangular huts made by the
Romans who dismantled parts of the original
structure to make stables. A lintel opening leads to
a large courtyard with a well from where you can
admire the masterpiece of this Bronze Age
settlement: a three-storey central keep rising 17.5
m and joined to three surrounding towers
enclosed by a triangular-shaped wall. The whole
structure was built in the 16th century BC. The

keep preserves its *tholos* dome roof and, below,
three niches lead to an encircling tunnel
connecting it to the surrounding towers. ,

In the courtyard, two flights of steps and a
staircase ascend to the first floor. Here, the ground
floor's tunnel-chamber pattern is repeated on a
slightly smaller scale. The spiral staircase continues
to the second floor where the base and lip of the
tholos dome remain, but its walls have collapsed,
turning it into a terrace. In its heyday, the fortress
rose to 25 m; you can make out traces of the
stairwell winding up to a terrace on the third level,
from where several other of Torralba's nuraghi are
visible. The Santu Antine ticket gets you in to the
town's **Museo della Valle dei Nuraghi** (via Carlo
Felice 143, T079-847296, daily 0900-sunset), which
has artefacts and pictures from Torralba's many
nuraghi and *tombe di giganti*.

Necropoli di Sant'Andrea di Priu

10 km east of Bonorva, T079-867894.
Jun-Sep Tue-Sun 1000-1300 and 1500-1900, or
by appointment, €2.

Ten kilometres south of Torralba on the SS131 is the
town of Bonorva, built on a plateau. Follow signs
from here towards Bono to reach the Neolithic
Necropoli di Sant'Andrea di Priu. Situated at the
end of a dirt road, the site preserves 18 *domus de
janas* tombs excavated by the Ozieri Culture from
the volcanic rock. The highlight is the **Tomba del
Capo**, which was reused as a Christian cult in the
Middle Ages. Some of the area's archaeological
finds can be seen at Bonorva's **Museo
Archeologico** (piazza Sant'Antonio, T079-867894,
Jun-Sep Tue-Sun 1000-1300 and 1500-1900, or by
appointment, €2 or €4 with Sant'Andrea di Priu).

Nuraghe Santu Antine.

Tip...

Call ahead for guided tours in
English. Be prepared to wait
during summer weekends
when the site gets crowded.

Suitably, Sardinia's most touristy town is also its most attractive. Colourful campaniles and sandstone palazzi preside over cobblestone streets inside its medieval walls, while the Mediterranean breaks against its seaside bastions on the west side. Yet, Alghero developed as a Catalan colony and is arguably the island's least 'Sardinian' town.

In the 12th century, the powerful Genoese Doria family wanted a foothold in Sardinia, so they transformed two tiny coastal villages – Castelgenovese (Castelsardo) and present-day Alghero – into fortified strongholds, naming the latter *Aleguerium* (algae). Aleguerium's strategic port attracted frequent raids. It was briefly taken over by Genoa's arch-rival, Pisa, in the 1280s and underwent 30 years of local riots before the Catalan-Aragonese eventually took control in 1353, renaming it *Alguer*. Rebellions continued until King Pere the Ceremonious sailed over a year later, expelled the unruly population to Sardinia's interior and repopulated his colony with obedient Iberians. Doria's ramparts came crumbling down and a taller, turreted wall sprang up as Alguer was named an official Aragonese royal city in 1501. The discovery of America led to the decline of Alguer's port and, even after the Savoyards took control in 1720, the population remained bound to Catalonia. The landward walls toppled in 1876 and, with its belt loosened, Alghero has since sprawled inland.

After nearly 400 years of Iberian rule, the *Algheresi* still doggedly maintain their Catalan heritage to such an extent that the town is referred to warmly by its Spanish cousins as 'Little Barcelona'. Street signs are written in both Italian (*'via'*) and Catalan (*'carrer'*) forms, Iberian-Gothic architecture abounds, recipes – such as the spicy *algherese* paella – mirror Spanish cuisine, and, most tellingly, an archaic form of Catalan is still spoken by old-timers and children alike.

Essentials

❶ Getting around You can only drive through Alghero's medieval centre from 0800 to 1030 and from 1430 to 1630 but its small size means it's easy to explore on foot. From via Cagliari, up to 19 AIFA buses run daily to Alghero Airport, 12 km away (30 mins), and frequent AO buses go along the coast, all the way to Capo Caccia (50 mins). There are also three daily buses from Alghero to the Sella & Mosca vineyards (20 mins).

❷ Bus station Stazione Bus, Giardini Pubblici, ARST T079-950179, FdS T079-950458.

❸ Train station Stazione Ferroviaria, via Don Minzoni, 2 km north of Alghero centre, T079-950785, trenitalia.com.

❹ ATM Banca Nazionale del Lavoro and MPS Banca are next to each other at No 5 and No 11 via Vittorio Emanuele.

❺ Hospital Ospedale Civile, via Don Minzoni, 2 km north of Alghero centre, T079-996200.

❻ Pharmacy Farmacia Bulla, via Garibaldi 13, T079-952115, Mon-Sat 0915-1300 and 1630-2000.

❼ Post office Poste Italiane, via Carducci 35, T079-972 0200, Mon-Fri 0800-1800, Sat 0800-1300.

❽ Tourist information The main office is at piazza Porta Terra 9, T079-979054, Mon-Sat 0800-2000, Sun 1000-1300. An additional office is located in the Torre di Porta Terra (see below).

Bonita, por mi fé, y bien assentada.

Beautiful, by my faith, and well fortified.

Spanish emperor, Carlos V about Alghero, 1541

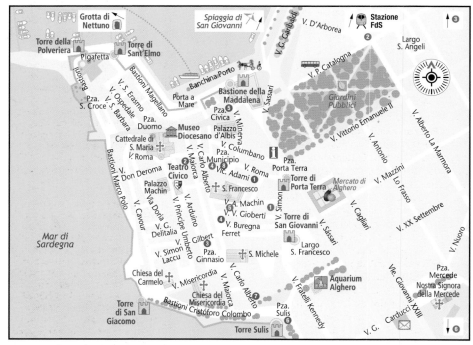

Alghero listings

❶ Sleeping
1 Aigua *via Machin 22 B&B*
2 Catalunya *via Catalogna 24*
3 La Mariposa *via Lido 22*
4 Mamajuana *Vicolo Adami 12 B&B*
5 San Francesco *via Machin 2*
6 Villa Las Tronas *Lungomare Valencia 1*

❶ Eating & drinking
1 Al Refettorio *Vicolo Adami 47*
2 Al Tuguri *via Maiorca 113*
3 Birreria Sant Miquel *via Ardoino 51*
4 Café del Corso *via Carlo Alberto 77*
5 Gelateria Arcobaleno *piazza Civico 33*
6 Il Pavone *piazza Sulis 3/4*
7 La Lepanto *via Carlo Alberto 135*
8 La Posada del Mar *Vicolo Adami 29*

Inside Alghero's walls

Alghero's medieval centre wears its age well. Beyond the arch of **Porta a Mare**, with its Aragonese coat of arms, the elegantly weathered **piazza Civica** gives a good first impression. The triangular square was home to Aragon's government and its most important families. Spanish Emperor Carlos V famously proclaimed, "You are all knights!" to the delight of the *Algheresi* from the second-storey window of the square's stately **Palazzo D'Albis** (No 32) in 1541.

Due west in piazza Duomo is Alghero's main religious landmark, the **Cattedrale di Santa Maria,** whose four oversized Doric columns nearly cover its façade. Like Cagliari's cathedral, Santa Maria is a medley of Renaissance, Baroque, and Gothic styles. The campanile and portal are from the original 1552 construction and modelled on the Gothic cathedral in Barcelona; they're best seen from via Principe Umberto behind the church. Nearby, the **Museo Diocesano d'Arte Sacra** (piazza Duomo, T079-975350, Sun-Tue 1000-1230, Thu-Fri 1030-1830, Sat 1000-1230 and 1600-1900, €4, €3 concessions) sits inside the Chiesa del Rosario. The museum holds Spanish silverware, woodcarvings and a marble statue of the Madonna della Miseracordia. However, the most interesting display is the collection of stamped lithographs of Sardinian Romanesque churches.

Four-storey Catalan-Gothic buildings hold their breath along the claustrophobically tight **via Carlo**

What the author says

One of Sardinia's most scenic coastal roads connects two of its most attractive medieval towns: Alghero and Bosa. For 42 km the Litoranea Panoramica offers spectacular views of the coast as it slaloms around volcanic cliffs, with the slick rock face on one side and the mountainous *macchia* on the other. This route can be undertaken as a leisurely drive or a full-day bike trip. However you travel, I recommend packing a bathing suit, looking for hidden beaches behind the hairpin turns and bringing your own supplies because there won't be any towns or houses in sight!

The first bathing spot, **Spiaggia La Speranza**, is 8 km south of Alghero. A bar/restaurant along its curling strand is your last chance to stock up on food or water before the 35-km stretch to Bosa. Watch for griffon vultures coasting on the *maestrale* winds as you twist south. Several watchtowers, and lots of goats, are visible as you descend around **Capo Marargiu**. Dirt paths often lead down to sheltered patches from the roadside parking spots; there's one 5 km north of Bosa near the Torre Argentina.

After spending the night in Bosa, serious cyclists who do not want to retrace the same route can take the SS292 inland road for 60 km back to Alghero, stopping at Padria, a hillside village with a **Museo Archeologico** (via Nazionale 1, T079-807018, May-Sep Tue-Sun 1600-1830, €1), and at **Villanova Monteleone**, whose morning farmers' market is a great place to pick up supplies.

Eliot Stein

Opposite page: Bastoni di San Marco, Alghero.
This page: The market at piazza Civica.

Alghero.

Alberto and **via Roma**, Alghero's main shopping arteries and site of the evening *passeggiata*. Beyond the sea of shop windows selling Alghero's blood-red coral jewellery, look for the 15th-century **Chiesa di San Francesco**. The church's original Gothic façade was redone in 1598 in Catalan Renaissance-Romanesque style, complete with two rose windows. The church's sandstone pillars, chapels and belltower are original and take centre stage for Alghero's Good Friday procession. Continue up via Carlo Alberto to the Baroque **Chiesa di San Michele** where a marble dove presides over the church's bare façade. Built by the Jesuits in 1589, the church is best known for its colourful majolica dome that dominates Alghero's skyline.

Along Alghero's walls

There were two main entrances to the Genoese medieval town. Alghero's wealthy Jewish community erected the **Torre di Porta Terra** land entrance in 1360, which was linked by a drawbridge to the Gothic arch now serving as a First World War memorial. Like in Cagliari's Castello

district, the gate closed each day at dusk and any Sardinian caught inside was subject to a harsh penalty. (The tower now serves as a tourist information office). The seaside entrance was the **Porta a Mare** (see page 249).

When the Catalans refortified Alghero in the 1500s, they ringed their royal city with a commanding wall and seven towers, which still remain. You can see remnants of the enclosing wall at the **Torre di San Giovanni**. Towards the sea, the 22-m **Torre Sulis** is Alghero's tallest tower and was named after the Sardinian patriot, Vincenzo Sulis, who was convicted of treason in 1799 and imprisoned inside for 21 years. The tower marks the beginning of the town's seafront bastion, a parapet that grips the town like a strong arm to keep it from falling into the Mediterranean, and creates Sardinia's most romantic *Lungomare* promenade. Each section is named after an explorer: Columbus, Marco Polo, Magellan and Pigafetta.

Bastioni Cristoforo Colombo leads west to the **Torre di San Giacomo**, affectionately called the *'Torre dels Cutxos'* (dogs' tower) by the *Algheresi* because the octagonal structure was used as a kennel for strays for much of the 20th century. From here, Bastioni Marco Polo heads north to **La Garitta** tower, which sailors used as a primitive lighthouse by placing a lantern inside, while the 18th-century **Torre de la Polveriera**, behind, held gun powder and weapons.

A few steps away, the **Torre di Sant'Elmo** is dedicated to the saint of navigators. The final tower, the **Torre della Maddalena** overlooking the port, has the best preserved remnants of Alghero's original interior bastions and now holds an outdoor theatre in its connecting rampart.

Outside Alghero's walls

Alghero's port offers daily boat trips from April to October to spot dolphins and tour Capo Caccia (see page 266). A cycling/jogging path shoots north from here towards the marina, where you can hire boats and to Alghero's city beach, **Spiaggia di San Giovanni**.

Across via Sassari from the Torre della Maddalena are the **Giardini Pubblici**, which have a large children's playground and makeshift carnival rides in warm months. Further south, the **Mare Nostrum Aquarium** (Via XX Settembre 1, T079-978333, Apr-Oct Sat 1500-2000, Sun 1000-1300 and 1500-2000. Oct-Apr hours vary, €8, €5 children), holds sharks, piranhas and a few reptiles and amphibians.

Around Alghero

The coast west from Alghero to Capo Caccia is known as the Riviera del Corallo after the rare red corallium rubrum that grows in the coast's dark caves. Fishermen have collected the stuff for centuries and it remains big business for jewellers. Divers should spend time around the Riviera, especially in Nereo's Cave, the largest underwater cave in the Mediterranean (see page 266) and everyone should make the trip to one of Sardinia's must-see sights, the Grotta di Nettuno. Before you head west, however, check out two contrasting attractions, north of town.

Necropoli di Anghelu Ruju

10 km north of Alghero towards Porto Torres, T079-994 4394, coopsilt.it. Easter-Oct daily 0900-1800, Nov-Easter daily 1000-1400. €3 or €5 with Nuraghe Palmavera.

Don't drive too fast after the turn-off for the airport 9 km north of Alghero or you'll miss the white, hand-written sign for one of the region's prime Neolithic attractions, Anghelu Ruju. The site preserves 37 *domus de janas* burial chambers, dug from sandstone by the Ozieri Culture between 3300 and 2900 BC and reused until 1500 BC by their successors. The earliest tombs were primitive caves, while the later ones appear as symmetrical T-shaped mass graves, where up to 30 men, women and children were buried, some partly cremated, others skinned beforehand.

Like ancient Egyptians, Sardinia's superstitious Nuraghic population designed these tombs to mirror the living quarters of those they eternally housed. Later tombs, such as those immediately to the right as you enter, had multiple rooms with carved beds, doorways and architraves. Many have geometric figures and bulls' heads engraved in the rock face: if you crouch down in Tomb 'A' you can make out six of these horned heads above the rectangular cut-out door. Bulls were regarded as a symbol of strength during this period, whose sacrificed blood had regenerative powers. Neolithic Sardinians carved bull heads on their tombs to represent the sacrifice of an individual's ancestors, believing it would spur fertility in the village, a practice still echoed in the Barbagie during Carnival (see page 171).

Necropoli di Anghelu Ruju.

Around the island

Sella & Mosca Cantina

Località I Piani, T079-997700, sellaemosca.com.
Tours Jun-Sep daily 1730 or by advanced
booking. Enoteca Jun-Sep daily 0830-2030,
Oct-May daily 0830-1830. Visitors should always
call ahead to check opening times.

Six hundred metres up the road from the
necropolis, you'll see the sign for Sardinia's most
renowned wine producer, Sella & Mosca. Set on
650 hectares of vineyards, the winery produces
nationally prized Torbato, Carignano, Vermintino
and Cannonau wines, as well as Sardinia's
esteemed *mirto* liquor and *filu e' ferru* grappa under
the label Zedda Piras, all of which are for sale at the
site's cantina.

The estate's lush gardens include its own
church and a former school for the labourers'
children. There's also a museum (summer only)
displaying vintage photographs by Vittorio Sella of
the company's early wine production. Another
museum houses artefacts found at the Anghelu
Ruju archaeological site, which was part of Sella &
Mosca's property until they donated it to the
comune.

Fertilia

Sandy beaches line the coast west of Alghero,
connected by bike paths that nearly reach as far as
Fertilia. The town ('Fertileville') was one of
Mussolini's imaginatively named land reclamation
schemes (see page 32) and was repopulated with
farmers from Ferrara, who built the austere dark
stone parish church and campanile. The place
resembles an army barracks, with an arcaded main
street that offers little relief from the otherwise
right-angled austerity.

Just inland is Alghero's airport (see page 271),
while on the coast to the west are two prime
beaches, **Le Bombarde** and **Lazzaretto**.

Nuraghe Palmavera

Less than a kilometre past Spiaggia Lazzaretto, the
crumbling remains of Nuraghe Palmavera nearly
tumble into the road. The village dates back to the
15th century BC and preserves two towers: the first
in limestone and the second in sandstone
surrounded by roughly 50 circular huts.
Archaeologists insist that another 150 huts lie
buried between the road and the sea and that, in
the village's golden age around the ninth century
BC, it housed 800 people. The reunion hut, where
the elders held court and performed religious
rituals, dates from this period. At its centre is a
remarkable model of a nuraghe, leading some
archaeologists to believe that the Bronze Age
towers became the subject of cult worship by
subsequent generations.

Porto Conte & Noah's Ark

The holiday community of Porto Conte is named
after the calm, crescent-shaped bay that stretches
from Punta Giglio in the east to Capo Caccia in the
west. A flat road rings the bay, going north around
pine and eucalyptus groves, and doubles as a
wonderful jogging or cycling route. The area's two
most popular beaches, **Mugoni** and **La Stalla** are
signposted right next to each other.

On their way to Capo Caccia, nature lovers
should stop off at the **Foresta Demaniale Le
Prigionette** (Km 5, SP55, T079-949060, Mon-Fri
0800-1600, Sat-Sun 0900-1700). The site of a former
prison, the park consists of 1,200 ha of protected
land and is nicknamed '*L'arca di Noè*' (Noah's Ark)
because of the diverse animals that have been
introduced here since the 1970s, turning it into a
virtual zoo of Sardinian fauna: deer from central
Sardinia, miniature horses from the Giara plateau
and albino donkeys from Asinara, among others.
Two hiking trails criss-cross between ilex trees,
heather and strawberry scrub and end at Cala della
Barca with views of Isola Piana.

Capo Caccia & the Grotta di Nettuno

South of Porto Conte, the road climbs past the placid Tramariglio and Dragunara bays and their Aragonese towers to the 107-m peak of Capo Caccia. Turn right at the 'Panoramica' sign to peer out over the windswept and barren **Isola Foradada** from the edge of Cala dell'Inferno (Hell's Cove). This is one of Sardinia's more dramatic and popular places to watch the sun set, so come early.

The road dead-ends at the ticket office for one of Europe's most renowned caves, the **Grotta di Nettuno** (T079-946540, tours every hour, Apr-Sep daily 0800-1900, Oct daily 0900-1800, Nov-Mar daily 0900-2000, closed during rain or rough seas, €10, €5 children). For the past 100 million years, nature has been hard at work battering Capo Caccia's limestone base with rough waves and constant winds to hollow out this spectacular 2.5-km cavern, and it makes visitors work hard too: to reach the cave's entrance you must either descend for 110 m down the steep 656-step Escala del Cabirol or arrive by boat from Alghero's port. The round-trip by boat takes about 2½ hrs and is operated by **Traghetti Navisarda** (T079-978961, navisarda.it), with departures hourly 0900-1700 from June to September, and at 0900, 1000 and 1500 only in April, May and October; purchase tickets (€12, €6 children) at the port.

Once inside the cave, the 200-m guided tour skirts the Lago Lamarmora, a saltwater lake fed by the sea and goes from the first chamber to the Smith Room, named after one of the cave's early explorers. Backlights allow you to marvel at a wonderland of stalactites, stalagmites and columns coloured from orange to a deep green, with nicknames like the 'Christmas Tree', 'Grand Organ' and 'Cupola'. The cavern shelters a small, sandy beach inside and saves its most delicate treasure for last: the Lace Room, where thousands of crystallized creations dangle from the ceiling like a stitched pattern.

The Nurra

North of Capo Caccia, the landscape flattens out into a fertile valley covered by farmland and eucalyptus trees, forming Sardinia's northwestern corner, the Nurra. Along the way, signs indicate Lago Baratz, Sardinia's only natural lake, where pine trees and sand dunes keep what little water there is from escaping to the sea. The region's star attraction, however, is a beach of jaw-dropping beauty, La Pelosa. Beyond its shelving shoreline lies the uninhabited Asinara national park, home to the world's only breed of albino donkey.

Stintino

Where Sardinia's northwestern tip narrows to a sliver lies the sunny fishing community of Stintino. The village takes its name from the Sardo word 'isthintinu' (narrow passage) and was founded in 1885, when 45 fishing families of Ligurian descent were displaced from their homes on Asinara island to make way for a state prison. Until 1972, the Stintinesi held an annual tuna mattanza (see page 109) but the industrial boom in Porto Torres in the 1970s and '80s warmed the surrounding waters,

Tip...

For a graphic visual of Stintino's traditional tuna slaughter, check out the mural at the bottom of via Asinara.

Around the island

changing the tuna's migration and effectively killing the industry. Like Carloforte (another Ligurian outpost), Stintino today is a medley of colourful, boxy houses on the water but the population hasn't kept up the traditional dialect or trade, and it's now tourists, not tuna, that drive the economy. Over 50,000 tourists descend on the area each summer to splash around Stintino's luminous beaches, so book ahead if you plan to come here in high season.

Stintino juts out from between two ports: the old Porto Minori for fishing boats and the newer Porto Mannu for yachts, where you can find information on excursions to Asinara (see page right). This is also where you'll find a trailer housing the **Museo della Tonnara** (Porto Mannu, T079-512209, May-Sep Tue-Sun 1800-2400, €1.55, €1 children), which recalls the glory days of the tuna trade and is cleverly modelled on the fishermen's six-chambered tuna nets, finishing in the *camera della morte* (deathbed).

La Pelosa.

La Pelosa

Throughout Italy, Stintino is synonymous with beaches. The most magnificent is La Pelosa, which lies 3.5 km north at Capo Falcone. Anyone who's ever posted a letter in Italy might already be familiar with the scene, as La Pelosa is one of two images – along with the Tuscan countryside – that the Italian post features on its stamps to illustrate Italy's natural beauty. A spherical patch of flour-white sand slowly shelves into the turquoise sea, changing hue with the varying depths. From the beach, you can wade out to a small island housing the 16th-century **Torre Pelosa** just offshore or look out towards Isola Piana in the distance. In the summer the place is mobbed, so you'll need to arrive extra early to grab a sliver of sand for your towel.

Isola di Asinara

Behind the deserted, *macchia*-blanketed Isola Piana is Isola di Asinara (donkey island), named after the world's only race of miniature albino donkeys which live here. At 17 km long by 6 km wide, Asinara is Sardinia's second-largest offshore island, yet aside from the donkeys, a few mouflon and pigs, it is completely uninhabited.

The island's remote location and harsh landscape of sharp cliffs and treeless shrub has shaped its odd history. It was used as a quarantine station for cholera victims in 1861, as a penal colony from 1885, and as a maximum security prison for Red Brigade and Mafia members until 1997 when it became a national park.

Today the park is a popular excursion for divers, trekkers and those looking to spot the snow-white, dwarf donkeys. Visitors dock at **Fornelli** at Asinara's southern point where guides are on hand to whisk tourists around on sightseeing trains or by bus to one of the park's three beaches at **Cala D'Oliva** in the northeast, where they can join other tours (see page 266).

Impretours run ferries from Stintino's Porto Mannu (T079-508024, Easter-Sep daily 0930 and

1530, €12) and from P orto Torres, near the Aragonese tower (T079-508042, 0830 and 1500, €12) to Asinara. Fara (T348-472 2562) runs buses from the dock at Fornelli to Cala D'Oliva; call ahead to reserve tickets. It's possible to tour Asinara without a guide but, in the summer with soaring temperatures and no shade, we don't recommend it. You should also bring your own food and water, as there are no shops.

Castelsardo & around

In the 12th century the Genoese Doria family dreamed of establishing a fortified settlement near Alghero to ensure political and economic control of northwest Sardinia. In hindsight, if they wanted to keep invaders out, they probably shouldn't have chosen one of the island's most dramatically beautiful settings as its location. Instead, they built Castelgenovese above a rocky promontory overlooking the Gulf of Asinara, with a medieval town rising like a wave up to a castle at its summit, and the sharp hillside breaking below. Sure enough, unwelcome visitors were soon knocking at the door and, by 1448, Castelgenovese had been renamed Castelaragonese after its new owners. Like in much of Sardinia, Aragonese rule led to a subsequent decline marked by rampant malaria outbreaks and pirate raids in the town. The Savoyards changed the town's name again to Castelsardo in 1769, and Ligurian immigrants introduced the town to its thriving fish and lobster industry. Today, Castelsardo remains understandably popular with visitors. A modern residential neighbourhood has grown up below the castle but the town's residents retain many of their age-old traditions, particularly the production of fine hand-woven baskets.

Five of the best

Souvenirs from northwest Sardinia

❶ A handmade knife from Pattada (see page 241).

❷ A bottle of wine from the Sella & Mosca cantina, especially La Cala Vermentino white, or Cannonau Riserva red (see page 252).

❸ A piece of coral or filigree jewellery from Alghero (see page 265).

❹ Ozieri's delicious sospiri almond and sugar sweets (see page 265).

❺ A hand-woven basket from Castelsardo (see page 265).

A local of Castelsardo hard at work weaving baskets.

Castelsardo.

Medieval Castelsardo

Visitors arrive in Castelsardo's lower, modern district, which is chock-full of restaurants and tourist emporiums. All roads lead up from the central piazza della Pianedda to the medieval district: you can either climb the steep steps up via Trieste or drive up via Nazionale.

Fortezza dei Doria crowns Castelsardo at its highest point. Built by the Dorias in 1102, the castle housed Eleonora d'Arborea when her brother, Ugone III, was killed in 1383, forcing her to take over as *giudicessa* of Arborea. The fortress has outlived its defensive purpose and now holds the Museo dell'Intreccio (T079-471380, Mon-Sat 0930-1300 and 1500-1830, €2, €1 children), dedicated to Sardinia's ancient basket- and wicker-weaving traditions. The castle culminates at the terrace with sky-high views of Castelsardo and the entire gulf below. Outside, it's not uncommon to see women sitting in their doorways weaving palm leaves into baskets.

Via Seminario connects the medieval district's two churches: the 16th-century Chiesa di Santa Maria, famous for its 13th-century black crucifix, and the Cattedrale di Sant'Antonio Abate, which is dwarfed by its octagonal campanile. The Dorias originally designed the soaring tower as a lighthouse and later topped it with a multi-hued majolica dome. The church's highlight is a Baroque painting above the main altar of the Madonna with six angels by the enigmatic 'Maestro di Castelsardo'. Sant'Antonio Abate's foundations rest on top of an early Romanesque structure, which is partially visible in the crypt as part of the Museo Diocesano Cripte (Jun-Aug daily 1030-1300 and 1830-2400, €2).

Roccia dell'Elefante

Three-and-a-half kilometres southeast of Castelsardo, where the SS134 and SS200 meet, you can't miss the red trachyte Elephant Rock, so called because its wind-eroded 'trunk' nearly hangs over the road. A closer look reveals several *domus de janas* tombs hollowed out of the Elephant's base by the Ozieri Culture in about 3500 BC. If you crouch down, you'll see two bull's horns carved into either side.

Nuraghe Paddaggiu & Valledoria

From the Elephant, take the SS200 exit towards the pleasant coastal town of Valledoria. Slow down as you ride under the overpass and look for a dirt path soon after on the left from which to admire Nuraghe Paddaggiu. You can't visit Paddaggiu

Left: Roccia dell'Elefante.
Above: Anglona.

(haystack, in Sardo), but a landscaping crew of gazing sheep provides a quintessentially "Sardinian" photo-op.

Seven kilometres on, the coastal beachtown of Valledoria is the best bathing option near Castelsardo – though the Castelsardesi just swim off their own rocky coast. A 10-km beach stretches east from here to Isola Rossa, changing names as it goes: the most popular section is **Baia Verde** near the town's entrance. Valledoria sits at the mouth of northern Sardinia's longest river, the Coghinas, which can be explored by kayak or canoe as a great way to beat the crowds (see page 266).

Anglona

Inland, the undulating farmland of the Anglona region was home to the first known Sardinians back in the Late Paleolithic Age (500,000 BC) but is sparsely populated today. With your own transportation you could easily see the following sights in a single day. Ten kilometres south of Castelsardo, Tergu's main attraction is the **Nostra Signora di Tergu** church. The site has always been a holy place – first as a Nuraghic temple, then a Roman temple, and later a monastery. The Pisans are responsible for the present medieval reincarnation: a 12th century Romanesque church

built with red trachyte and outlined in white limestone. Two columns frame the façade's rose window, and a square campanile backs the structure. On via Nazionale is a massive limestone boulder containing a series of *domus de janas* burial tombs from the third millennium BC. The Spanish converted the mound into a prison and, when they left, it was used as a residence, right up until 2001. Today, the site houses an ethnographic display (via Nazionale 23, T349-844 0436, web.tiscali.it/sedini, Jun-Sep daily 0900-1300 and 1500-1800, or by appointment, donations welcome).

Continue east on the SS134 past Bulzi and look for the 12th-century Pisan-Romanesque **Chiesa di San Pietro di Simbranos** in an abandoned field to the left. A bas-relief on the façade shows a Benedictine abbot standing between bearded monks with his arms raised in prayer. Evidence of the area's earliest Paleolithic inhabitants is on display in Perfugas at the **Museo Archeologico e Paleobotanico** (via Sauro, T079-564241, Jun-Sep Tue-Sun 0900-1300 and 1600-2000, Oct-May Tue-Sun 0900-1300 and 1500-1900, €3). The village also has a late Nuraghic well temple in its centre.

Sleeping

Sassari

Frank Hotel €€
*Via Diaz 20, T079-276456,
frankhotel.com.*
Frank is the cheapest hotel in town and caters to the business crowd. Aesthetically, it's stuck in the '80s (note the crank phone in the hallway) but the rooms are perfectly fine and the breakfast buffet is small but appetizing. The bathroom is shoehorned in a closet-sized space and has a shower that's guaranteed to flood your floor.

Vittorio Emanuele €€
*Corso Vittorio Emanuele 100/102, T079-235538,
hotelvittorioemanuele.ss.it.*
This is Sassari's nicest hotel, conveniently located a short walk from the train and bus stations. Set in a refurbished building on Sassari's main avenue, the rooms all come equipped with air-conditioning and private bath. The lobby's art gallery and the vaulted wine cellar add a touch of class.

Casa Chiara €
Vicolo Bertolinis 7, T079-200 5052, casachiara.net.
This is a great and affordable B&B in the centre of the medieval district. The second-floor of an 18th-century *palazzo* has been restored to offer three rooms sharing two baths. Guests may also use the kitchen.

The Logudoro

Hotel Liberty €
*Piazza dei Poeti, Pattada, T079-755384,
libertyhotelpattada.it.*
Pattada's finest hotel has 11 modern rooms in an attractive art nouveau building from the 1920s. Each has a bright tiled bathroom, TV and air-conditioning. The restaurant downstairs makes its own *Pattadese* pasta and the local owner can point potential knife buyers in the right direction.

Alghero

Villa Las Tronas €€€€
Lungomare Valencia 1, T079-981818, villalastronas.com.
Four-night minimum in summer.
Alghero's most prestigious hotel hosted Italian royalty until the 1940s and still feels like a palatial villa. Set on a rocky bluff jutting into the sea, Las Tronas retains the trappings of its regal past: antique beds, oriental rugs and mahogany chests. Add lush gardens, a pool and a spa, encircled by sweeping views of the sea, and this place is something else!

Hotel Catalunya €€€
Via Catalogna 24, T079-953172, hotelcatalunya.it.
This hotel has a no-fuss business-class feel about it but, with 128 air-conditioned rooms, you're likely to find space here when there's none elsewhere. Request a view towards Alghero's historic district.

Aigua €
Via Machin 22, T339-591 2476, algua.it.
This completely restored B&B in Alghero's historical district has three cosy apartments, each with air-conditioning and private bathroom, plus a shared downstairs kitchen. The delightful location and charm more than make up for its low wooden ceilings and lack of lift.

Hotel San Francesco €
Via Machin 2, T079-980330, sanfrancescohotel.com.
This unique and central hotel is housed in a former 14th-century convent. The rooms have everything you need and not much else but many overlook the attractive cloistered courtyard below, where breakfast is served.

Mamajuana €
Vicolo Adami 12, T339-136 9791, mamajuana.it.
Found up a flight of steps on one of the old town's cobblestone side streets, this old building has been done-up and has four sunny rooms overlooking piazza Municipio. Never mind the small bathrooms and scant breakfast served out of a vending

machine, you can't beat the price and the location.

Camping
La Mariposa €
Via Lido 22, T079-950360, lamariposa.it.
Mar-Sep only.
One kilometre north of Alghero, La Mariposa is Sardinia's oldest campsite but remains one of its better ones. In addition to spaces for tents and campers, guests may book bungalows and small villas. The private beach, Internet access, bike rentals, kite, diving and windsurfing centre ensure the hours fly by.

Around Alghero

El Faro €€€€
Località Porto Conte, 10 km west of Alghero towards Punta del Giglio, T079-942010 elfarohotel.it.
Apr-Oct only.
Set on a dramatic rocky outpost at the end of Porto Conte, this resort's stylish rooms overlook the calm bay below and face Capo Caccia. Guests have use of two pools and a spa, plus diving, sailing and other excursions.

Punta Negra €€€€
Between Fertilia and Porto Conte, T079-930222, hotelpuntanegra.com.
Apr-Oct only.
The elegant property borders its own private beach and has a pool and tennis courts. It's also

affiliated to diving and windsurfing outfitters. All rooms have balconies but you'll want one with a view of the bay.

Agriturismo Porticciolo €
Località Porticciolo, Porto Conte, T079-918000, agriturismoporticciolo.it.
Signposted where the SS127 meets the road around Porto Conte, Porticciolo has cute bungalow-style apartments, each with its own kitchenette, upstairs loft, bathroom and air-conditioning. Meals are served in an enormous wooden dining room where guests gorge themselves on four courses by an open hearth.

The Nurra

La Pelosetta €€€
Località Capo Falcone, Stintino, T079-527188, lapelosetta.it.
May-Oct only.
This sand-coloured building is steps away from La Pelosa with a view that's worth every penny. In addition to well-equipped standard rooms, guests may reserve apartments by the week.

Silvestrino €€
Via Sassari 14, Stintino, T079-523007, hotelsilvestrino.it.
Mar-Nov only.
Silvestrino is a comfortable hotel that doesn't go overboard when it comes to amenities, so spend a few euros more and request air-conditioning. The panoramic

Eating & drinking

terrace and the top-floor rooms have great views of the twin harbours but the restaurant is the stand-out attraction.

Ostello Cala d'Oliva €
Località Cala d'Oliva, Isola di Asinara, T346 173 7043, sognasinara.com.
May-Oct only.
Asinara's park cooperative runs the island's only accommodation: a restaurant and modest hostel that's better suited to the adventurous than those seeking comfort. The hostel has a large terrace facing the sea and 110 beds, divided into rooms of up to five people, each with its own shower.

Castelsardo & around

Hotel Riviera €€
Via Lungomare Anglona 1, Castelsardo, T079-470143, hotelriviera.net.
The Riviera is located below the rising old town across the street from Castelsardo's small beach. The modern rooms offer plenty of comfort and the restaurant downstairs is one of Castelsardo's best and most expensive seafood options.

Casa Doria €
Via Garibaldi 10, Castelsardo, T349-355 7882, casadoria.it.
If you can haul your bags up to Castelsardo's medieval district, the Casa Doria is an attractive option at one of Castelsardo's highest points. Three (rather dark) rooms share two bathrooms but the highlight is the upstairs breakfast room, with its thatched roof, fireplace and seaside views of the Gulf of Asinara.

Eleonora d'Arborea €
Via Garibaldi 19, Castelsardo, T347-605 4828, residenzaeleonoradarborea.it.
An elegantly restored B&B housed in a 13th-century building. There are three rooms and, while you can't go wrong with any of them, the best is the top-floor apartment with its own kitchen and balcony. Owner Martino is local and owns the food shop downstairs.

Camping
La Foce
Via Ampurias 1, Valledoria, T079-582109, lafoce.eu.
May-Sep only.
La Foce is set around eucalyptus trees at the mouth of the Coghinas river and steps from the beach. The bungalows and villa lodging options are quite refined. New Kayak Sardinia operates from here.

Sassari

Il Cenacolo €€€€
Via Ozieri 2, T079-236251.
Mon-Sat 1300-1430 and 2000-2230.
A chic affair with stiff white tablecloths and flickering candles by night. Seafood is Cenacolo's speciality, with several dishes incorporating *bottarga* or mussels.

L'Antica Hostaria €€€€
Via Cavour 55, T079-200066.
Mon-Sat 1300-1430, 2000-2230.
This rust-red restaurant is run by two brothers and is Sassari's finest and most intimate eatery. Choose from mouth-watering bass served in broccoli sauce, rabbit filled with porcini mushrooms and thyme in a pumpkin sauce or orzo with shrimp.

Trattoria Da Antonio €€€
Via Arborea 2B, T079-234297.
Mon-Sat 1230-1430 and 1930-2245.
A rustic atmosphere pervades this revamped warehouse. Pasta is nowhere in sight but there are lots of *secondi* to choose from. The *cordula con piselli* is a *Sassarese* speciality: cow's intestines with onions and peas in a sauce.

Trattoria L'Assassino €€
Vicolo Ospizio Cappuccini 1A,
T079-235041.
Mon-Sat 1230-1500 and
2000-2230.
The Assassin is hidden in an alley
near via Tola and loved by locals
for its quality and fair prices. If
there's two of you, opt for the
'Sassareseria' and sample eight
typical dishes from Sassari for
€18. The homemade *pane
carasau* bread is addictive.

Pizzeria Cocco €
Via Rosello 25, T079-238052
Mon-Sat 1000-1300 and
1700-2100.
A take-away in Sassari's historic
district with folded *pizzettas* and
typical chickpea *faine*.

Cafés & bars
Caffè Roma
Via Roma, T079-201 3003.
Mon-Sat 0700-2130.
Café by day, swanky bar by night
with modish types spilling out of
its backlighted yellow interior
onto the street.

Mocambo Caffè
Via Roma 97, T348-999 8375.
Mon-Sat 0730-2200.
A popular morning spot serving
the standard bar fare plus
delicious fresh orange juice.

The Logudoro

L'Opera €€
Piazza Garibaldi, Ozieri,
T079 787026.
Daily 1230-1430 and 1930-2245.

A surprise in the centre of Ozieri:
a casual restaurant serving surf
and turf inside a converted
two-storey ballroom with
frescoes covering the ceiling. The
gnochetti sardi are tasty but stay
away from the *agnello*.

Alghero

Al Tuguri €€€€
Via Maiorca 113, T079-976772.
Mon-Sat 1930-2300.
Al Tuguri is one of Alghero's most
famous luxury seafood
restaurants and has intimate
seating on three wood-panelled
levels. Mullet, sea urchin, bass,
squid, prawns and lobster are all
served with Iberian flair, and
there's delicious *crema catalana*
for dessert.

Il Pavone €€€€
Piazza Sulis 3/4, T079-979584,
Mon-Sat 1300-1500 and
2000-2230.
The Peacock is an *Algherese*
staple, with elegant patio seating
that overlooks the Torre Sulis.
Choose from fish or meat,
accompanied by Alghero's
famous Sella & Mosca wine.
Service is impeccable.

La Lepanto €€€€
Via Carlo Alberto 135,
T079-979116.
May-Sep daily, Oct-Apr
Tue-Sun.
Chef Moreno Cecchini is one of
Sardinia's most famous seafood
chefs, although locals complain

this place is not what it was since it came onto the tourist radar. Lobster is the star attraction: try it doused in orange sauce or, even better, with olive oil.

Al Refettorio €€€
Vicolo Adami 47, T079-731126.
Mon-Sat 1230-1430 and 1900-2330.
This new kid on the *carrer* is Alghero's restaurant of the moment. There's chic indoor seating with mood lighting or outdoor dining under a covered walkway. The mixed grilled seafood is a meal in itself, and the *paella algherese* is delicious. The restaurant doubles as a great wine bar with lots of munchies.

La Posada del Mar €€€
Vicolo Adami 29.
Mon-Sat 1230-1500 and 1900-2230.
Tables spill out onto the cobblestones from this upscale eatery. Choose from fixed menus at €18 and €28, or à la carte. The pasta and prawns dashed with saffron is good, but locals recommend the sea urchin.

Cafés & bars
Birreria Sant Miquel
Via Ardoino 51.
Tue-Sun 0900-1600 and 1900-0200.
Tables outdoors, chess boards indoors and lots of beer on tap. There are also wine, cocktails and sandwiches available.

Café del Corso
Via Carlo Alberto 77, T079-975596.
Daily 0800-0200.
The cascading oleanders and outdoor seating render this one of Alghero's most popular cafés, and the busy pedestrian thoroughfare makes for good people-watching.

Gelateria Arcobaleno
Piazza Civico 33.
Feb-Oct Thu-Mon 1100-2300, Tue-Wed 1300-2300.
Very hyped, but this small gelateria lives up to its reputation as Alghero's best.

Around Alghero

Sa Mandra Agriturismo €€€
Località Sa Segada, Fertilia, T079-999150.
Daily by reservation 1300-1500 and 1900-2200.
Rita, Mario and their two children operate this top-notch restaurant along the SP44 road north of the airport. All dishes come directly from the family's 100-ha farm and a typical meal is so plentiful (and delicious) that it's hard to pace yourself.

The Nurra

Silvestrino €€€€
Via Sassari 14, Stintino, T079-523007.
Fri-Wed 1930-2230.
Outdoor seating under a veranda facing the water and attention to detail by head chef Efisio Denegri make this Stintino's best seafood restaurant. Try the lobster soup and *cozze gratinate* mussels accompanied by a glass of Sella & Mosca wine.

Capo Falcone €€€
Località Capo Falcone, Stintino, T079 527037.
Daily 0900-2400, food served 1200-1500 and 1930-2300.
Located high above the cape, this restaurant/pizzeria has a two-level terrace overlooking La Pelosa beach. With a view like this, the food is often an afterthought, but the open grill serves some delicious steaks, and the seafood selection is impressive.

Cafés & bars
Lu Fanali
Lungomare Colombo 89, Stintino, T079-523054.
Daily 0730-2230, food served 1230-1430 and 1930-2200.
This cafè/pizzeria/bar has sublime patio seating directly on the water and serves snacks, salads, seafood and sweets.

Entertainment

Castelsardo

Il Cormorano €€€€
Via Colombo 7, T079-470628.
Wed-Mon 1930-2230.
Locals say the Pinna brothers serve some of the best seafood dishes around. Especially popular is the marinated tuna, linguine with sea urchin, and spaghetti with Castelsardo lobster.

La Guardiola €€€€
Piazza del Bastione 4,
T079-470428.
Tue-Sun 1230-1400 and 1930-2300.
Castelsardo's most upscale restaurant occupies much of its finest real estate on piazza del Bastione. Whether you get a table inside or on the terrace, you're guaranteed amazing views of the coast. Pasta and meat dishes here are fine, but the Guardiola is known for its seafood.

La Trattoria €€€
Via Nazionale 20, T079-470661.
Tue-Sun 1230-1430 and 1930-2230.
Pictures of shaggy old-time shepherds adorn the walls in this sophisticated but relaxed eatery. Chef Maria Giuseppa whips up *pane carasau* topped with onions, penne with crab and fantastic *zuppa gallurese* (by reservation).

Sassari

Clubs
Sergeant Pepper
Via Asproni 20, T079-282805.
Fri-Sun 2300-0400.
Sassari's most central disco plays mainly Latin and salsa music on Friday, and live hip-hop or house music on Saturday and Sunday.

Tumbao
Largo Pazzola 11, T349-332 7913.
Thu-Sat 2200-0300.
This club tucked into Sassari's historic district is private, but the owners are tourist-friendly. The bar is popular with the university crowd and plays a variety of music, from Latin to pop to jazz to Sardo folk.

Festivals & events
On the second to last Sunday in May, thousands of Sardi in traditional dress convene in Sassari for the **Cavalcata Sarda**, a parade through the streets, followed by music and dancing.

Gay & lesbian
Time
Via Civitavecchia 3/G.
Tue-Sat 2100-0300.
A gay-friendly wine bar in downtown Sassari.

Porto Torres & around

Festivals & events
In early May pilgrims from throughout northwestern Sardinia walk to Porto Torres' San Gavino church for **Festha Manna**, to pray for the three martyred saints, Gavino, Proto and Gianuario.

The Logudoro

Festivals & events

Ozieri commerates the summer solstice with a bonfire on 23rd June. It also celebrates the **Festa della Madonna del Rimedio** at the end of September to thank the Virgin for ridding the town of the plague. The religious festival is followed by the Su Cantaru and *Cantareddu* choral and poetry competition.

Alghero

Children

Trenino Catalano
Porta a Mare, T336-691836.
€5, €3 under-9s.
A tourist train whisks families through Alghero's historic district with (somewhat unintelligible) descriptions of the town's sights in English on this 20-minute tour.

Clubs
El Tró
Lungomare Valencia 3, T079-973 3000.
Fri-Sat 2300-0500.
A lively disco within walking distance of downtown Alghero. This attractive club is set on a rock jutting into the water, which helps justify its popularity (especially with tourists), high entrance fee and drink prices.

Festivals & events
Known as **San Christus dei Jermans Blancs**, Alghero's Easter rites are steeped in Catalan influence. On the Tuesday before Easter, the *Processione dei Misteri* (Passion of the Christ) leaves from San Francesco church, followed by the parade of a 17th-century wooden cross. On Good Friday, four men remove the nails from a statue of Jesus and on Easter Sunday, it is paraded through the streets. Other events on the calendar include the **Sagra del Riccio Mare** (sea urchin harvest) in early March and an international classical music festival, **Estate Musicale**, in July and August.

Performance
Teatro Civico
Piazza Vittorio Emanuele, T079-973 1057.
Built in 1826, this is Sardinia's only wooden theatre and hosts frequent theatre productions and concerts.

Around Alghero

Clubs
Il Ruscello
Località Angeli Custodi, T079-953168.
Jun-Sep Thu-Sat 2300-0500.
One of the northeast's most popular discos is found 10 km north of Alghero toward Olmedo. The open-air club has two dance rooms separated by a large garden and specializes in house, techno and pop music.

The Nurra

Clubs
L'Isolotto
Via Cala di Rena, Stintino, T079-523088.
May-Sep Fri-Sat 2400-0500.
L'Isolotto is also a bar/pizzeria but it's mainly known as Stintino's only disco. DJs spin dance music by the club's outdoor pool overlooking the sea.

Castelsardo & around

Festivals & events
Easter is a decidedly Spanish-themed affair in Castelsardo. On Good Friday, hooded men enact a mock funeral for Christ, while on Easter Monday, the **Lunissanti** procession travels from Castelsardo to Tergu for a torch-lighting ceremony at Nostra Signora church.

Shopping

Antica Salumeria Mangatia
Via Università 68, T079-234710.
Mon-Fri 0830-1330 and
1700-2000, Sat 0830-1330.
Sells a myriad of fresh cheeses,
pastas and meats from around
the island, including *panadas*
packed with meat from
Montiferru's *bue rosso* bulls.

The Logudoro

Pasticceria Pinna Pietro
*Via Pastorino 35, Ozieri,
T079-787451.*
Mon-Sat 0900-1200 and
1630-1900.
Ozieri is known for its handmade
desserts, especially *sospiri* (sighs),
made from almond paste and
covered in sugar, chocolate or
myrtle.

Piero Fogarizzu
*Via Belvedere, Pattada,
T079-754137.*
By appointment only.
Piero comes from four
generations of *pattadese*
knife-makers and is considered
one of Sardinia's top craftsmen.
He typically works only by
custom order and pays for
shipping within Italy.
International shipping costs are
split with the customer.

Alghero

DeFilippi's
Via Roma 41, T079-978100.
Apr-Oct daily 0930-2100,
Nov-Mar daily 0930-1300 and
1630-2000.
Lots of blood-red coral in
necklace, earring and bracelet
form plus watches and turquoise
jewellery. English-speaking staff.

Explora
Via Carlo Alberto 65, T079-981991.
Mon-Sat 0930-1300 and
1630-2000.
There's a little of everything
Sardinian in this one-stop
souvenir shop: crafts, wine,
sweets, cheese, *bottarga*, cork,
knives… you name it, it's here!

Il Labirinto
*Via Carlo Alberto 119,
T079-980496*
Daily 0900-1330 and 1500-2100.
A classic bookshop with a few
English-language novels and
some beautiful black-and-white
photography books showing
Sardinia in the 1950s.

Castelsardo

Tutto Artigianato
Via Roma 31, T079-471266.
Mon-Sat 0900-1330 and
1500-2000.
A wonderful place to purchase
Castelsardo's trademark
handmade baskets. Upstairs,
hand-woven rugs from
throughout Sardinia are sold.

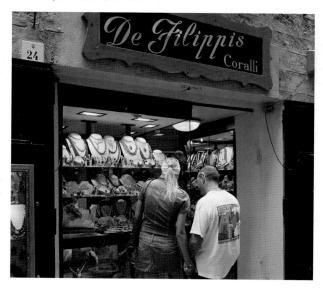

Activities & tours

Alghero

Andrea Jensen
T338-970 8139, ajsailing.com.
€75 per person, €35 children.
Cruise around coastal Alghero aboard a 1930s yacht. The bilingual crew pick you up from the port in the morning, whisk you around Capo Caccia, past prime dolphin-spotting waters where you stop for snorkelling and lunch made fresh on the boat, before sailing back to town. With a usual quota of just 12 people, this is spectacular!

NautiSub
Via Garibaldi 45, T079-952433, nautisub.com.
Bilingual staff run full- and half-day dive trips to Capo Caccia and Nereo's Cave, all starting from €38.

Pintadera
Vicolo Adami 41, T079-917064, pintadera.info.
Wine tasting, Italian courses and cooking lessons in the heart of Alghero.

Stroll & Speak
Via Cavour 4, T339-489 9314, strollandspeak.com.
Learn Italian from locals while walking around Alghero.

Around Alghero

Capo Galera Diving Center
Località Capo Galera, southwest of Lazzaretto, T079-942110, capogalera.com.
This well-established dive operator runs dozens of training courses and submersions around the Rivieria del Corallo, including the fantastic Nereo's Cave. Single dives start at €20. Keen divers will want to stay at the centre's fabulous villa hotel overlooking the sea.

The Nurra

Asinara Diving Center
Porto dell'Ancora, Stintino, T079-527000, asinaradivingcenter.it.
Locals say this is your best bet for diving in Asinara's protected marine park. It also offers dives around Capo Falcone and runs courses for adults and children as young as eight.

Windsurfing Center Stintino
Località L'Approdo, Stintino, T079-527006, windsurfingcenter.it.
This top-notch outfitter is on Le Saline beach, offering windsurfing, sailing and diving lessons, boat hire and day-long excursions to Asinara aboard three 40-foot catamarans.

Transport

New Kayak Sardinia
Camping La Foce,
Via Ampurias 1, Valledoria,
T338-125 8403,
newkayaksardinia.it.
This outfit offers guided or individual kayak, canoe and paddle-boat excursions down the River Coghinas (by reservation). The three routes last between three and six hours (€19-22) and cut through the north coast's undeveloped countryside, past Roman ruins, juniper trees and canyons.

Sassari

There are frequent daily ARST buses to **Porto Torres** (30 mins) and **Alghero** (30 mins), plus up to seven daily to **Torralba** (50 mins-1hr 40 mins), one to **Olbia** (1 hr 30 mins), four to **Bosa** (2 hrs 15 mins) and two to **Cagliari** (3 hrs 30 mins). Up to four daily trains run from Sassari to **Cagliari** (2 hrs 50 mins to 3 hrs 45 mins), 10 to **Alghero** (30 mins) and seven to **Olbia** (2 hrs). Most routes require passengers to change at Ozieri-Chilivani.

Alghero

Up to 15 ARST buses travel daily from Alghero's via Catalogna to **Sassari** (1 hr), eight to **Porto Torres** (1 hr) and two to **Bosa** (1 hr). Up to 11 daily trains go to **Sassari** (35 mins) where you can change for trains to **Cagliari**.

Castelsardo

Up to 14 daily ARST buses travel from Castelsardo to **Sassari** (1 hr) and four stop at **Valledoria** (25 mins) en route to **Santa Teresa di Gallura** (1 hr 40 mins).

Contents

Practicalities

Getting there

Air

From UK and Ireland

Alitalia-Air One fly regularly to Cagliari from London-Heathrow by way of Rome, touching down in Sardinia in five hours. British Airways flies direct from London-Gatwick to Cagliari between April and October. Ryanair run a brisk trade, flying from Liverpool, London Stansted and East Midlands to Alghero, from Edinburgh, Dublin and Manchester to Cagliari, and from Birmingham to Olbia. Jet2 offers flights to Olbia from Edinburgh, Leeds and Manchester. ThomsonFly flies to Alghero from Birmingham and to Alghero and Olbia from London Gatwick. EasyJet goes from London Luton to Cagliari.

From North America

The cheapest option from North America is to book a transatlantic flight into a European city that has discount flights to one of Sardinia's three airports (see below) – whichbudget.com or europebyair.com are both good resources. Note: you may have to transfer airports within the city you fly into and you should be sure to check the connecting airline's luggage requirements beforehand. The most convenient options are either to book a flight with Eurofly from New York into Rome, Palermo or Naples and take one of the many daily flights into Sardinia, or to fly with AerLingus, which has cheap flights to Dublin from numerous US and Canadian cities, and then hop on a low-cost carrier to Sardinia.

From the rest of Europe

Flights to Sardinia from the Italian mainland are operated by the joint company Alitalia-Air One, Meridiana, Ryanair and Volare. Flying tends to be relatively expensive, with fewer flights outside the high season of May to October. The cheapest fares are generally found with Meridiana, Ryanair and Volare.

Alitalia-AirOne, EasyJet, Meridiana, Ryanair, ThomasCook, Transavia and TUI have flights to Cagliari and Alghero from several major European cities outside Italy. AirBerlin, EasyJet, jet2, Ryanair, SkyEurope, ThomasCook, Transavia and TUI fly to Olbia. Check the company websites and whichbudget.com for specific routes.

Airport information

Cagliari Elmas Airport (T070-211211, sogaer.it) is 6 km north of Cagliari. Departures are on the top level and Arrivals on the ground floor, where you will also find a tourist booth and many car hire offices. There's a taxi stand outside Arrivals. A white or blue public bus departs every 15-20 minutes for piazza Matteoti in central Cagliari; buy tickets on the ground floor of the airport.

Olbia Airport (T0789-563444, geasar.it) is located 5 km south of Olbia and serves the northeast. This newly revamped, compact airport has a tourist information booth where you can buy tickets for the bus journey into Olbia (buses 2 or 10, every 30 mins 0730-2000). There's a taxi stand outside and car hire firms operate from a separate building.

Alghero Airport (T079-935124, aeroportodialghero.it) is 12 km north of Alghero and serves the northwest. This is the smallest of Sardinia's three airports. The Arrivals hall has car hire outlets and a tourist booth, where an assistant can tell you about buses into Alghero or Sassari. Taxis are parked outside and there's a private Logudoro service (logudorotours.it/orari.php), which runs buses to Macomer, Oristano and Cagliari; buy tickets on board.

Sea

The main Sardinian ports are Porto Torres (northwest), Olbia (northeast) and Cagliari (south) and the slightly smaller Arbatax (east) and Golfo Aranci (northeast). Travelling overland to Sardinia will involve a ferry crossing, taking between five and ten hours, from either France (Toulon, Savona, Marseille) or mainland Italy (Genoa, Livorno, Naples, Civitavecchia, Piombino). There are also services connecting Sardinia with Corsica (Bastia, Ajaccio, Propriano and Bonifacio) and Sicily (Palermo and Trapani). Note that some services from mainland France travel via a Corsican port.

While ferries to Sardinia take considerably longer than flights, they are usually more comfortable, with cabins and full amenities. However, with so many low-cost airlines in operation, flights are often the cheaper option. The cheapest and quickest ferry service from continental Europe is from Civitavecchia to Olbia, Golfo Aranci or Arbatax (4 hrs 30 mins, roughly €50 per person).

The French company **SNMC** (T0825-888088 or T020-7491 4968, snmc.fr) sails from French ports. Italian operators (with UK agents) sailing from both France and Italy include **Grand Navi Veloci** (T020-8343 5810, gnv.it), **Tirrenia** (T020-7244 8422, tirrenia.it) and **Corsica and Sardinia Ferries** (T0825-095095, corsica-ferries.co.uk). For more information on routes and timetables, consult the company websites or **aferry.to**.

Rail

To reach Sardinia by train, you can catch a fast TGV to Marseille from either Lille (5 hrs) or Paris (3 hrs) or a sleeper train from these stations to Nice, followed in each case by a ferry (see above). If you're travelling from the UK to France by **Eurostar** (eurostar.com), bear in mind that you'll need to cross Paris from the Gare du Nord to the Gare de Lyon to board the TGV or sleeper services, whereas in Lille all services use the same station. Alternatively, travel through the Italian mainland with **Trenitalia** (trenitalia.it) before picking up a ferry from one of the ports on the west coast. Whichever route you choose, allow several hours for a safe connection between the train and ferry. Buy tickets through **Rail Europe** (T0870-584 8848, raileurope.co.uk, raileurope.com) or **SNCF** (voyages-sncf.com). For comprehensive information on rail travel throughout Europe, consult **seat61.com**.

Road

Car

Driving through France to Toulon and taking a ferry for the 370-km passage to Porto Torres in the north of Sardinia is the most direct road route from the UK but will still take over 20 hours, including the ferry crossing. Unless the journey through France is an important part of your holiday, booking a discount flight and hiring a car in Sardinia is usually the more practical option.

Bus/coach

There are no scheduled European bus or coach services to Sardinia but several organizations occasionally hire buses and vans for parties travelling between mainland Italy and Sardinia. Check **nicosgroup.it**, **logudorotours.it** and **gruppoturmotravel.com**.

Getting around

Rail

In general, rail travel in Sardinia is inexpensive, comfortable and slow. Since train lines are limited, we recommend hiring a car to reach most destinations. A rail service operated by Trenitalia runs year-round, twice a day between Cagliari in the south and Porto Torres in the northwest (4 hrs, €16) with more frequent services from Cagliari to the main stations en route: Oristano, Ozieri and Sassari. Two comparable branch lines shoot off this route, one heading west from Decimomannu to Iglesias (40 mins, €2.80), and one east from Ozieri-Chilivani to Golfo Aranci (90 mins, €5.65). Tickets can be booked at **trenitalia.com** or at the station via counter service or ticket machines. Even if you plan on travelling exclusively by train, don't bother buying a pass as a surcharge is often required, making single tickets better value.

Remember, you must validate train tickets at the yellow stamping machines before boarding.

The **Trenino Verde** (see page 184) offers summer tourist train services along four routes that are slow but very beautiful: Mandas–Arbatax (June-September), Isili–Sorgono (June-September), Macomer–Bosa (July-August) and Sassari–Palau (June-September). Buy your tickets at the station before boarding.

Road

Car

Sardinia's roads, when paved, are generally in good condition. However, due to the island's mountainous topography, few roads are straight and flat. Lanes are narrow, and dual-carriageways (eg the SS131) and rural roads are not lit at night and can be very dark. The SS131 is Sardinia's main thoroughfare and connects Cagliari to Oristano

(1 hr), Abbasanta (1 hr 30 mins), Sassari (2 hrs 30 mins) and Porto Torres (2 hrs 30 mins). The SS131dcn shoots east from Abbasanta to Nuoro (30 mins) and Olbia (1 hr 30 mins).

Speed limits are 110 kph on dual carriageways and 50 kph in towns. Limits are 20 kph lower on dual carriageways when the road is wet.
Automobile Club d'Italia (T06-49981 aci.it) provides driving information and offers roadside assistance with English-speaking operators on T116.

Many small towns have a single-lane main thoroughfare that has to deal with two-way traffic, so slow, cautious driving is recommended. Be aware that there are restrictions on driving in historic city centres, indicated by signs with black letters ZTL (*zona a traffico limitato*) on a yellow background. If you pass these signs in a vehicle, you are liable for a fine, although guests of town centre hotels are sometimes entitled to an official pass – contact your hotel or car hire company – that allows access to the hotel. Parking spaces with white lines are free, while those with blue lines require payment at nearby electronic metres, which are indicated with a "P" (roughly €1 an hour).

EU nationals taking their own car into Italy need to have an International Insurance Certificate (also known as a *Carte Verde*) and a valid national or EU licence. Those holding a non-EU licence may need to take an International Driving Permit with them. Unleaded petrol is *benzina*, diesel is *gasolio*.

Since July 2007 on-the-spot fines for minor traffic offences have been in operation; typically they range from €150 to €250 (always get a receipt). Note the following legal requirements: the use of mobile telephones while driving is not permitted; front and rear seatbelts must be worn, if fitted; children under 1.5 m may only travel in the back of the car. Italy has very strict laws on drink driving – the legal limit is 0.5g of alcohol per litre of blood – so steer clear of alcohol entirely to be safe. If your car breaks down on the carriageway, you must display an emergency triangle and wear a reflective jacket in poor visibility. Car hire companies should provide both of these, but check the boot when you pick up your car.

Car hire

Hiring a car in Sardinia is a relatively hassle-free process. It's always best to hire with a reputed agency, and the least expensive option throughout Sardinia is **Thrifty** (thrifty.it). Other agencies include **Hertz** (hertz.com), **Dollar** (dollar.com) and **Budget Car Rental** (budget.com). Car hire comparison websites and agents are a good place to start a search for the best deals. Try **rentalcargroup.com** or **carrentals.com**.

Car hire is available in several town centres but better rates are generally found at Sardinia's three airports (see page 270). You will probably wish to book the car before you arrive in the country; this is certainly advisable for popular destinations and at busy times of year. Check in advance the opening times of the car hire office.

Check what the hire company requires from you. Some companies may occasionally ask for an International Driving Licence, alongside your normal driving licence; others are content with an EU licence. You'll need to produce a credit card for most companies who will block a damage fee of €800-1,000 on to your card; this becomes unblocked if the vehicle is returned undamaged. If you book ahead, make sure that the named credit card holder is the same as the person renting and driving the car to avoid any problems. Most companies have a minimum age limit of 21 years and require that you've held your licence for at least a year. Some have a young driver surcharge for those under 25. Confirm insurance and any damage waiver charges and keep all your documents with you when you drive.

Bicycle

Drivers in Sardinian towns and cities are unaccustomed to sharing roads with cyclists, so limit your cycling to the open countryside where roads are rarely busy. Bikes can be hired at many of Sardinia's major tourist destinations between May and September; prices vary depending on the quality of the bike but are usually under €30 a day. There are a number of companies offering cycling tours of the island (see page 69).

Bus/coach

ARST (arst.sardegna.it) and **FdS** (ferroviesardegna. it) are the island's two state-run bus/coach companies. The privately owned **Turmo Travel** (gruppoturmotravel.com) also has widespread services, while **FMS** (ferroviemeridionalisarde.it) operates in the southwest. Buses are usually reliable but are slow and time consuming. If you're travelling without your own vehicle, you are advised to use both buses and trains to maximize your chances of reaching a given destination. A helpful resource is **getaroundsardinia.com**.

Directory

Customs and immigration

UK, EU and US citizens do not need a visa, but will need a valid passport to enter Italy. A standard tourist visa for those from outside the EU is valid for up to 90 days.

Disabled travellers

Like the rest of Italy, Sardinia is a bit behind when it comes to catering for disabled travellers and access is sometimes difficult or ill thought-out. Contact a specialist agency before departure for more details, such as **Accessible Italy** (accessibleitaly. com), Society for **Accessible Travel and Hospitality** (sath.org) or **Cagliari's Associazione Italiana Assistenza Spastici** (T070-379 1010).

Emergency numbers

Ambulance T118; Fire service T115; Police T112 (with English-speaking operators), T113 (*carabinieri*); Roadside assistance T116.

Etiquette

Bella figura – projecting a good image – is important to Sardinians. Take note of public notices about conduct: sitting on steps or eating and drinking in certain historic areas is not allowed. Spitting in public is considered disrespectful. Covering arms and legs is necessary for admission into some churches – in rare cases even shorts are not permitted. Punctuality is apparently not important in Sardinia, so be prepared to wait on occasion.

Families

Whether for a traditional beach break or an afternoon in a gelateria, children are well catered for in Sardinia. The family is highly regarded and *bambini* are indulged. Do note that sometimes lone parents or adults accompanying children of a different surname may need evidence before taking children in and out of the country. Contact your Italian embassy for current details: in London T020-7312 2200, in Washington DC T202-612-4400, in Dublin T353-1-660-1744, in Ottawa T613-232-2401, in Canberra T612-6273-3333.

Practicalities

Health

Comprehensive medical insurance is strongly recommended for all travellers to Italy. EU citizens should also apply for a free **European Health Insurance Card** (ehic.org), which replaced the E111 form and offers reduced-cost medical treatment.

Late-night pharmacies are identified by a large green cross outside; call T1100 for the addresses of the three nearest. The accident and emergency department of a hospital is the *pronto soccorso*.

Insurance

Comprehensive travel and medical insurance is strongly recommended for all travellers to Italy – the EHIC is not a replacement for private insurance. You should check any exclusions and that your policy covers you for all the activities you want to undertake. Keep details of your insurance documents separately; emailing yourself with the details is a good way to keep the information safe and accessible. Ensure you have full insurance if hiring a car, or, if you're taking your own car, contact your current insurers to see if you require an international insurance certificate.

Money

The Italian currency is the Euro (€). There are ATMs throughout Sardinia that accept major credit and debit cards. To change cash or travellers' cheques, look for a cambio. Many restaurants, shops, museums and art galleries will take major credit cards, though a €10 minimum is usually required. Paying directly with debit cards such as Cirrus is more difficult in many places, so withdrawing from an ATM and paying cash may be the best option.

Police

While it appears that there are several different types of police in Italy, the polizia (T113) and the *Carabinieri* (T112) are the most visible. The *polizia* are the 'normal' police under the control of the Interior Ministry, while the *Carabinieri* are a de facto military force. However both will respond if you need help.

Post

The Italian postal service (poste.it) has a not entirely undeserved reputation for unreliability, particularly when handling international shipments. Sardinia is worse. Passports are usually required when sending international packages (such as boxed souvenirs), and it's highly recommended that you insure your shipment and receive a tracking number. Overseas post will require *posta prioritaria* (priority mail) and a postcard stamp will cost from €0.60. You can buy *francobolli* (stamps) at post offices and *tabacchi* (look for T signs).

Safety

The crime rate in Sardinia is generally low, but rates of petty crime are higher than in much of the UK or USA. The ports around Cagliari and Olbia are reputed to be seedy at night but with common sense you shouldn't have problems. It is always advisable to take general care at night or when travelling: don't flaunt your valuables; take only the money you need and don't carry it all in one wallet or pocket. Pick-pockets and bag-cutters operate on public transport, so try not to make it obvious which stop you're getting off at, as it gives potential thieves a timeframe in which to work. Car break-ins are common, so always remove valuables and secure other luggage in the boot. Beware of

0781; Oristano 0783; Bosa 0785; Nuoro 0784; Ogliastra 0782; Sassari and Alghero 079; Gallura 0789. You need to use these local codes, even when dialling from within the city or region. The prefix for Italy is +39. You no longer need to drop the initial '0' from area codes when calling from abroad. For directory enquiries call T12.

Time difference

Italy uses Central European Time, GMT+1.

Tipping

Only the more expensive restaurants will necessarily expect a tip, although everywhere will be grateful for one: 10% is generous. You might leave a few spare coins at a café or restaurant that has provided especially good service or that has allowed you to spend an unusually long time at a table. Taxis may add on extra costs for luggage but an additional tip is always appreciated. Rounding-up prices always goes down well, especially if it means avoiding having to give change.

scams, con artists and sellers of fake goods: you can be fined for buying fake designer goods. In general, don't take risks you wouldn't at home. Take extra care not to drive or act aggressively or to offend locals in any way in rural Sardinia – especially in the province of Nuoro. While banditry targeting tourists has vanished, the *Nuoresi* are not known for backing away from a fight.

Tourist information

Sardinia's regional tourism office is located in Cagliari (viale Trieste 105, 070-606 7255, regione. sardegna.it, Mon-Fri 0900-1230 and 1530-1730). Useful websites include **ciaosardinia.com, hellosardinia.com, sardiniapoint.it, sardegna.com** and **sarnow.com**.

Telephone

The dialling codes for the main towns on the island are: Cagliari and around 070; Iglesiente and Sulcis

Voltage

Italy functions on a 220V mains supply and the standard European two-pin plug.

Language

People in Sardinia tend to speak less English than in other parts of Italy. In hotels and bigger restaurants, you'll usually find English is spoken but the further you go from the tourist centres, the more trouble you may have, unless you have at least a smattering of Italian. Alghero is probably the most English-friendly town; throughout much of the interior, you'll struggle to find an English speaker.

Sardinia's first language, Sardo, is spoken in much of the island but, with the exception of the very elderly, all Sardinians also speak Italian. Ironically, Sardinian Italian is often much easier than mainland Italian for foreigners to understand, as Sardinians tend to emphasize consonants and detach their words, so their speech may sound less garbled than Italian elsewhere. For more on Sardo, see page 39.

Stress in spoken Italian usually falls on the penultimate syllable. Italian has standard sounds: unlike English you can work out how it sounds from how it's written and vice versa.

Vowels

a like 'a' in cat
e like 'e' in vet, or slightly more open, like the 'ai' in air (except after c or g, see consonants below)
i like 'i' in sip (except after c or g, see below)
o like 'o' in fox
u like 'ou' in soup

Consonants

Generally consonants sound the same as in English, though 'e' and 'i' after 'c' or 'g' make them soft (a 'ch' or a 'j' sound) and are silent themselves, whereas 'h' makes them hard (a 'k' or 'g' sound), the opposite to English. So ciao is pronounced 'chaow', but chiesa (church) is pronounced 'kee-ay-sa'.

The combination 'gli' is pronounced like the 'lli' in million, and 'gn' like 'ny' in Tanya.

Basics

thank you   *grazie*
hi/goodbye   *ciao* (informal)
good day (until after lunch/
mid-afternoon)   *buongiorno*
good evening (after lunch)   *buonasera*
goodnight   *buonanotte*
goodbye   *arrivederci*
please   *per favore*
I'm sorry   *mi dispiace*
excuse me   *permesso*
yes   *sì*
no   *no*

Numbers

one	*uno*	17	*diciassette*
two	*due*	18	*diciotto*
three	*tre*	19	*diciannove*
four	*quattro*	20	*venti*
five	*cinque*	21	*ventuno*
six	*sei*	22	*ventidue*
seven	*sette*	30	*trenta*
eight	*otto*	40	*quaranta*
nine	*nove*	50	*cinquanta*
10	*dieci*	60	*sessanta*
11	*undici*	70	*settanta*
12	*dodici*	80	*ottanta*
13	*tredici*	90	*novanta*
14	*quattordici*	100	*cento*
15	*quindici*	200	*due cento*
16	*sedici*	1000	*mille*

Gestures

Italians are famously theatrical and animated in dialogue and use a variety of gestures.

Side of left palm on side of right wrist as right wrist is flicked up   Go away

Hunched shoulders and arms lifted with palms of hands outwards   What am I supposed to do?

Thumb, index and middle finger of hand together, wrist upturned and shaking
  What are you doing/what's going on?

Both palms together and moved up and down in front of stomach   Same as above

All fingers of hand squeezed together   To signify a place is packed full of people

Front of side of hand to chin   'Nothing', as in 'I don't understand' or 'I've had enough'

Flicking back of right ear   To signify someone is gay

Index finger in cheek   To signify good food

Questions

how?   *come?*

how much?   *quanto?*

when?   *quando?*

where?   *dove?*

why?   *perché?*

what?   *che cosa?*

Problems

I don't understand   *non capisco*

I don't know   *non lo so*

I don't speak Italian   *non parlo italiano*

How do you say ... (in Italian)?
  come si dice ... (in italiano)?

Is there anyone who speaks English?
  c'è qualcuno che parla inglese?

Shopping

this one/that one   *questo/quello*
less   *meno*
more   *di più*
How much is it/are they?
  quanto costa/costano?
Can I have ...?   *posso avere ...?*

Travelling

one ticket for...   *un biglietto per...*
single   *solo andate*
return   *andate ritorno*
does this go to Mantova?
  questo va per Mantova?
airport   *aeroporto*
bus stop   *fermata*
train   *treno*
car   *macchina*
taxi   *tassi*

Hotels

a double/single room
una camera doppia/singola
a double bed   *un letto matrimoniale*
bathroom   *bagno*
Is there a view?   *c'è una bella vista?*
Can I see the room?   *posso vedere la camera?*
When is breakfast?   *a che ora è la colazione?*
Can I have the key?   *posso avere la chiave?*

Time

morning *mattina*
afternoon *pomeriggio*
evening *sera*
night *notte*
soon *presto/fra poco*
later *più tardi*
What time is it? *Che ore sono?*
today/tomorrow/yesterday *oggi/domani/ieri*

Days

Monday *lunedi*
Tuesday *martedi*
Wednesday *mercoledi*
Thursday *giovedi*
Friday *venerdi*
Saturday *sabato*
Sunday *domenica*

Conversation

alright *va bene*
right then *allora*
who knows! *bo! / chi sa*
good luck! *in bocca al lupo!* (literally, 'in the mouth of the wolf')
one moment *un attimo*
hello (when answering a phone) *pronto* (literally, 'ready')
let's go! *andiamo!*
enough/stop *basta!*
give up! *dai!*
I like ... *mi piace ...*
how's it going? (well, thanks) *come va?* (bene, grazie)
how are you? *come sta/stai?* (polite/informal)

Index

Index

Index

Credits

Footprint credits

Text editor: Sophie Jones
Assistant editor: Alice Jell
Picture editor: Rob Lunn
Layout & production: Davina Rungasamy
Maps: Compass Maps Ltd

Managing Director: Andy Riddle
Commercial Director: Patrick Dawson
Publisher: Alan Murphy
Editorial: Sara Chare, Ria Gane,
Jenny Haddington, Felicity Laughton,
Nicola Gibbs
Cartography: Sarah Sorensen,
Kevin Feeney, Emma Bryers
Design: Mytton Williams
Sales & marketing: Liz Harper,
Hannah Bonnell
Advertising: Renu Sibal
Business Development: Zoë Jackson
Finance & Administration: Elizabeth Taylor

Print

Manufactured in Italy by EuroGrafica
Pulp from sustainable forests

Footprint feedback

We try as hard as we can to make each
Footprint guide as up to date as possible
but, of course, things always change. If
you want to let us know about your
experiences – good, bad or ugly – then
don't delay, go to footprintbooks.com
and send in your comments.

Every effort has been made to ensure that
the facts in this guidebook are accurate.
However, travellers should still obtain
advice from consulates, airlines etc about
travel and visa requirements before
travelling. The authors and publishers
cannot accept responsibility for any loss,
injury or inconvenience however caused.

Publishing information

FootprintItalia Sardinia
1st edition
© Footprint Handbooks Ltd
May 2009

ISBN 978-1-906098-58-2
CIP DATA: A catalogue record for this
book is available from the British Library

* Footprint Handbooks and the Footprint
mark are a registered trademark of
Footprint Handbooks Ltd

Published by Footprint

6 Riverside Court
Lower Bristol Road
Bath BA2 3DZ, UK
T +44 (0)1225 469141
F +44 (0)1225 469461
www.footprintbooks.com

Distributed in North America by

Globe Pequot Press

All rights reserved. No part of this
publication may be reproduced, stored in a
retrieval system, or transmitted, in any form
or by any means, electronic, mechanical,
photocopying, recording, or otherwise
without the prior permission of Footprint
Handbooks Ltd.

The colour maps are not intended to have
any political significance.

BIBLIO RPL Ltée
G – DÉC. 2009